Ecologies of Architecture

Essays on Territorialisation

Andrej Radman

EDINBURGH
University Press

Edinburgh University Press is one of the leading university presses in the UK. We publish academic books and journals in our selected subject areas across the humanities and social sciences, combining cutting-edge scholarship with high editorial and production values to produce academic works of lasting importance. For more information visit our website: edinburghuniversitypress.com

Edinburgh University Press Ltd
The Tun – Holyrood Road, 12(2f) Jackson's Entry, Edinburgh EH8 8PJ

First published in hardback by Edinburgh University Press 2021

Typeset in 10/14 Warnock Pro by
Servis Filmsetting Ltd, Stockport, Cheshire, and
printed and bound by CPI Group (UK) Ltd,
Croydon, CR0 4YY

A CIP record for this book is available from the British Library

ISBN 978 1 4744 8301 8 (hardback)
ISBN 978 1 4744 8302 5 (paperback)
ISBN 978 1 4744 8303 2 (webready PDF)
ISBN 978 1 4744 8304 9 (epub)

Contents

List of Figures and Tables

All figures and tables, unless otherwise specified, are the author's.

Acknowledgements

This book is the product of research conducted by the Theory Group at the Faculty of Architecture and the Built Environment, Delft University of Technology. It was fuelled by the discussions at the architecture theory doctoral seminars that I chaired at TU Delft together with colleague and friend Stavros Kousoulas, with the indispensable assistance of Robert A. Gorny. The first series of seminars was launched in 2014 with the pilot *Ecologies of Architecture*; the second (2015) dealt with the *Affective Turn*; the third (2016) explored the concept of *Futurity*; the fourth (2017) was devoted to the Guattarian *Chaosophy*; the fifth (2018) explored the *Feminist Ethics of Sustainability*; and the Simondonian sixth series (2019) tackled *Architecture's Mode of Existence*. The current series (2020) runs under the name of *Everybody Loves Ruyer: The Architecture of Neo-finalism.*

I have benefited from the stimulating intellectual milieu of the local Deleuze Circle, in particular Rosi Braidotti, Sjoerd van Tuinen and Rick Dolphijn. The work was inspired by three Annual National Deleuze Conferences I had the pleasure of hosting with Deborah Hauptmann, Marc Boumeester and Stavros Kousoulas, respectively: *Asignifying Semiotics: or How to Paint Pink on Pink* (2013) at TU Delft; *A Grin without a Cat* (2017) at AKI Academy of Art and Design, University of the Arts ArtEZ; and *Architectures of Life and Death* (2019) at TU Delft.

Thanks are extended to the global circle, namely Hélène Frichot, Peg Rawes, Momoyo Homma, Bodil Marie Stavning Thomsen, Greg Seigworth, Gary Genosko, Constantin Boundas, Andrew Ballantyne, Dan Smith, John Protevi, Paulo de Assis, Henrik Oxvig and Sanford Kwinter, as well as other innumerable generous interlocutors.

I am grateful to Christian Girard for his meticulous feedback on the typescript and to Heleen Schröder for proofreading. I owe a big thank you to Carol Macdonald for her generous editorial guidance and support. Finally, I gratefully acknowledge the financial support of my institution.

My endeavour would not be possible or sensible without the love of my life Tatjana Zagajski and our children Paula and Karlo.

This book is dedicated to the memory of my friend, Nenad Šironja, who passed away on 27 April 2017.

I would like to thank the publishers for permission to reprint material from the following chapters:
Chapter 1: 'Figure, Discourse: To the Abstract Concretely'
This essay first appeared in *Cognitive Architecture: From Bio-politics to Noo-politics*, edited by Deborah Hauptmann and Warren Neidich (Rotterdam: 010 Publishers, 2010), 430–51. It was subsequently reprinted with permission in *Deleuze and Guattari on Architecture (Critical Assessments in Architecture, Volume II)*, edited by Graham Livesey (London: Routledge, 2015), 317–39.
Chapter 2: 'Architecture's Awaking from Correlationist Slumber: On Transdisciplinarity and Disciplinary Specificity'
This essay first appeared in *Footprint* 6, no. 10/11, *Architecture Culture and the Question of Knowledge: Doctoral Research Today*, edited by Deborah Hauptmann and Lara Schrijver (Delft: DSD in partnership with Stichting Footprint and Techne Press, 2012), 129–41.
Chapter 3: 'Northern Line'
This essay, co-authored with Deborah Hauptmann, first appeared in *Deleuze and Architecture*, edited by Hélène Frichot and Stephen Loo (Edinburgh: Edinburgh University Press, 2013), 40–60.
Chapter 4: 'Sensibility is Ground Zero: On Inclusive Disjunction and Politics of Defatalisation'
This essay first appeared in *This Deleuzian Century: Art, Activism, Society*, edited by Rosi Braidotti and Rick Dolphijn (Leiden & Boston: Brill/Rodopi, 2014), 57–86.
Chapter 5: 'Architecture of Immanence'
This essay first appeared in *Architecture & Situation*, Vol. 4, edited by Ella Chmielewska, Tahl Kaminer and Dorian Wiszniewski (Edinburgh: Architecture, University of Edinburgh, 2014), 18–19.
Chapter 6: 'The Impredicative City: or What Can a Boston Square Do?'
This essay, co-authored with Marc Boumeester, first appeared in *Deleuze and*

the City, edited by Hélène Frichot, Catharina Gabrielsson and Jonathan Metzger (Edinburgh: Edinburgh University Press, 2016), 46–63.

Chapter 7: 'Space Always Comes After: It is good when it comes after; it is good only when it comes after'

This essay first appeared in *Speculative Art Histories: Analysis at the Limits*, edited by Sjoerd van Tuinen (Edinburgh: Edinburgh University Press, 2017), 185–201.

Chapter 8: 'Zigzagging: Bound by the Absence of a Tie'

This essay first appeared in in *The Dark Precursor: Deleuze and Artistic Research*, edited by Paulo de Assis and Paolo Giudici (Leuven: Leuven University Press (Orpheus Institute Series), 2017), 182–91.

Chapter 9: '3D Perception ≠ 2D Image + 1D Inference: or Why a Single Precise Shot Would Often Miss the Target, whereas a Series of Imprecise Shots Will Eventually Lead to a Hit'

This essay first appeared in *What Images Do*, edited by Henrik Oxvig, Jan Bäcklund, Michael Renner and Martin Søberg (Aarhus: Aarhus University Press, 2018), 145–55.

Chapter 10: 'Double Bind: On Material Ethics'

An abridged version of this essay first appeared in *Schizoanalysis and Ecosophy: Reading Deleuze and Guattari*, edited by Constantin V. Boundas (London: Bloomsbury, 2018), 241–56.

Chapter 11: 'Involutionary Architecture: Unyoking Coherence from Congruence'

This essay first appeared in *Posthuman Ecologies: Complexity and Process after Deleuze*, edited by Rosi Braidotti and Simone Bignall (London: Rowman & Littlefield, 2019), 61–86.

Preface: Transversality at Work

Rosi Braidotti

THESE ARE DIFFICULT times for materialist thinkers, as public opinion is caught in specular and equally fallacious dichotomies: on the one hand, the mythologised half-truths and renaturalised hierarchies of ethno-nationalists, conspiracy theorists and crypto-fascists. And on the other, the denaturalised habits of thought of social constructivists, with their binary oppositions between nature and culture, bodies and technology, matter and thought, *zoe* and *bios*, the environment and politics. A social pathology of sick holism confronts the old habit of prioritising the social. Both genuflect to triumphant human exceptionalism. There is hardly any room left for critical thinkers to breathe in; no common ground or shareable milieu for thinking in critical and clinical frames.

Reading Andrej Radman's work is an antidote against these simplifications: he is a neo-materialist critical thinker committed to setting up a different agenda, in a rigorous yet collaborative tone, proposing an affirmative set of alternative ethical values. Radman proposes a process ontology, in the form of a general ecology that questions all those binary poles and connects them transversally. In an eco-sophical move, he moreover inserts technology into the equation. Emphasising an originary kind of technicity, which makes all humans always already mediated, Radman undoes biological determinism, while carefully avoiding any form of cognitive or moral relativism.

The 'matter' of matter-realism is delinked from the pernicious Cartesian grid that opposed it to mind, cognition and the generative potency of thought. In a switch to critical Spinozism, negotiated via the philosophy of Deleuze and Guattari, but also with contemporary genetics and neural sciences, Radman defines matter as vital, intelligent, self-organising, but also heterogeneous and post-naturalistic. At the core of it all, technologically mediated hetero-genesis composes multiple materialist ecologies that do not depend on any organicist's vision of nature. Belonging is about becoming alongside multiple relations and forces, of the environmental, social and affective or psychic kind.

The assumption is that all substance is one and that all living entities are modulations within a common matter. This means that we all pertain to the totality of all living things and that the matter we are composed of is vital, intelligent and self-generating. As the perceiving and thinking subjects that observe and account for the world, we are situated within it, not external or transcendent. Made of combinations of the same substances as all other matter, we humans interact and exchange within networks integral and immanent to the world. But this does not amount to a 'flat ontology' (*pace* the object ontologists) that fails to differentiate or recognise the specific qualities, propensities and degrees of potency of each bound entity, organism and species. Quite the contrary: matter is differentiated internally by processes of non-dialectical differing that result in speciation and mutual specification. To be immanent to matter means to be situated along differential, not identical locations: we are embodied and embedded differently and our embrained bodies and embodied brains are capable of very different things. Given the parallelism mind–body, minds cannot be differentiated independently of the bodies of which they are ideas or representations. They are structured by ontological relationality, which is the power to affect and be affected by one another. This differential materialism also embraces the non- and the in-human entities as constitutive components of subjectivity defined as the heterogeneous assemblage of elements.

An undifferentiated vitalist system that would form flat equivalences across all species, all technologies and all organisms under one common Law, on the other hand, is a vulgar form of naturalised mechanism. This undifferentiated and yet hierarchical system was the error of the organicist philosophies of Life developed in the first half of the twentieth century. They were complicitous with the necro-political project of historical European fascism. Deleuze and Guattari are committed to exposing the homicidal logic of this spurious glorification of naturalised hierarchies. In so doing, they accomplish the denazification of European philosophy, as Foucault famously stated. They extract the idea of vital matter from the racist, anti-Semitic murderous regimes of fascism and colonialism. What Radman defends is a neo-materialist philosophy of immanence that lifts the categorical divides between concepts that have structured the philosophies of modernity and their bellicose use of the architecture of scientific rationality for the purpose of conquest and domination.

This grounded or embedded differential materialism posits a pacifist relational ontology as its core. Ethically, it rests on radical perspectivism, honouring a multiplicity of locations and windows of perception for each organism. All living matter is animated by a constitutive desire to go on becoming, flowing and reaching across. All living organisms can be defined by the ontological desire to persevere in their existence. This desire is a transversal force that expresses the constitutive freedom of all entities and their relational ability to connect with innumerable human and non-human others. Relationality is onto-logical and extends transversally through the multiple ecologies that constitute contemporary subjects. These entail different modes and relations of power, that encompass ecologies of architecture, institutional instances, subjective and affective and psychic landscapes, as well as transversal mediated assemblages. This heterogeneous view of vital materialist subjectivity includes relations to a multitude of human and non-human others (both organic and technological).

Thinking consequently becomes a 'thisworldly' activity – grounded in the project of composing *a* life, in the radical immanence of its specificity – haecceity, or degree of intensity. What is ethically desirable is the composition of a middle ground, composed by alliances and collaborative connections of both human and non-human agents. These are heterogeneous multiplicities, interacting through networks of natural, social, political and affective relations. Ethics starts with the recognition of these transversal subject assemblages – 'we, posthuman subjects' – that actualise the unrealised or virtual potential of what 'we' are capable of becoming. The critical project is about becoming other-than the Homo Universalis of humanism or other-than the Anthropos of anthro-pocentrism. It is about a multiplicity of nomadic differences activated for the construction of alternative ways of becoming (post)human.

Transcendentalist claims to exceptionalism are therefore cut down to size, through an emphasis on immanence and the recognition of our mutual inter-dependence. We – who are not One and the same – are definitely in this world together – in the combination of breathtaking technological developments, but also the injustices, the epidemics and other environmental devastations, strug-gling alongside each other. In such a context, rejecting human exceptionalism is a way of embracing the immanence of a Life that we do not own, a Life that is not restricted to hegemonic 'Man', but includes his multiple, disposable and despised others. It calls for differential, materially embedded accounts of the respective prices 'we' are prepared to pay for being and staying alive here and now. Radman proposes a generous philosophy on other-than and more-than-human love for life as a generative process of interdependence. Thinking as a relational gesture emerges from the thick materiality of interacting with these multiple forces – it is an immanent and outward-bound activity, not transcen-dental and anthropocentric.

The term 'transversality' appears systematically throughout the journey Andrej Radman maps out for us. Transversal thinking is the expression of post-human subjects that are heterogeneous assemblages of human and non-human entities, within a neo-materialist vital ontology. The relational capacity to affect and be affected by others is not confined within our species, but includes all non-anthropomorphic elements, starting from the air we breathe. Transversality challenges linearity in that it has to steer a course across the zigzagging trans-positions of a *zoe*-geo-techno-mediated world. Notably amidst the convulsions of cognitive capitalism, the deterritorialisations of the posthuman convergence and the eternal return of familiar patterns of social injustice and exclusion.

There is a qualitative aspect to the transversal transferral of information across the categories that Radman proposes, as well as a higher degree of res-onance between them. They connect the better and faster to move across and out of their points of origin. This is an affirmative deterritorialisation that does not aim at pitching the knowledge claims on to immediate disciplinary, political or financial targets. It is curiosity-driven, gratuitous and experimental. This is minor science at work, in the most affirmative sense of the term, proposing daring and illuminating combinations. The point of this transversality is not only to honour the multiple sources of knowledge production in our posthuman times, but also to desegregate the domains by blurring disciplinary and even interdisciplinary boundaries. Radman's encyclopaedic knowledge is crucial to this aspect of the project, which increases synergy between the three cultures of the Humanities, Social Sciences and Natural Life Sciences. The qualitative leaps of transversal ways of thinking and knowing come with a high ethical requirement: a transformation of how we think about the world, but also of how we inhabit it. Such a radical change, based on the immanent material structure of the subject, requires the acknowledgement of ontological relationality: that is to say, of our interconnection to both social and environmental entities, to mul-tiple belonging and shared processes of transformation. At some basic genetic level 'we' living entities are in *this* together.

Transversally connected subjects are allied but differentiated. Agreeing to common belonging to a planetary home but abandoning the notion of a uni-tary humanity as One and the same. Accepting the materially embedded social grounding of their differences, they can act in common to potentiate their shared vision and enact collective transformations. Striving together for alter-native ways of designing multiple heterogeneous ecologies of belonging. Thus, affirming the basic point that, all other differences notwithstanding, 'we' are in *this* together, though we are not-One-and-the-same.

Introduction:
Under the Pixels, the Beach!

Ecology is about [the weaving of co-evolutions]
without a transcendent common interest,
without an arbiter distributing the roles,
without a mutual understanding.
(Isabelle Stengers, 2018)[1]

Discrete perception,
like discrete ideas,
are as mythical as the Jack of Spades.
(James Jerome Gibson, 1986)[2]

Four Emergent Domains

Why *Ecologies of Architecture*, instead of just Architecture? Why territorialisation? To be worthy of the event. As Gilles Deleuze put it, the opposite of the
concrete is not the abstract. It is the discrete, and so is the digital by definition.[3]
To reduce architecture to its ontic (manifest and calculable) effect is to deprive
it of its real-yet-incorporeal pathic affect. They are two unequal and irreducible co-constitutive 'halves': the actual properties and the virtual capacities. To
paraphrase Gregory Bateson, remaining committed to 'architecture proper' is
analogous to studying the anatomy of half a chicken – it makes no sense. To
speak of ecology – beyond greenwashing – is to uphold irreducibility, embrace
non-entailment and thus make sense. Sense is never found; it does not come
ready-made. Sense-making is a matter of 'technicity' in Simondonian terms.[4] It
is a force of psychosocial invention and cultural transformation which does not

exclude relations with non-humans and the greater cosmos. While dimensionality is about what happens, of the order of percept, directionality is about what is going on in what happens, of the order of affect.

Following Félix Guattari, the two halves will not do. They could be mistaken for dialectics. *Pace* his prodigious *Three Ecologies*, even a triad would be an all-too-facile upgrade. Instead, in the most detailed account of his theory – *Schizoanalytic Cartographies* – Guattari proposes a fourfold built around two axes: the horizontal axis of reference and the vertical axis of consistency.[5] Any architectural collective enunciation worthy of its ecological attribute can be said to consist of quadruple ontological domains: Territory (**T**) and Universes of Value (**U**) as non-discursive, and energetic and semiotic Flows (**F**) and Machinic Phylum (**P**) as discursive. These are four dimensions of the assemblages that are always articulated together. Although there is no order of priority, let us start from the endo-consistent/endo-referential *existential* Territory. This is the substance-of-content, as opposed to the form-of-content as the deterritorialised exo-consistent/endo-referential Universes of value. Their difference is *modal*. By contrast, the difference between territorialisation and coding is *real*. The exo-consistent/exo-referential Phylum as a form-of-expression is but a decoded endo-consistent/exo-referential Flow as a substance-of-expression. The informatics of the *possible* **U-P** is inconceivable without the energetics of the *real* **T-F**. Likewise, the *virtual* **T-U** is sterile without the *actual* **F-P** (Tables I.1, I.2).

Most of our recent techno-scientific history, architecture included, is marked by its preference for the material and efficient causality. *Ecologies of Architecture* in general and territorialisation in particular follow the Stoic lead in rectifying this bias against the supposedly crypto-vitalist formal and final causalities. Every actual state of affairs produces an incorporeal effect that, in turn, becomes a quasi-cause.[6] In other words, the arrows of causality do not flow in one direction only, as vulgar mechanism would have it. There is a 'downward causation' –

Table I.1 The four ontological domains.

Form of Expression	Possible		Form of Content
	Phyla Universes		
Actual	**P** | **U**		**Virtual**
	F | **T**		
	Flows Territories		
Substance of Exp.	**Real**		Substance of Cont.

Source: author.

Table I.2 The four quasi-causalities.

Formal Causality	Exo-Consistency		Final Causality
Exo-Reference	Machinic P	Incorporeal U	**Endo-Reference**
	F	T	
	Energetic	Existential	
Material Causality	**Endo-Consistency**		Efficient Causality

Source: author.

neo-finalism[7] – which determines the degrees of freedom at the level of actuality. This high level of abstraction calls for an illustration. Brian Massumi offers a persuasive case, that of love.[8] Love is arguably both an effect and a quasi-cause par excellence. It is irreducible to the lovers and holds them in its power. It is the whole not *of* the parts, but *alongside* them.

The Guattarian meta-modelling rests on the primacy of action, or action on action, to be more precise.[9] That activity is not subject to deterministic causality is good news for designers whose focus lies on what could have been otherwise.[10] What eventually does happen becomes the 'rule', as in the copula of 'concrete rules and abstract machines'.[11] In other words, values do not exist outside the constitutive problematic fields that give them sense. That action is never exerted on the object is possibly the greatest ethological lesson for architecture students who are encouraged to stay with the problem instead, as Donna Haraway would put it.[12] One never designs an artefact (a piece of architecture), but constructs the phase space (*Umwelt*) so as to engender a new territory. In other words, the problem always has the solution it deserves. While engineering is solution-oriented, architecture plays with the virtual without actualising it (as yet) to tease out a creative potential. As a matter of fact, architecture remains 'unrealised' by default, because we never know what it can do. Territorialisation cannot occur without the quasi-causality of the finalist Universes of reference, the material Flows and the formalist Phyla.

We cannot afford to dismiss that which remains opaque to our representational regimes. As Deleuze and Guattari insisted, the fundamental (cosmo) political question is still precisely the one that Spinoza saw so clearly (and that Wilhelm Reich rediscovered): why do people fight for their servitude (as stubbornly) as though it were their salvation?[13] It is for this reason that the book stages an architectural encounter between affordance theory, affect theory and process-oriented philosophy. These kindred ontotopological approaches dispense with any foundational appeal to the subject understood in Cartesian terms as the sovereign author of its actions or in phenomenological terms as a 'transcendental field'. Under radical empiricism, as defined by William James, relations are immediately real and really experienced.[14] Moreover, every experience exceeds its empirical conditions.[15] The question is not who it is that connects and universalises, but how one becomes through separation (transduction) and individuation – 'belonging in becoming'.[16] Consequently, what constitutes (architectural) thinking is not the application of acquired concepts, but the process of destratification. Counter-effectuation applies both to epistrata ($T>U$) and parastrata ($F>P$).[17] Crucially, it applies to the city and the countryside, 'a glaringly inadequate term for all the territory that is not urban'.[18] Vice-diction takes us from what was formerly known as the base of fact (what is) to the 'superstructure' of value (what ought to be), from causes to 'becauses'. This is where resingularisation of desire and values may occur: that is, where a different action may be motivated. In a nutshell, to think is to destratify (far from equilibrium: that is, far from stratifications).[19] Such an approach constitutes a necessary antidote to the supposed axiological neutrality of what Bruno Latour calls 'factishism', including the most recent 'dataism' defined as the pure presence of data, amnesic of the singularities and prone to self-fulfilling prophecies including 'homophily' (love of the same).[20] The wet dream of dataists is to resuscitate Laplace's demon: that is, to determine the present state of the universe as the effect of its past and the cause of its future. By contrast, *Ecologies of Architecture* aims to avoid the algorithmisation of desire that can short-circuit the future.[21] 'An effect of existential consummation and superabundance of being' will be the only and inevitable criterion of truth once architects find themselves carried away by a process of eventisation.[22]

> The architect would thus have to be capable of detecting and exploiting processually the catalytic points of singularities that can be incarnated in the sensible dimensions of the architectural apparatus as well as in the most complex of formal compositions and institutional problematics.[23]

Destratification is always followed by restratification. Consequently, every territorialisation is in fact (and in value!) reterritorialisation. This means that the basic grain of reality cannot be found in the finite or the indefinite (infinite regress). *Ecologies of Architecture* is about the 'unlimited finity' that can only exist collectively, not distributively. Matter and energy are finite, yet the 'lure of the virtual' is unlimited, because boundary conditions continue to mutate and produce different enabling constraints and modes of existence.[24] A Whiteheadian

Table I.3 The four architectural technicities.

Decoding	**Infinite / Informatics / Irreversible**		Deterritorialisation
Discursive	Skyscraper **P**	Congestion Culture **U**	**Non-Discursive**
	F	**T**	
	Elevator	Bachelor Machine	
Coding	**Finite / Energetics / Reversible**		Territorialisation

Source: author.

'fallacy of misplaced concreteness' arises from under- and overdetermination.[25] How far up do you go along the mereological ladder opting for the concept that is all-too-inclusive and disregarding the singularity of the 'parts' (**F** and **T**)? Conversely, how far down do you go along the path of individuation merely describing the given without the enquiry into how the given is given, or if it could have become otherwise (**P** and **U**)? What is needed is the right granularity, not an unmarked universality or idiosyncrasies of singular situations.[26] A way out of the deadlock is to consider a different form of universality, one that is no longer grounded on commonality (representation).

Take the positive example of Rem Koolhaas's *Delirious New York*, with the apt subtitle *A Retroactive Manifesto* (Table I.3). Manifestos should not be written if not *ex post facto*.[27] Beneath the manifesto, the beach! The purely contingent invention of the elevator – the vertical Flow (**F**) – fuelled a rare new architectural *dispositif* (formerly known as typology) of the skyscraper. This Machinic Phylum (**P**) made way for the unprecedented 'culture of congestion'. The new Universe of Value and Reference (**U**) engendered the Territory of a Metropolitan Subject (**T**). There was never an explicit plan for this unprecedented form of life to take shape. It is but a resolution of (or concrescence in) the highly saturated field, also known as the plane of immanence. The sub-ject does not pre-exist. Rather, it is secondary in relation to the point of view and should have been super-ject all along. This is the heart of (Leibnizian) radical perspectivism.

In the above example of technicity, the skyscraper is the form-of-expression and the culture of congestion is the form-of-content. The former is the actually possible, the latter is virtually possible. Otis's invention is the substance-of-expression and the naked boxer '*eating oysters with boxing gloves . . . on the* nth *floor*'[28] is the substance-of-content. The elevator is actually real, and the 'bachelor machine' is virtually real. The four delirious domains are fully contingent. Yet once they lock in through heteropoietic reconfiguration of boundary conditions, they become metastable. Multiplicity is plastic where the condition does not outweigh the conditioned. Producing path-dependencies does not render the Chreod logically necessary.[29] This neologism – coined by the developmental biologist Waddington – denotes the contingently obligatory path of any becoming. All actual causes (T and F) produce virtual effects (U and P) that in turn constrain the degrees of freedom at the level of actuality (T and F). To realise that all forms of life are effectuated transversally is a bitter pill to swallow for the 'bounded individual' – a pet figure of liberal humanism. That there are no libertarians in a pandemic, or otherwise, is a lesson learned.[30]

> In the spring of 2010, a dust cloud from a minor volcanic eruption in Iceland, a small disturbance in the complex mechanism of the life on the Earth, put to a standstill the aerial traffic over most of Europe [energetic F]. It was a sharp reminder of how, despite all its tremendous activity of transforming nature, humankind remains merely another of many living species on planet Earth [existential T]. The very catastrophic socioeconomic impact of such a minor outburst is due to the fragility of our technological development, in this case air travel [machinic P]. A century ago, such an eruption would have passed unnoticed. Technological development makes us more independent from nature and at the same time, at a different level, more dependent on nature's whims [referential U]. And the same holds for the spread of coronavirus: if it had happened before Deng Xiaoping's reforms, we probably wouldn't even have heard about it.[31]

The metastable dynamics cannot be captured once and for all. Put simply, the (posthumanist) subject continues to be modulated by emergent enabling constraints. This calls for schizoanalytic cartography to tie the multiplicity (or Ruyerian 'absolute form') to the variables which determine its own mutation. No more, no less. The entanglement of Territory, Flux, Phyla and Values/References is fully relational, anexact yet rigorous. The 2020 pandemic has already transformed the fourfold diagram. It is, as yet, impossible to qualify it as a mere state of exception, or the new normal. However, we can tentatively suggest the following updated version of ontological domains: actually real Covid-19 flow (F); actually possible Camp/Bunker System (P); virtually possible Quarantine *Ritornello* (U); virtually real Epidemiological and Immunological Commons (T). Yet, keeping the (perceived) danger either contained (camp), or conversely at bay (bunker), only seemingly reinvigorates the Westphalian model. As Yuk Hui cautions, the pandemic renders explicit the immanence of an infodemic where a nation state extends technologically and economically beyond its physical borders to establish new ones (mereotopology).[32]

At long last, ecology must be unyoked from nature.[33] It is shorthand for irreducibility and non-entailment: process and product, form and structure, operation and structure, content and expression, form and substance, value and fact, abstract and concrete, virtual and actual, smooth and striated, relays and domains, beach and pixels. To freely take sides, as so many architects do, would be to commit an error of category. The virtual is not transcendent. It is a product of immanence. Sense is not given. It has to be made. This is the gist of 'agential realism'.[34] Data (including big data) is not information. Information is a difference that makes a difference. By the same token, Territory is emergent yet constructed.[35] The built environment accumulates and transmits successive epigenetic experiences from one generation to another.[36] Thanks to a degree of mnemonic detachability (from the genetic register), habits are enforced, modulated and transmitted through habitats and vice versa. We design our territories and they design us in turn. In the words of Benjamin Bratton from his *Terraforming* manifesto: 'It's not just that we use technologies to survive, but that we evolved in symbiotic relationship with the technical cascades that shaped us, and we are nothing without them.'[37] To illustrate the problem of irreversibility, Guattari offers what is by today's standards a cruel experiment involving an octopus conducted live on French television.[38] There were two glass tanks, one with clean seawater and the other with polluted seawater and a healthy thriving octopus. As the octopus was moved from polluted to clean water it curled up, sank to the bottom and died. We can agree with Guattari that now, more than ever, nature cannot be separated from culture. This is the ecological principle of trophic cascade that compels us to think 'transversally': that is, we have to think of affordance, affect and politics as co-constitutive.

Eleven Essays on Territorialisation

The book is composed of eleven essays published in the course of the second decade of the third millennium. Their focus may vary, but the ecological affective tonality is palpable throughout.

Chapter 1 'Figure, Discourse: To the Abstract Concretely' makes a case for the concept of multiplicity that premises a radically new relationship between one and many with no primacy of either. What we have is one world with two modes of reality: the actual and the virtual, in constant chiasmic eventful interaction.

Chapter 2 'Architecture's Awaking from Correlationist Slumber: On

Transdisciplinarity and Disciplinary Specificity' opposes the scientific point of view that regards architecture as not rigorous enough. It is a bias that has tangible consequences for research and education (assessment) alike. However, this perceived weakness may turn out to be architecture's main strength, a result of the symbiosis between its *beaux-arts* and polytechnic traditions (aberrant nuptials). Yes, it is possible to be both anexact and rigorous. What distinguishes architecture from other disciplines and makes it the material-discursive technicity par excellence is the interplay between the abstract means and concrete ends. Architecture requires both intellectual and practical tools to work effectively in a paradoxical environment that is immersed in the incorporeal world of images and abstract notations, yet intimately connected to the corporeality of material and forces.

Chapter 3 'Northern Line' draws on Deleuze and Guattari's reading of the concept of the 'Northern Line' as a theoretical disposition towards the differential difference in contrast to the dialectical difference. The latter operates in terms of opposition, negation and, *ipso facto*, resistance correlative to a molar notion of power (*pouvoir*) and not, as the former, at the (molecular) level of 'desiring assemblages'. The chapter shows that the 'Northern Line' provides an aesthetic reading – neither distributed nor organised around the mind, nor oriented towards cognition – that is capable of escaping architecture's long-standing dependence on representationalism.

Chapter 4 'Sensibility is Ground Zero: On Inclusive Disjunction and Politics of Defatalisation' endeavours to rebut a long-standing philosophical and psychoanalytic tradition of inscribing the subject as primarily grounded in thought or language. As such, the fetishist self-identical subject is deluded into being the epicentre of various experiences and understandings, separate from the constellation of intensities that it undergoes.

Chapter 5 'Architecture of Immanence' lays out the expectations from the machinic or eco-logical architecture, not as a reactive and thus reactionary, but a positive determination beyond ex-futurism and neo-archaism. It might just hold the secret of how to go beyond the totality derived from the parts and the totality from which the parts emanate, to produce an architecture of immanence.

Chapter 6 'The Impredicative City: or What Can a Boston Square Do?' draws upon schizoanalytic cartography to concentrate on the perception which occurs not on the level at which actions are decided but on the level at which the very capacity for action forms. If representation is a means to an end (tracing), cartography is a means to a means (intervention). The goal-oriented human action cannot be used as the design criterion, because the freedom of action is never a de facto established condition; it is always virtuality.

Chapter 7 'Space Always Comes After: It Is Good When It Comes After; It Is Good Only When It Comes After' argues that the royal road to the understanding of space is through the non-intentional, non-reflexive and non-conscious. It is through population thinking that we will undergo a biopolitical apprenticeship in spatialisation.

Chapter 8 'Zigzagging: Bound by the Absence of a Tie' unpacks Deleuze and Guattari's 'machinic' conception of consistency which is determined neither by the naïve 'organic' autonomy of the vitalist whole, nor by the crude reductionist expression of the whole in the sum of its mechanical parts. Machinism entails the dark precursor's zigzagging between the immanent limits of empathy and abstraction, nature and culture, the extensive and the intensive, signification and significance, as well as the political and the libidinal.

Chapter 9 '3D Perception ≠ 2D Image + 1D Inference: or Why a Single Precise Shot Would Often Miss the Target, Whereas a Series of Imprecise Shots Will Eventually Lead to a Hit' draws on what Deleuze diagnosed as the historical crisis of psychology caused by the 'ontological iron curtain' between the mind and the body, which keeps the images in consciousness separated from the movements in space. Such a dualist position is not attainable, for there has never been such a thing as a bounded body coupled to the world. The 'movement-image' as a pure event is antecedent to the formation of the border between the inside and the outside. To escape the pernicious 'reversed ontology' whereby the cart of representation is placed before the horse of morphogenesis, we need to draw on the 'reversal (of the reversal)'. The realist account of metastable structures as being produced out of material flows requires that we put the event before and beyond meaning and organism altogether. Images cannot be reduced to their all-too-human semiotic function in a cultural system.

Chapter 10 'Double Bind: On Material Ethics' champions the neologism ethico-aesthetic in order to underline the inseparability of action and perception. The chapter argues that it is practice and experimentation that actively shape the subject. Until recently the sentient was considered as a mere supplement to the sapient. The ranking order in major philosophical systems clearly reveals a historical bias towards the cognitive over the affective. But it is in the manner of such lowly supplements to end up supplanting what they are meant to subserve.

Chapter 11 'Involutionary Architecture: Unyoking Coherence from Congruence' is devoted to the involutionary relation of the forces from within with the forces from without. It starts from the premise that the interior as a given needs to be set aside until the issue of how the given is given has been addressed. Only then will it be possible to make sense of the superfold's (eternal) giving. When the explanatory ladder is turned upside down, what has figured as an explanation – namely interiority as a datum – becomes that which begs the question.

Six Constructive Relays

In a desperate attempt to catch up with forms of contemporary media culture, architects tend to perpetuate earlier notions of culture as representation rather than culture as modes of existence. Architecture has yet to break with the conception of culture as reflection still firmly embedded in its parochial concepts. When a society manipulates its matter it is not a reflection of culture, it is culture. To speak of *Ecologies of Architecture* is to break with judgement in favour of experience. Experimentation comes before interpretation.[39] One cannot understand a system unless one acts on it. If to think differently we have to feel differently then the design of built environment has no other purpose but to transform us. It qualifies as a major psychotropic practice. The introduction concludes with a list of key ecological concepts:[40]

1 Pedagogy of the Senses

Posthuman or non-anthropocentric architecture ought to focus on the encounter between thought and that which forces it into action.[41] While accepting multiple nested scales of reality, *Ecologies of Architecture* challenges the alleged primacy of the 'physical' world. What we engage with is the world considered as an environment and not an aggregate of objects. The emphasis is on the encounter, where experience is seen as an emergence which returns the body to a process field of exteriority.[42] Sensibility introduces an aleatory moment into thought's development, thus turning contingency into the very condition for thinking. It is the encounter that compels the thought, and not vice versa.

2 Radical Perspectivism

The eco-logical perspectivist assault on the ego-logical representational thinking inevitably impinges upon the identity of the subject. Where Kant founded the representational unity of space and time upon the formal unity of consciousness, the difference fractures consciousness into multiple states not predicable of a single subject. In other words, the difference breaks with the differentiation of an undifferentiated world in favour of the homogenisation of a milieu or *Umwelt*.[43] Perspectivism is not to be confused with relativism. To paraphrase the anthropologist Viveiros de Castro, different life forms do not see the same world in different ways (cultural relativism), but rather see different worlds – coping possibilities – in the same way.[44] Relativity of truth does not equal truth of the relative.

3 Anti-Hylomorphism

Ecologies of Architecture relies on schizoanalytic cartography to overturn the theatre of representation into the order of desiring-production. The ultimate ambition is to debunk hylomorphism – where form is imposed upon inert matter from without and where the architect is seen as a god-given inspired creator and genius – and to promote the alternative immanent morphogenetic approach that is at once more humble and more audacious. There lies a (r)evolutionary potential in creating the 'new', defined as the circulation of decoded and deterritorialized flows. These flows resist the facile co-option by overcoding as an illegitimate overstretching of conceptual resources that make the word 'visionary' so banal.[45]

4 Asignifying Semiotics

To speak of univocity of expression is to break with equivocity of the hegemonic linguistic sign.[46] Action and perception are inseparable, as are forms of life and their environments. If objects of knowledge are separated from objects of existence, we end up with a duality of mental and physical objects – bifurcation of nature – that leads to an ontologically indirect perception. By contrast, the premise of *Ecologies of Architecture* is that perceptual systems resonate with information, where information is defined as a difference that makes a difference. This 'direct realism' is grounded on the premise that, from the outset, real experience is a relation of potential structure rather than a formless chaotic swirl on to which structure must be imposed by cognitive process (sapience). The world is seen as an ongoing open process of mattering, where meaning and form are acquired in the actualisation of different agential virtualities.

5 Epigenetic Turn

Architecture ought to reclaim its vanguard position within the epigenetic turn which embraces technicity as constitutive of (post)humanity, and not just the other way around.[47] Experience is not an event in the mind. Rather, the mind emerges from interaction with the environment. The predominant homeostatic notion of structure in architectural thinking has to give way to the event-centred ontology of relations. The metastability of existence (formerly known as sustainability) is to be mapped in the very act of becoming. If representation is a means to an end (classification), schizoanalytic cartography is a means to a means (abduction).[48]

6 Niche Constructionism

The virtual as a proto-epistemological level of potentialisation (priming) is already ontological.[49] It concerns change in the degree to which a subject is enabled vis-à-vis its (built) environment. Their reciprocal determination commits contemporary architecture to ecology in general and ethico-aesthetics in particular. Only recently have biologists conceded the effect that niche construction has on the inheritance system.[50] They confirmed that a subject does not only passively submit to the pressures of a pre-existing environment, but also actively constructs its existential niche. The implications for the discipline of architecture, considering its quasi-causal role in the weaving of co-evolutions, remain significant and binding.

Notes

1. Stengers, 'The Challenge of Ontological Politics', 91.
2. Gibson, *The Ecological Approach to Visual Perception*, 240.
3. Deleuze, *Cours Vincennes*, 'Sur Kant: Synthesis and Time' (14 March 1978). 'Sous les pixels, la plage!' is a play on words on the famous slogan from the May 1968 protest movement in France, 'Sous les pavés, la plage!' ('Under the paving stones, the beach!'). The slogan meant that it was possible to escape a regimented life.
4. Simondon, *On the Mode of Existence of Technical Objects*.
5. In contrast to the triangle and the binary form, the 3+N entities are sufficiently unstable, opening up to the multiple (multiplicity as a critique of structuralism). See: Guattari, *Schizoanalytic Cartographies*.
6. Grosz, *The Incorporeal*, 140; emphasis in the original.
7. 'The main obstacle to the adoption of a finalist or neofinalist philosophy . . . stems from a deep-rooted prejudice, according to which the visible and tangible matter is *all the same* more real than senses, ideas, and values.' Ruyer, *Neofinalism*, 140. See also: Massumi, *99 Theses on the Revaluation of Value*.
8. Massumi, 'Immediation Unlimited', 509.
9. The coupling of two morphodynamic systems is known as a 'teleodynamic process'. See: Deacon, *Incomplete Nature*, 264–325.

10. Activity is synonymous with freedom. See: Ruyer, *Neofinalism*, 147–8: 'The notion of 'functioning' implies that there exists in the first place a static, material, or substantial structure that moves but can also remain at rest. In contrast, true action, free action, implies that no material or mental substance is posited at the origin.'

11. Deleuze and Guattari, *A Thousand Plateaus*.

12. Haraway, *Staying with the Trouble*.

13. Deleuze and Guattari, *Anti-Oedipus*, 29.

14. Heft, *Ecological Psychology in Context*.

15. The capacity to surpass the given is referred to as 'absolute survey'. See: Ruyer, *Neofinalism*.

16. Massumi, *Parables for the Virtual*, 79. See also: Simondon, *On the Mode of Existence of Technical Objects*, 242. 'Knowledge by way of intuition is a grasping of being that is neither *a priori* nor *a posteriori*, but contemporaneous with the existence of the being it grasps.'

17. Deleuze and Guattari, *A Thousand Plateaus*, 53. 'Forms relate to codes and processes of coding and decoding in the parastrata; substances, being formed matters, relate to territorialities and movements of deterritorialization and reterritorialization on the epistrata. In truth, the epistrata are just as inseparable from the movements that constitute them as the parastrata are from their processes.'

18. Guattari's 'four unconsciousnesses' – corporeal (T), subjective (U), material (F) and machinic (P) – are not exclusive to the city. They both pertain to the 'ignored realm' of the countryside, albeit differently. See: Koolhaas, 'ignored Realm', in AMO and Koolhaas, eds, *AMO/Rem Koolhaas: Countryside*, 2–3 (3). 'Currently, countryside discourse is polarized between attempts to keep "as is" and to change "everything". What we wanted to collect is *evidence of new thinking*, new ways of paying, . . . cultivating, . . . building, . . . remembering, . . . exploring, . . . acting, old ways of contemplating and being, new ways of using new media, . . . owning, relating, . . . protecting, . . . planting, . . . farming, . . . fusing, . . . harvesting, that are taking place *beyond a metropolitan consciousness*'; emphasis added.

19. Guattari, 'Les Quatres Inconscients'. Cf. Kwinter, *Far from Equilibrium*. See also: Dosse, *Gilles Deleuze and Félix Guattari*, 264.

20. Rouvroy, 'Adopt AI, Think Later: The Coué Method to the Rescue of Artificial Intelligence'.

21. If decoding were impossible (F>P), the left-hand side of the diagram would sediment to discrete quantities that could be calculated and could fit into a pre-ordered structure. Such overcoding precludes the articulation of (non-programmed) collective enunciation as a political practice. See: Zuboff, *The Age of Surveillance Capitalism*.

22. Thesis from Guattari's essay 'Architectural Enunciation', where he directly addresses

the role of the architect. See: Guattari, *Schizoanalytic Cartographies*, 231–39 (39).

23. Ibid., 39.

24. Deacon, *Incomplete Nature*.

25. Whitehead, *Process and Reality*.

26. Protevi, *Life, War, Earth: Deleuze and the Sciences*, 125–36.

27. Koolhaas, *Delirious New York*. See also: Koolhaas, 'Salvador Dali'.

28. Ibid., 155; emphasis in the original.

29. As Sanford Kwinter explains, a Chreod refers to an invisible but not imaginary feature in an invisible but not imaginary landscape on which a developing form gathers the information and influence necessary for it to make itself what it is. See: Kwinter, 'A Discourse on Method', 40–5. Cf. Waddington, *The Strategy of the Genes*, 29.

30. In the words of Kim Stanley Robinson: 'Margaret Thatcher said that "there is no such thing as society", and Ronald Reagan said that "government is not the solution to our problem; government is the problem". These stupid slogans marked the turn away from the postwar period of reconstruction and underpin much of the bullshit of the past forty years. We are individuals first, yes, just as bees are, but we exist in a larger social body. Society is not only real; it's fundamental. We can't live without it. And now we're beginning to understand that this "we" includes many other creatures and societies in our biosphere and even in ourselves. Even as an individual, you are a biome, an ecosystem, much like a forest or a swamp or a coral reef. Your skin holds inside it all kinds of unlikely coöperations, and to survive you depend on any number of interspecies operations going on within you all at once. We are societies made of societies; there are nothing but societies. This is shocking news – it demands a whole new world view.' Robinson, 'The Coronavirus Is Rewriting Our Imaginations'.

31. Žižek, *Pandemic!*, 55.

32. Hui, 'One Hundred Years of Crisis'.

33. Shaviro, *Discognition*, 216–23. See also: Bratton, '18 Lessons of Quarantine Urbanism'. Refusal to engage and embrace the intrinsically 'artificial' reality of our planetary condition, on behalf of a return to 'nature', has led to catastrophic denial and neglect.

34. Barad, *Meeting the Universe Halfway*.

35. According to Massumi, the concrete surface of architecture and the abstract surface of perception are reciprocal. In other words, the abstract and the concrete go together, processually, with the major consequence that 'This *forbids any distinction between "raw" experience and enculturated experience* [nature / nurture] – as it [forbids] any empirical distinction between the physical . . . on the one side and the cognitive on the other. Cultural factors associated with "higher" cognitive oper-

ations are already materially entering into effect . . . they are as already-abstract as they are still-bodily.' Massumi, *Architectures of the Unforeseen*, 92; emphasis in the original.

36. Stiegler, *Technics and Time, 1*.

37. Bratton, *The Terraforming*, 50.

38. Guattari, *The Three Ecologies*, 42–3.

39. Sauvagnargues, *Artmachines*.

40. For a more extensive list of concepts, see: Radman and Kousoulas, 'Twenty Theses on Ecologies of Architecture'. See also: Radman, 'Ecologies of Architecture'.

41. Braidotti, *The Posthuman*.

42. Hayles, *The Unthought*.

43. Uexküll, 'A Stroll through the Worlds of Animals and Men'. Cf. Uexküll, *Theoretical Biology*.

44. Eduardo Viveiros de Castro, 'Cosmological Deixis and Amerindian Perspectivism', 478.

45. See: Koolhaas, '?', in *AMO / Rem Koolhaas: Countryside*, 324–51 (350).

46. Hauptmann and Radman, *Asignifying Semiotics*.

47. The epigenetic turn calls for a re-examination of the status of Lamarckism. In contrast to Darwinism, Lamarckian inheritance is the idea that an organism can pass on to its offspring characteristics that it acquired during its lifetime.

48. Magnani, *Abductive Cognition*.

49. Clark, *Being-There*.

50. Odling-Smee, 'Niche Inheritance'.

Figure, Discourse:
To the Abstract Concretely

If you want the correct explanation
Why embryos grow into men
The Alsatian begets an Alsatian
A hen's egg gives rise to a hen
Why insects result from pupation
Why poppies grow out of a seed
Then just murmur 'canalization'
For that is the word that you need.

Chorus
Then three cheers for canalization
Oh, come on now, hip hip hooray
A stiff dose of canalization
Will drive all your troubles away.[1]

THE GREATEST DISCOVERY of contemporary psychology was to include the environment in the study of the psyche. Only recently have biologists considered the effect of the 'niche construction' on the inheritance system.[2] It is high time for the discipline of architecture to do the same, albeit from the opposite angle. James Jerome Gibson's contribution is indispensable in his tying of perception to potential action (degree zero of perception). His focus on the before (things are named) ranks him among the pioneers of the noosphere. Brian Massumi has cautioned against the military and right-wing monopoly over the 'soft power' of *Noo-politik* where perception is targeted not on the level at which actions are decided but on the level at which the very capacity for action is forming:

This is a point before 'knowability' and 'actability' are differentiated from one another. At that point modulation of perception is directly and immediately a change in the parameters of what a body can do . . . This antecedent level of capacitation of potentialisation is proto-epistemological and already ontological in that it concerns changes in the body's degree and mode of enablement in and towards its total situation or life environment. Any application of force at this level is an onto-power, a power through which being becomes.[3]

The first step is to acknowledge that – with or without us – matter does matter. This is what Charles Sanders Peirce refers to as 'firstness'. Then there are relations or 'secondness'. Crudely put, the dyad marks the difference between the (intrinsic) properties and (extrinsic) capacities. Finally, there is also the 'centre of indetermination' or 'thirdness' where an interval between perception and action is inserted. This is the brain. It is crucial to remember that secondness presupposes firstness and that thirdness incorporates both firstness and secondness.[4] This is to say that the first-order isomorphism and linearity inherent to the representational thought is dismissed as utterly reductionist: it is neither about the appearance of the essence, nor is it about the apparition of the sense (conditions of possibility) but about the reciprocal determination of the virtual and the actual.[5]

In *What is Philosophy?* Gilles Deleuze and Félix Guattari distinguish between three (brain) becomings: philosophy, science and art. What seems to be the essential difference between them is the direction they take with regard to becoming.[6] Science and philosophy take opposite directions. Science follows the downward stream of actualisation (dynamic genesis, differenciation), whereas philosophy chooses to go upstream as in counter-actualisation (static genesis, differentiation). Art does something completely different. It preserves the infinite in the finite. Architecture as a discipline needs to transect all three planes. Only then can we rightfully claim that the culture of hylomorphism has given way to the life-affirming creative morphogenesis.[7] If form is not to be imposed from the outside (by decree or architectural plan) but rather teased out of the potentiality of the plane (of immanence), a more humble and yet empowering disposition is required. This chapter will attempt to offer a discourse on this utterly non-discursive practice.

Architecture

In April 2009, the Harvard Graduate School of Design organised a conference on ecological urbanism where Rem Koolhaas delivered a keynote lecture.

Through a historical overview stretching from Vitruvius to the Renaissance and Enlightenment to the present day, Koolhaas identified two opposed design outlooks vis-à-vis nature – those of dominance and submission. At the midpoint of the lecture a graph depicting a downturn in the stock market 'broke the symmetry':

> What about architecture? What the crisis will mean for us is an end to this regime. For those who did not realise this is a collection of masterpieces by senior architects in the last ten years. A skyline of icons showing mercilessly that an icon can individually be plausible but collectively they form an utterly counterproductive and self-cancelling landscape. So, that is out! [The audience laughs.][8]

The message could not be clearer. No more false dialectics between 'natural' Wright and 'cultural' Mies! It won't do. Slide One – Falling Water. Slide Two – Farnsworth. Slide Three – an anonymous vernacular (*sic*) house seen through thermal vision goggles. How are we to interpret the third image? Is this yet another attempt to shift our attention from cultural form towards urban sub-stance? In an interview with Robert Venturi and Denise Scott Brown, Koolhaas notes how in their *Learning from Las Vegas* (1977) a shift from substance to sign arose precisely when he himself was trying to decipher the impact of substance on culture in what was to become *Delirious New York: A Retroactive Manifesto for Manhattan* (1978).[9] But now the wager seems to be raised, in that the clas-sical logic of taxonomy is displaced from the visible into the invisible domain. This effectively ends the linear (retroactive) causality between the content and form; in other words, drawing homologies between the (discrete) engendered and the (continuous) engendering is but a resuscitation of the representational approach. Its tautological nature simply precludes any account of emergence.[10]

The non-representational alternative requires a great leap of imagination. It requires no less than an entirely new logic which is to complement the old logic of discreteness. Thinking the continuum calls for a 'logic of sense' where 'sense' in Deleuze could be said to stand for significance (conditions of real, not merely possible experience). A whole new vocabulary needs to be invented, as well as a new set of conceptual tools. Geometry becomes indispensable. Apart from being a branch of mathematics, geometry has always been a mode of rationality. Bernard Cache argues that it should at last be taken as a cultural reference.[11] This is no trivial matter, as we rely upon a 'different rationality' where the law of the excluded middle is vehemently rejected (where Schrödinger's cat is both dead and alive).[12] The geometry which fits the purpose has been with us for over a hundred and fifty years and is called topology. Its current appeal for architects merely at the formal level is more than obvious and rather sad, as it rarely goes beyond mimesis.[13]

The new conceptual tools are legacies of esteemed rheologists – a term we may now retrospectively apply – such as Gottfried Wilhelm Leibniz (differential calculus), Carl Friedrich Gauss and his disciple Bernhard Riemann (manifold), Henri Poincaré (phase space) and Felix Klein (Erlangen Programme), to name but a few.[14] To adopt a topological approach to architecture and urbanism is to think in terms of capacities (to affect and be affected), rather than mere (intrinsic) properties. As Gregory Bateson maintained, capacity is always relational (secondness): 'It makes no sense whatsoever to try to understand the anatomy of half a chicken.'[15] By publicly denouncing the dialectic between nature and nurture (submission and dominance), Koolhaas tacitly repudiated the 'paranoid critical method' as exemplified by his famous Daliesque diagram. The amorphous blob (limp conjectures) supported by the Cartesian crutch (of rationality) from *Delirious New York* still relied on the 'retroactive reasoning' from the domain of the visible. It approached the obscure from the clear.

Koolhaas's anti-dialectical stance resonates strongly with the thesis Deleuze outlines in his book on Francis Bacon. Deleuze distances himself from both (natural) abstract expressionism and (cultural) abstraction à la Kandinsky.[16] After all, Jackson Pollock is notorious for his statement that he does not paint from nature but that he *is* nature.[17] Following the 'logic of sensation', Deleuze opts for a 'third way' through the concept of the 'Figural' (as opposed to figurative) of Francis Bacon who is 'working with sensations as material'.[18] The architect too might be said to be in the business of the 'distribution of the sensible'.[19] Certainly, these considerations call for a radical rethinking of media specificity at both the material and immaterial intersections of aesthetics and politics. It is precisely this attitude of cutting across previously held dichotomies (nature/culture, matter/thought, aesthetics/politics) that provides Bacon with the 'goggles' to access the virtual. It is arguably for the same reason that Koolhaas conspicuously aligns his current work with that of a true architectural maverick – Buckminster Fuller. Naturally, this is not the first time that the founding partner of the Office for Metropolitan Architecture (OMA) is rethinking his strategies. Another of his widely published and very influential diagrams was revamped, at least verbally, on the occasion of the 2007 Intelligent Coast conference in Barcelona. Asked to comment on the Dubai urban strategy he replied that it was about an 'ongoing developers' orgasm' of total saturation. He seems to have taken seriously Jeffrey Kipnis's criticism of the OMA Masterplan for the Urban Design Forum in Yokohama where they similarly proposed a programme that was to guarantee round-the-clock activity.[20] Such a guarantee no longer holds, as Koolhaas is well aware that, although anything is possible in the world of design, this might not be the case in the design of the world.[21] The manifold does indeed contain remarkable (singular) points, but it also includes ordinary ones. It is a matter of consistency, of holding. Any- and everything do not go.

Through its 'anexact yet rigorous' approach to the genesis of form, OMA offers an emancipating alternative to both Minimalist and Parametricist claimants to the status of contemporary architectural avant-garde. It continues to avoid the Scylla of the all-too-autonomous 'critical' white cube and the Charybdis of the all-too-complacent 'high performance' blob. Most important of all, it fosters the affective turn, which is addressed below.

Ecologies

More often than not, architecture as a discipline has sought legitimacy from without. It is high time for a genuine change of heart triggered by the realist/materialist approach of ecological perception which embraces the complementarity of people and their environment. This coupling was a life-long project of the psychologist J. J. Gibson, whose contribution to a broader radical empiricism is still underappreciated.[22] The discipline of architecture should regain self-confidence and do what it does best. When a society manipulates its matter it is not a reflection of culture – it *is* culture. Architecture is a non-discursive practice. Formed materiality (territorialisation) and its expressivity (coding) are irreducible and must not be confused with the 'specialised lines of expression', such as genes and words. Marcos Novak, who often does the wrong things ('melting all that is solid into air') for all the right reasons, precisely hits the mark with a statement implicitly related to Kant's *Critique of the Power of Judgement* (1790): 'There is meaning before language, meaning before taxonomy, meaning before discourse, . . . beauty is multi-modal formalism, is a very, very deep thing – the mind and the body are not separate and the whole thing is about not being mimetic.'[23] It is therefore possible to argue that the third *Critique* does not simply 'complete' the other two, but in fact provides them with a ground. In the words of Brian Massumi:

> Alfred North Whitehead characterized his philosophy of process as a 'critique of pure feeling'. William James, with whose thought Whitehead aligned his own, considered a notion of 'pure experience' an indispensable starting point for philosophy practiced as what he termed a radical empiricism. In both of these formulae, what the qualifier 'pure' asserts is a world of experience

prior to any possibility of apportioning reality along a subject/object divide or positioning it in preconstituted time and space coordinates. These, on the contrary, are understood as emergences from feeling. The world, for Whitehead and James, is literally made of feeling. Often misunderstood as a solipsism or anything-goes voluntarism, these approaches on the contrary see themselves as rigorous philosophies of determination, no less than of novelty of emergence and creative formation.[24]

In order to avoid parochial anthropocentrism a true realist cannot but separate ontology from epistemology. There is simply much more to the world than catches the eye (and other senses). Or – to put it even more simply – reality is in excess to the phenomenal. Content is bigger than form: 'How many fingers?' asked Gregory Bateson, raising his hand at a public lecture in anticipation of the wrong answer. 'Five', the puzzled audience readily answered. 'Wrong', Bateson replied with perverse delight. The answer is 'No', because the five fingers are but a derivative of the four bifurcations that allow for a numberless set of relations.[25] This is a standard Batesonian lesson about the inevitable tautology inherent in our predominant epistemology. We seem to be condemned to misplacing concreteness. According to Whitehead, one commits this fallacy when mistaking an abstract belief, opinion or concept about the way things are for a concrete reality. In other words, by the time we perceive Bateson's five fingers through 'presentational immediacy', 'causal efficacy' will have kicked in, passing below the threshold of consciousness (the very same consciousness that works so hard to ensure its superior role). Our bodily experience is primarily an experience of the dependence of presentational immediacy upon causal efficacy and not the other way around.[26] The 'physical world' is therefore a concept. This, of course, is as counter-intuitive as Deleuze's positing of difference before identity in his metaphysics, or Gibson's emphasis on the movement at the basis of perception. To put it bluntly, consciousness is overrated, as Katherine Hayles rightly claims:

> In the posthuman view . . . conscious agency has never been 'in control'. In fact the very illusion of control bespeaks a fundamental ignorance about the nature of the emergent processes through which consciousness, the organism, and the environment are constituted. Mastery through the exercise of autonomous will is merely the story consciousness tells itself to explain results that actually come about through chaotic dynamics and emergent structures . . . emergence replaces teleology; reflexivity replaces objectivism; distributed

cognition replaces autonomous will; embodiment replaces a body seen as a support system for the mind; and a dynamic partnership between humans and intelligent machines replaces the liberal humanist subject's manifest destiny to dominate and control nature.[27]

There is possibly one thing even more damaging to creativity – provided that we are interested in the problem of the new and not merely in bare repetition – and it is meta-consciousness. Consciousness about consciousness supplants the ontological problem of creation with the epistemological problem of foundation. Goethe knew how 'unproductive' this was, argues Jochen Hörisch in his *Theoretical Pharmacy*.[28] So did the main protagonists of *Delirious New York* who, despite their outstanding intelligence, acknowledged the necessity of keeping a distance from their own self-awareness. It is this particular attitude of the first generation of New York architects, according to Koolhaas, that allowed the aspirations of the collective to coincide effortlessly with those of a client: 'I had the idea that this was something we would never see again. That we were condemned to consciousness.'[29]

Individuation

According to Deleuze, affect is distinct from affection. Affection, such as feeling, emotion or mood, relates to the status of the body caused by the encounter. Since affection has to be enveloped by the human body, it is subject to biographical or social mediation (we do not know what meaning is being created for each individual). An affect, by contrast, is an intensity. As such, it belongs to a non-extensive non-metric and consequently non-representable realm.

Rendering palpable the intensive process deserves the three cheers from the opening poem. That is why Sanford Kwinter considers the Chreod the greatest achievement of twentieth-century thought (Figure 1.1). This neologism of Conrad Waddington's denotes the necessary path of any becoming. Of course, there is hardly anything necessary about it once we appropriate the reciprocal determination between the actual and the virtual. It is a 'figure of time'. A good illustration is Goethe's *Urpflanz*, although the term is misleading insofar as its prefix signifies an origin. The genius of Goethe lay in his ability to see the (morphogenetic) Chreod beyond the actuality of the plant. In other words, if Bateson had a chance to hold this flower in his hand and ask Goethe 'How many petals?' he would most certainly answer – 'No. It is the wrong question.'

There is a strange paradox with this new materialism which has in comparison to its opposite – idealism – turned out rather formalist as a project. But this

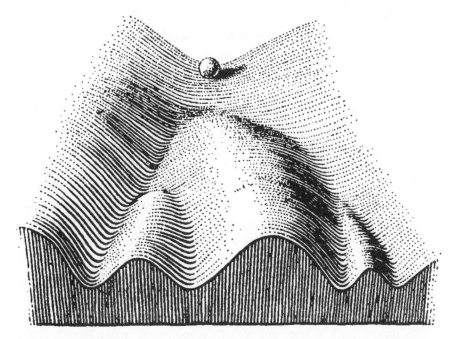

Figure 1.1 Conrad Waddington's epigenetic landscape, later to become the Chreod, a visual analogy of the stable pathways of development diagrammed as a (morphogenetic) pinball machine, with the (morphic) ball.

Source: Waddington, *The Strategy of the Genes*, 29.

is not the pejorative formalism where the process and the product are conflated. It is the 'good' formalism in the tradition of the 'greatest formalists such as Goethe and Foucault', explains Kwinter:

> The very idea that the figure . . . might enfold within it a resonant, transmissible logic of internal control, one that can be at once dissociated from its material substrate *and* maintained in communicative tension with it, was once an assertion of great contentiousness. The moment of its rigorous demonstration became one of the watersheds, not only of modern aesthetics, but of modern science and philosophy as well.[30]

The shift from the generic to genetic approach should be good news for architects, since they are good at handling form(ation). However, the radically new logic of becoming presupposes the existence of both the 'form of content' and 'form of expression'. The bad news is that there is no 'form of forms' to bridge the gap.[31] The virtual and actual need to be always thought together, as Brian Massumi rightly insists, the virtual and actual need to be always thought together. The virtual is neither an input nor an output but rather a throughput. This throughput is the fuel of individuation as proposed by Gilbert Simondon. It is an intensive horizontal process that unfolds the 'universal singular' into the actual (individual singular), in contrast to the vertical axis of the general/ particular. However, one needs to avoid the nominalist trap of claiming that only the particular exists. The real battlefield is at the level of a 'difference that makes a difference', to cite Bateson once again. This is the level of a problem, a genuine reservoir of potentiality (pure difference) of 'static genesis' with a temporal form of *aiōn*.[32] In contrast, to operate exclusively at the level of 'dynamic genesis' – the unfolding of *chronos* – is futile. This is perhaps why Walter Benjamin considered both art deco (aestheticisation of technology) and futurism (technologisation of aesthetics) failures.[33] The criticism equally applies to the data fetishism of today, which is also fixated on actuality (presentational immediacy). It also explains why Deleuze, as previously mentioned, questions both the (too slow) 'code' of Kandinsky and the (too rapid) 'chaos' of Pollock. Bacon's work offers an alternative. It is seen as diagrammatic in the true Foucauldian sense: it does not render *the* visible, but it renders visible, as Paul Klee would have it. Phenomenology with its maxim 'back to phenomena' will obviously not suffice here. It is for this very reason that Deleuze is keen to appropriate the term expressionism. As Steven Shaviro explains: 'phenomena are generated out of the encounter between subject and object in Kant – but if one is willing to let rocks, stones, armies, and Exxon join in the fun of being excluded from the in-itself, then we can say that phenomena are positively generated out of *all* encounters between objects'.[34] Phenomenology remains human, all too human, and therefore – in spite (or perhaps because) of its anthropocentrism – ultimately anti-human and even suicidal, as Claire Colebrook argued.[35] The Spinozian principle of a *conatus* is narrow in its disregard for the long-term (ecological) consequence of striving for self-preservation.[36] For phenomenology (Husserl), consciousness is always *of* something, whereas for Deleuze qua Bergson it *is* something. Correlationism of how I as a subject perceive that object over there is to be met with the same rigour of Batesonian scepticism.

With the thesis of univocity, Deleuze finally dispels all dualisms: 'being is said of all things in the same sense'. The question is how to think relation that is exterior to its terms (thirdness). This could not be done from the so-called third space of 'lived experience', which was alleged to counteract instrumental rationality and the consequent mathematisation of life. The postmodern potion of Dionysus's passion to complement the modernist Apollo's cool did not work either. All these attempts never left the realm of Bateson's five fingers. The strategy of defamiliarisation (including the discourse on the sublime) also reached its limits.[37] It was promising in the attempt to circumvent straightforward re-cognition (are they five fingers or something else?), but it failed to meet the requirement of the second part of Bateson's answer, namely, engendering an alternative (space for) life. Sadly, it remained at the level of indulging in object fetishisation. In contrast, Kwinter's 'radical anamnesis' requires remembering not the past that has happened but the past that has not happened although it might have.[38] This marks a cardinal difference between the mere possible (always retroactive hypostatisation) and the reservoir of pure potentiality of the (ideal yet real) virtual.

Superior Empiricism

Even materialism needs to eventually come to terms with the 'spiritual'. Deleuze's answer is neither *transcendental* empiricism nor transcendental *empiricism* but *transcendental empiricism*. The formation and form, the emerging and the emerged, pertain to two modes of a single reality. Everything starts from the sensible but is subsequently extended into the intelligible. This is what Deleuze means by a 'pedagogy of the senses'. The convergence of thought and matter is diagrammed in *The Fold* as two floors of a baroque house. It is important to stress yet again that there is no structural homology between the two floors: the horizontal common rooms with 'several small openings' (the five senses) and the vertical closed private room decorated with a 'drapery diversified by folds'.[39] To borrow Daniel Dennett's powerful metaphor, there is no homunculus sitting in the Cartesian theatre (where all the evidence is gathered). The form of expression and the form of content do not share a form. There is no meta-form. There is only folding and unfolding of progressive different/ciation. What connects the two is a process.

Deleuze's main adversary in this respect is not Plato but the great systemiser Aristotle, who 'operates' between the general and the particular on the basis of resemblance, that is, representation.[40] But for Deleuze there is more resemblance between a racehorse and a racing car than between a racehorse and a plough horse.[41] Universality does not explain anything; it itself requires an explanation. In the 'flat ontology', genera are as contingent as the particular species. There is no logical relationship between the 'individual singular' of the five fingers and the 'universal singular' or the manifold (pinball machine) that engenders them.

The Aristotelian syllogism, which has not lost a scintilla of its prestige over the past two millennia, is still indispensable for discrete (binary) logic. So is Euclidean mathematics for metric space, as well as Newtonian physics for isotropic space. But when it comes to the logic of continuity it was Leibniz who provided the much-needed conceptual tools. More recently, Deleuze recognised the creative potential of science in general, and differential calculus in particular, to deal with becoming. The three-hundred-year-old mathematical convention allowed for the treatment of relations independently of their terms. The emphasis shifted from signification to significance or to the distribution of singularities structuring the manifold. The clear emerges from the obscure. The five fingers emerge from a topological body plan, the very same plan that unfolds into a flipper or a wing.[42]

The long-lasting legacy of privileging *epistēmē* over *technē* needs to be rethought, as Bernard Stiegler repeatedly advocates. The Second Law of Thermodynamics is to the sciences what Shakespeare is to the humanities. It is most unfortunate that the self-appointed guardians of disciplinary boundaries are working hard to keep the realms separate. It is equally damaging to privilege linguistic theories on account of their academic prestige, given the limitations of the representational approach. The humanities are bankrupt when it comes to dynamic far-from-equilibrium systems. They cannot but commit the fallacy of 'tracing' – conflating the process with the product. If we carry on merely relying on the 'agency of mapping' we will continue to see Bateson's five fingers.[43] Thinking needs to go in the opposite direction (counter-actualisation) towards the virtual and 'mapping of agency'.

Old habits die hard. For that reason, the best way to approach (visual) perception is through non-visual senses. Charles Sanders Peirce proposes a thought experiment: a pitch-black cave with no gravity where one relies upon one's own proprioception (joint sense), sense of smell and temperature sensing.[44] Note that these senses only operate locally through an interval of change with no reference to extrinsic space. Through navigation, one starts to distinguish zones in the gradient field and their thresholds (there are no clear-cut boundaries). Eventually one is able to identify invariants as the three series start to relate (proprioception, smell and temperature). Gradually we witness the concrescence of extensive and therefore mappable space which is born out of topological, intensive space of sensation. Smooth space has turned into striated. Massumi stresses that the striated Euclidean geometry in no way contradicts the topological one. They are enfolded. The nesting of geometries according to their respective resilience to transformation or level of generality (Euclidean > projective > affine > topology) is explained by Manuel DeLanda in *Intensive Science and Virtual Philosophy.*[45] This is an important point often overlooked by eager proponents of the topological turn in architecture. What is truly remarkable is that the order of movement and space is reversed. Points in space do not pre-exist their connection. The logic of sensation leads to the logic of relation. Movement does not happen in space. Rather, space is a derivative of movement.

Brian Massumi emphasises the stark contrast between Peirce's cave and the most famous cave parable – that of Plato. Curiously enough, in Plato's version the beholders are immobilised by chains and therefore compelled to rely exclusively on their vision, wondering whether (mediated) appearances might be but illusions. In the Peircean version there is no room for doubt, since everything results from one's unmediated interaction (contemplative vs participative space). In the short essay 'Factory', Vilém Flusser makes a similar assertion: '*homo faber* becomes *homo sapiens sapiens* because he has realised that manufacturing means the same thing as learning – i.e. acquiring, producing and passing on information'.[46]

Stillness of the beholder is the *sine qua non* of most optical illusions. This is not a minor issue. There is a long-standing dispute between two great experts in the field of visual culture which mirrors the cave parable: that of J. J. Gibson and Ernst Gombrich.[47] For Gibson it is evident that pictorial representation is a contingent (chronologically late) discovery. To put it bluntly: (3D) space comes first, (2D) images follow. In contrast, Gombrich believes that pictorial representation mirrors the representational architecture of the mind. He thus spends a substantial part of his career trying to account for depth in the pictorial surface (3D out of 2D). In Gibson's sensorimotor (kinaesthetic and synaesthetic) understanding of perception 'the problem of depth' does not arise at all. According to him we do not see images anyway! One needs to bear in mind that the geometry of information must be kept independent from the geometry of the receptor surface (retina in the case of visual perception). Only then will we not succumb to the first-order isomorphism fallacy of equating optics with perception. This is what ecological perception is about.

Stradivarius Syndrome

Pictorial representation is an extension of the elaboration of perception, and not the other way around. Action and perception form a continuum of experience. This is especially pertinent to architecture, given that its basic medium is *ipso facto* the 'field of experience' rather than geometry, CAD, design, critique or any formalisable field.[48] Implications for the discipline are enormous and still highly unappreciated, as we are just beginning to feel the loosening of the linguistic grip. Ironically, even the social sciences have been more eager to turn towards the realist and materialist paradigm. If shaking off the 'linguisticality of experience' and losing the scare quotes around the word real was difficult enough, tackling the nature of (graphic) representation will prove even more difficult. This means that the current reliance on mapping could be fatally over-stated. Gilbert Ryle distinguishes between propositional (symbolic and discrete) knowledge of *that* and (performative and continuous) knowledge of *how*.[49] One cannot learn to swim by reading a manual. It requires entering into a relation with water and trying out different ways of propulsion through one's own idio-syncratic bodily movement and eventually acquiring a unique style. Where does this leave us with the discoveries of Kevin Lynch's 'cognitive mapping'?[50] The fact that my wife cannot map a city has no bearing on her capacity to navigate it more effectively than a 'trained professional' such as myself. You walk the walk or talk the talk, you do not talk the walk. The sentiment is best reflected by Reyner Banham: 'So, like earlier generations of English intellectuals who taught themselves Italian in order to read Dante in the original, I learned to drive in order to read Los Angeles in the original.'[51]

In his book *The Craftsman* Richard Sennett blames the famous violin-maker Antonio Stradivari for failing to transmit knowledge to his disciples. Again, the problem lies in the failure to distinguish between the encyclopaedic factual (propositional) and the knowing-how-to-make-a-violin knowledge.[52] Curiously, there is a similar naïveté among a substantial part of the artificial intelligence (AI) community, who refuse to reject the 'input-output' view of cognition in favour of the embodied, embedded, extended, enactive and affective (4EA) approach to the mind.[53] The same cleavage seems to be at the core of Danny Boyle's *Slumdog Millionnaire* from 2008, where the main protagonist unexpect-edly wins a popular quiz-show by knowing *how* rather than knowing *that* (the answer is a, b, c or d).

We have long witnessed the most unlikely alliance between Cartesians and cybernetics. Katherine Hayles blames it on a pathological fear of death (soul as software lives on). Hubert Dreyfus argues in his polemic with Marvin Minsky that if the AI community had ever read Maurice Merleau-Ponty they would not have wasted as much time on the disembodied (symbolic) approach. In the sub-sequent reprint, his masterpiece *What Computers Can't Do* was renamed *What Computers Still Can't Do*.[54] According to Dreyfus the fallacy rests on both episte-mological and ontological assumptions. The epistemological assumption is that all activity (by animate or inanimate objects) can be formalised (mathematically) in the form of predictive rules or laws. The ontological assumption is that reality consists entirely of a set of mutually independent atomic (indivisible) facts. It is because of the epistemological assumption that experts in the (symbolic) AI field argue that intelligence is the same as formal rule-following. The ontological assumption leads them to argue that human knowledge consists entirely of internal representations of reality. Sadly, placing images in consciousness and movement in space happens to be the predominant modus operandi of the architectural community. We have yet to distinguish between hodological and Euclidean space. Luckily, at least for the cognitive sciences, symbolic computing is gradually being superseded by the more promising connectionist approach where training (and thus embodiment) plays a major role.[55]

There is an uncanny resemblance between the two public disputes: Gibson vs Gombrich and Dreyfus vs Minsky. Strictly speaking, they are not disputes at all. They are perfect illustrations of Thomas Kuhn's paradigm shift, where the proponents operate in different contrast spaces with a different logic, as in the example provided by DeLanda:

Priest: Why did you rob the bank?
Prisoner: There was more money there than in a post office.[56]

The true ambition is always measured at the level of the (virtual) problem rather than the (actual) solution. Already in the seminal *Difference and Repetition* Deleuze posited that problems/ideas were extra-propositional and sub-representative. It is plausible that Whitehead is the *éminence grise* of Deleuze's *Fold*. His replacement of the subject by the superject (as well as prehension for relational understanding) resonates with Hume's theory of subjectification. Hume sees the subject as coagulation (Whitehead's concrescence, Peircean thirdness, Deleuzian folding) in the field of sensation.[57] He foregrounds habitual association as the basic (sensorimotor) mechanism. Perceiving is neither pre-senting nor representing, but enacting perceptual content. This is how mind is brought to nature. Memory is seen as the low-intensity replica of raw sensation. Henri Bergson agrees that memory is content retrievable, as opposed to the communicational model where data is address retrievable. This is the major obstacle of symbolic computing. Take googling, where both textual and graphic content is retrievable only through the address. Try to find an image you have seen earlier. This is impossible unless you remember the name. The signifier is of course arbitrary. DeLanda wittingly proposes that you either believe that the Inuit people distinguish between twenty-nine kinds of snow because they have twenty-nine different names for it ('linguisticos') or that the synonyms have started to accumulate because local conditions require that the population interact with the snow on a daily basis (materialists). Surely, there was a world long before the word. Environment is always seen as meaningful. We cannot put the cart before the horse. The relationship between stimulus information and the environment is therefore natural (motivated) rather than arbitrary.

When René Magritte writes 'This is Not a Pipe' in the caption below the image of a pipe he is hinting at the peculiar nature of representation. In the same vein, Robin Evans reminds architects that they do not make buildings but drawings for buildings.[58] Lars Spuybroek is thoughtful in stressing the arbitrariness of the convention of architectural representation (horizontal programme vs vertical appearance) and the need to get to grips with the continuum of experience.[59] Action and perception are inseparable. Curiously, he is less attentive to the difference (in kind) between the actual experience of space and the virtual space of experience. As Bernard Cache cautioned in the seminal 'Plea for Euclid', not a single architect seemed to realise that the Mobius house had already been built back in the seventies, albeit in Euclidean geometry. He meant Centre Pompidou by Richard Rogers and Renzo Piano.[60] To presume that the non-metric topological geometry of experience needs to be maintained in (striated) actuality at any cost is a common misunderstanding of the contemporary 'avant-garde'. What is forgotten is that there is no structural homology between the realms of the sensible and intelligible. In other words, Magritte would need the caption 'This is Not a House' not only below the image of a house but also in front of an erected (actualised) house, as it were. We do not yet know what a house (body) can do, to paraphrase Spinoza.[61] It is certainly impossible to make any judgement on the basis of its geometry, just as we could not study the anatomy of half a chicken in any meaningful way. Things themselves are bearers of ideal events that do not always coincide with their properties. The leeway was already identified by the ancient Stoics: it's not where the form stops (outline) but rather where the action stops (affect). Lars Spuybroek is therefore as wrong about the stupidity of the straight line as Le Corbusier was about the stupidity of the curved line, which he notoriously took as the sheer index of a donkey's movement.[62] This is especially pertinent as it occurs at the opposite pole from that of *concentration*. To quote Walter Benjamin from 'The Work of Art in the Age of Mechanical Reproduction' (1935): 'Architecture has always represented the prototype of a work of art the reception of which is consummated by a collectivity in a state of *distraction*.'[63] However disadvantageous this may seem for the architectural profession, it will not prove to be the case once we fully grasp the affective turn and its implications for architecture. Quite the contrary, it might turn out to be the royal road to the understanding of space.

Ex Uno Plura

According to Dennett, 'If you make yourself really small you can exteriorise everything.'[64] This monadic attitude has been gradually superseded by the nomadic, as the advanced fields of neuro- and cognitive science recognise the porosity and contingency of the boundary between the inside and the outside (that is, in Evan Thompson, Andy Clark and Alva Nöe). However, one should not dismiss the importance of autonomy at certain levels, and not just for practical purposes. This is why Deleuzian deterritorialisations are always followed by reterritorialisations, or why they ought to be. It is just as much about the striated as it is about the smooth (yet another lesson disregarded by the so-called avant-garde). It may well be that the rhetoric of 'We Build Our Cities and in Return They Build Us' is to be taken literally.[65]

Humans operate in a very restricted portion of reality.[66] Technology, in the broad sense of the term, including epigenetics and its sedimentation, epiphylogenetics (buildings), expands the realm of sensibility.[67] It acts as scaffolding, as Andy Clark argues. This is also known as Baldwinian Evolution or evolution by other (epigenetic) means.[68] Coping with the world – thanks to the co-evolution of the environment and the animal (human) – is quite effortless. We do not need any representational schema in order to assess the opportunities and risks that the environment offers or provides. One does not see the shape first, re-cognise its (necessary and sufficient) properties for belonging to the category with the essence of 'chairness' before one eventually decides to use it for sitting. What one sees, according to Gibson, is the (proto-epistemological) affordance, that is, the 'sit-on-ability' as an event. It is indeed possible to turn neo-Kantian in rare cases of brain damage, as reported by Merleau-Ponty (the Schneider example), and one then has to go through all the rational steps (this is my arm, I am now going to raise it . . .).[69]

Human beings have the marvellous capacity to zero in on the matter of concern precisely because they do not need to calculate or represent anything. Ego-logy gives way to eco-logy at a meso scale that is commensurate with life. This approach is as opposed to the 'ghost in the machine' as it is to neuro-reductionism. To try to capture the whole of 4EA experience through the late (in terms of evolution) graft of linguistic theories or the more current input/output processing is certainly appealing (in terms of formalisation) but wrong because there is simply no structural homology between the analogue and digital. Zeno's paradox still haunts us. This is not unrelated to Moravec's paradox: it is comparatively easy to make computers exhibit adult-level performance on intelligence tests or a game of checkers. However, it is difficult or impossible to give them the perception and mobility skills of a 1-year-old.[70]

Gibson's second important concept is that of the extraction of 'formless invariants' in perception (over time!). The key is to trace permanence in the face of change (of position or perspective or both). Topology is helpful yet again in addressing a second (or higher) degree order of abstraction: how the change changes. This is closely related to his insight into occlusion, that is to say, accretion and deletion in the visual field. At any rate, clear-from-the-obscure seems to be the recurrent pattern of *mathēsis universalis*. Clear and stable actuality is emerging from the field of potentiality – the virtual. The maxim *E Pluribus Unum* (out of many – one), whereby imperfect reincarnations all stem from a single perfect essence, needs to give way.[71] Multiplicity provides for a radically new relationship between one and many, with no primacy of either. What we have is one world with two modes of reality: the actual and the virtual in constant chiasmic eventful interaction.

Notes

This essay first appeared in *Cognitive Architecture: From Bio-politics to Noo-politics*, edited by Deborah Hauptmann and Warren Neidich (Rotterdam: 010 Publishers, 2010), 430–51. It was subsequently reprinted with permission in *Deleuze and Guattari on Architecture (Critical Assessments in Architecture, Volume II)*, edited by Graham Livesey (London: Routledge, 2015), 317–39.

1. The song 'Magic Words', sung to the tune of 'Mush Mushalorum' by Conrad Weddington's colleagues on the occasion of his fiftieth birthday. Published in the obituary and subsequently reprinted in the biography by Alan Robertson, *Conrad Hal Waddington*, 583.

2. Odling-Smee, 'Niche Inheritance'. The epigenetic turn calls for a re-examination of the status of Lamarckism. In contrast to Darwinism, Lamarckian inheritance is the idea that an organism can pass on to its offspring characteristics that it acquired during its lifetime.

3. Brian Massumi has argued that the US Defence Advanced Research Projects Agency (DARPA) is aware of this. These effects are not to be confused with subliminal influence but taken as existential operations creating pragmatic fields of potential action and thought that modulate without directly causing the outcome. Massumi, 'Perception Attack'.

4. Peirce, *Philosophical Writings of Peirce*, 74–97. Deleuze bases his 'movement-image analysis' on Peirce's semiotics. See: Deleuze, *Cinema 1*. However, in the subsequent volume on the 'time-image' Deleuze dispenses with the sensorimotor schema. See: Deleuze, *Cinema 2*.

5. Deleuze, *Nietzsche and Philosophy*, 3.

6. Deleuze and Guattari, *What is Philosophy?*, 155–6.

7. Hylomorphism is a compound word composed of the Greek terms for matter (*hylē*) and form or shape (*morphē*). It was the central doctrine of Aristotle's philosophy of

nature, denoting a model of the genesis of form as external to matter, as imposed from the outside on an inert material. In contrast, the Stoics' *spermatikos logos* (immanent principle of organisation) requires a different, experimental attitude of partnership with matter. There simply are no methodologies to follow. It is therefore puzzling to find the following as the concluding lines of an otherwise outstanding book: 'As Deleuze understands it, living contemplation proceeds at an immeasurable distance from what is merely lived, known or decided. Life lives and creation creates on a virtual plane that leads forever out of our actual world.' So far so good, but then Hallward concludes: 'Few philosophers have been as inspiring as Deleuze. But those of us who still seek to change our world and to empower its inhabitants will need to look for our inspiration elsewhere.' See: Hallward, *Out of This World*, 164.

8. Ecological Urbanism: Alternative and Sustainable Cities of the Future conference. The conference, held on 3–5 April 2009, brought together design practitioners, students and theorists, economists, engineers, environmental scientists, politicians and public health specialists with the goal of reaching a more robust understanding of ecological urbanism and what it might be in the future; <http://ecologicalurbanism.gsd.harvard.edu> (accessed 15 October 2018).

9. 'I sensed in your book a pair of architects who, in spite of their love of architecture, were horribly fascinated by its opposite – while I was becoming fascinated by architecture, coming from its opposite.' See: Rem Koolhaas and Hans Ulrich Obrist, interview with Robert Venturi and Denise Scott Brown, 'Re-Learning from Las Vegas', 150.

10. Foucault employs 'archaeology' to demonstrate how scientific knowledge is dependent on the prevailing epistemes of a culture at particular moments in time. Foucault, *The Order of Things*.

11. Peter Macapia's 'Interview with Bernard Cache', where Cache and Macapia discuss several conceptual changes in the contemporary use of geometry in the field of architecture.

12. A term taken from Scott Lash's book of the same title, *Another Modernity*.

13. The same concern is expressed by Kwinter in 'A Discourse on Method', 46.

14. Rheology is the study of the deformation and flow of matter. The term – inspired by Heraclitus's famous expression *panta rhei*, 'everything flows' – was coined by Eugene Bingham, a professor at Lehigh University in 1920.

15. In his contribution to *Questions of Taste*, Barry Smith in fact upholds Gregory Bateson's view of the properties of opium: it does not contain a 'dormitive principle'. It is the entering into a differential relation of the two series (organism and substance) that produces an effect. See: Smith, 'Objectivity of Taste'.

16. Deleuze, *Francis Bacon*, 73–7.

17. As quoted by Lee Krasner in an 'Interview with Dorothy Strickler'. In Krasner's words, 'When I brought Hofmann up to meet Pollock and see his work which was before we moved here, Hofmann's reaction was – one of the questions he asked Jackson was, do you work from nature? There were no still lives around or models around and Jackson's answer was, "I am nature" And Hofmann's reply was, "Ah, but if you work by heart, you will repeat yourself." To which Jackson did not reply at all.' The meeting between Pollock and Hofmann took place in 1942.

18. In his first major philosophical work, *Discourse, Figure* (1971), Lyotard distinguished between the meaningfulness of linguistic signs and the meaningfulness of plastic arts. He argued that, because rational thought or judgement is discursive and works of art are not, certain aspects of artistic meaning require a different treatment. Gilles Deleuze was highly influenced by Lyotard's criticism of the adequacy of both structuralism and phenomenology, which led him to opt for a kind of expressionism. Similar concerns are anticipated by the American philosopher of art Susanne K. Langer, best exemplified by her *Feeling and Form*.

19. 'The distribution of the sensible' is a reference to the subtitle of a book by Jacques Rancière, who reassesses the centrality of aesthetics to politics. See: Rancière, *The Politics of Aesthetics*.

20. It is rather ironic that Kipnis, who is versed in dynamic systems theory, would not demonstrate the same scrutiny when in 2002 he curated the 'Mood River' exhibition 'examining the impact of design on contemporary life' at the Wexner Center for the Arts in Columbus, Ohio. This aesthetically pleasing show was the perfect example of what Deleuze would condemn as the fallacy of 'tracing' (bad formalism of conflating the form with the formation).

21. The maxim is borrowed from the subtitle of the book by Bruce Mau and the Institute Without Boundaries, *Massive Change: It's Not about the World of Design. It's about the Design of the World.*

22. His major work is *The Ecological Approach to Visual Perception*.

23. Novak even uses the term 'beauty', which has virtually been banned from architectural discourse. See: Novak, 'Alloaesthetics and Neuroaesthetics'.

24. Massumi, 'The Critique of Pure Feeling'.

25. Bateson, 'Lecture on Epistemology'.

26. Whitehead, *Process and Reality*.

27. Hayles, *How We Became Posthuman*, 288.

28. The ontological problem of *creation* was thus superseded by the epistemological problem of *foundation*. See: Hörisch, *Theorie-Apotheke*, 201.

29. Bouman and Van Toorn, *The Invisible in Architecture*, 442–53.

30. Kwinter, 'Who's Afraid of Formalism?'.

31. This intricate interdependence has been the fulcrum of my own architectural prac-

tice in partnership with Igor Vrbanek, <https://radurb.blogspot.com> (accessed 5 April 2020).

32. Considered in the mutual immanence of the differential relations that compose it, structure is *static*, indifferent to the measurable space-time and the discrete magnitudes that characterise individuated actuality.

33. Buck-Morss, *The Dialectics of Seeing*, 144–5.

34. See: Shaviro, 'Object-Oriented Philosophy'. See also: Shaviro's book that furthers this research, *Without Criteria*.

35. Keynote lecture by Claire Colebrook at the 7th European Feminist Research Conference (Utrecht, 4–7 June 2009): Gendered Cultures at the Crossroads of Imagination, Knowledge and Politics. Under the title 'Sexuality and the Politics of Vitalism' Colebrook declared a shift in knowledge paradigms away from linguistic, intellectual and cognitive approaches to experience accompanied by turn to embodiment, affect, vitality and the dynamism of knowledge. According to Colebrook, many of these vitalist appeals to corporeal and transhuman life, for all their claims to radicalism and posthumanism, harbour highly normative masculinist, organicist and Western presuppositions regarding proper life. By examining the ways in which the crisis of our imagined future has enabled a return to life, she put forward the case for a counter-vitalism that is also anti-organicist.

36. In his essay 'Atmospheric Politics' Peter Sloterdijk recalls the term 'environment', which was first used by the biologist Jakob von Uexküll exactly a hundred years ago (*Umwelt und Innenwelt der Tiere*), as one of the most significant discoveries of the twentieth century which would influence the development of *ecology*. The military was once again quick to tap into the latest discovery of the inextricable tie between the organism and its environment, albeit in a sinister way – new WWI chemical warfare targeted the environment instead of the soldiers, thus revolutionising killings which happened in a mediated way and no longer by direct action on the body. One should therefore extend the notion of *corporeality* in a threefold way, as Arie Graafland proposes in 'Looking into the Folds', 157. 'The territorial body of the planet and ecology, the social body or socius, and our human body.'

37. The term 'defamiliarisation/ostranenie' was coined by the Russian formalist Victor Shklovsky, 'Art as Technique' (1917): 'The purpose of art is to impart the sensation of things as they are perceived and not as they are known. The technique of art is to make objects "unfamiliar", to make forms difficult, to increase the difficulty and length of perception because the process of perception is an aesthetic end in itself and must be prolonged. *Art is a way of experiencing the artfulness of an object; the object is not important.*' Ibid., 12.

38. Kwinter, *Far from Equilibrium*. In the essay that is the key to the book, the 1996 'Radical Anamnesis', Kwinter concludes, 'Through (selective) memory the future

becomes possible, a future that the past could not think and that the present – alone – dares not.' Ibid., 142.

39. Deleuze, *The Fold*, 5.

40. Deleuze's 'battle with the Hegelian power of re-cognition and the negative, culminating in self-awareness as absolute knowledge' is explained by Patrick Healy in *The Model and Its Architecture*, 84.

41. Deleuze writes in *Spinoza, Practical Philosophy*: 'You will not define a body (or a mind) by its form, nor by its organs or functions [but by its] capacity for affecting or being affected. . . . For example: there are greater differences between a plow horse . . . and a racehorse than between an ox and a plow horse. This is because the racehorse and the plow horse do not have the same affects nor the same capacity for being affected; the plow horse has affects in common rather with the ox.' Ibid., 124.

42. The basic idea is that of a common source of form, a 'body plan' which, through different foldings and stretchings during embryological development, is capable of generating a wide variety of specific forms. See: DeLanda, 'Uniformity and Variability'.

43. Corner, 'The Agency of Mapping'.

44. Peirce, *Reasoning and the Logic of Things*, brought to my attention by Brian Massumi's superb interpretation, 'The Virtual', at the Experimental Digital Arts lecture (EDA, 2000).

45. DeLanda, *Intensive Science and Virtual Philosophy*, 18.

46. Flusser, *The Shape of Things*, 50.

47. The 'Gombrich/Gibson Dispute' (on picture perception) is accessible from the Gombrich Archive. To my mind it is every bit as current as when it started in 1971.

48. The 'field of experience' thesis was put forward by Brian Massumi, 'The Diagram as Technique of Existence', 42–7.

49. Ryle, *The Concept of Mind*, 25–61. The introduction to the 2000 edition was written by Ryle's student Dan Dennett.

50. Strong ocularcentric reduction of experience is evident in the very title: Lynch, *The Image of the City*.

51. Banham, *Los Angeles*, 5.

52. Sennett, *The Craftsman*, 75–9.

53. The key is to expand the explanatory framework. For more information on ways of thinking about cognition that depart from standard cognitivist models, see John Protevi's '4EA' blog.

54. Dreyfus, *What Computers Can't Do* (1972); *What Computers Still Can't Do* (1992). Nöe's book which reiterates some of Dreyfus's basic arguments could be seen as a natural sequence (What Computers Will Never Do?): Nöe, *Out of Our Heads*.

55. The term hodological space is derived from the Greek word *hodos*, path, way. In

contrast to the mathematical concept of space as presented on maps, plans and so on, hodological space is based on the factual topological, physical, social and psychological conditions a person is faced with on the way. Connectionism is a set of approaches in the fields of artificial intelligence, cognitive psychology, cognitive science, neuroscience and philosophy of mind, that models mental or behavioural phenomena as the emergent processes of interconnected networks of simple units.

56. DeLanda, *Intensive Science and Virtual Philosophy*, 129–30. In this regard compare the contrasting analyses of fragmentation vs unity of Mies's Barcelona Pavilion (1929) by Hays and Evans respectively. Hays, 'Critical Architecture'; Evans, 'Mies van der Rohe's Paradoxical Symmetries', in *Translations from Drawing to Building*.

57. The subject emerges from the world, the world does not emerge from the subject. The American pragmatist William James insisted that we are sad because we cry and that we are scared because we run and not the other way around. His major work is James, *The Principles of Psychology*, Vol. 1 and 2.

58. In his essay from 1986, *Translations from Drawing to Building*, 154, Robin Evans writes: 'Before embarking on the investigation of drawing's role in architecture, a few more words might be spent on language; more particularly, on the common antilogy that would have architecture be like language but also independent of it. All things with conceptual dimension are like language, as all grey things are like elephants.'

59. Spuybroek, *The Architecture of Continuity*, 78.

60. Cache, 'Plea for Euclid', 40.

61. See: Doucet and Cupers, eds, *Footprint*, issue 4, dedicated to *Agency in Architecture*. In his contribution, Scott Lash expresses his concern about the teleological over-tone of the notion of agency. The 'problem of agency' in Foucault is tackled by Nealon, *Foucault beyond Foucault*, 101–2: 'In Foucault's work there's quite literally nothing but agency. There are in fact many more forms of "agency" than there are "agents". Sexuality, surveillance resistance: these things are verbs or deployments of force, or at least that's what they are before they become attached to nouns, subjects, or states of being.'

62. Both statements figure as unfortunate cases of the mode of representational think-ing. Fortunately, Le Corbusier was never as consistent as Lars Spuybroek. Brian Massumi's advocating of the 'topological architecture . . . as in a way of continuing its process in its product' in his otherwise indispensable *Parables for the Virtual* proves that the very proponents of the new materialism sometimes fail to live up to their own standards. Sadly, he commits the 'fallacy of misplaced concreteness' after 190 pages of pure 'critique of pure feeling'.

63. Benjamin, 'The Work of Art in the Age of Mechanical Reproduction', 245–55; emphasis added.

64. For Dennett's account on the inadequacy of the predominant impoverished theories of experience, such as phenomenology, see: Dennett, *Consciousness Explained*.

65. A socialist realist slogan also attributed to Churchill. On (re)territorialisation, see: Grosz, *Chaos, Territory, Art*: 'Territory is produced, made possible, when something, some property or quality, can be detached from its place within a regime of natural selection and made to have a life of its own, to resonate, just for itself. Territory is artistic, the consequence of love not war, of seduction not defence, of sexual selection not natural selection.' Ibid., 69.

66. $1/(3 \times 10^{35})$ is the (very very small) fraction of the electromagnetic spectrum that we detect and call 'reality'. From: Hughes, *Sensory Exotica*.

67. Stiegler, *Technics and Time, 1*, 134–79.

68. Wolfe, 'De-Ontologizing the Brain'.

69. Merleau-Ponty centres his critique on the pathological case of Schneider, a German soldier wounded in WWI. Schneider was able to perform 'concrete movements' (e.g. lighting a lamp) but not 'abstract' movements (e.g. extending his arm parallel to the floor) without watching his limbs; he could not describe the position of his limbs when they were stationary, etc. See: Merleau-Ponty, *Phenomenology of Perception*, 130, 181.

70. The principle was articulated by Hans Moravec, Rodney Brooks, Marvin Minsky et al. in the 1980s.

71. According to the media theorist Roy Ascott, 'during the 20th century there was much ado about *e pluribus unum*, out of many, one: a unified culture, unified self, unified thought, unity of time and space. Now at the start of the 3rd millennium, it could be the reverse.' He is advocating the syncretic approach of bringing together disparate entities – material and non-material – and their philosophic, religious and cultural customs and codes. See: Ascott, 'Syncretic Strategies'.

2   Architecture's Awaking from
     Correlationist Slumber:
     On Transdisciplinarity and
     Disciplinary Specificity

PoMo Relativism

SLAVOJ ŽIŽEK'S DIAGNOSIS of the struggle for intellectual hegemony between postmodern cultural studies and the cognitivist popularisers of 'hard' sciences is still relevant, a decade on.[1] The so-called third culture covers a vast range of theories: from evolutionary theory to quantum physics and cosmology, the cognitive sciences, neurology, chaos and complexity theories, studies of the cognitive and general social impact of the digitalisation of everyday life, to auto-poetic systems.[2] The theorists and scientists involved have been endeavouring to develop a universal formal notion of self-organising emergent systems. These systems apply to 'natural' living organisms and species, as well as social 'organisms' such as markets and other large groups of interacting social agents.[3] On the other hand, there are cultural theorists whose pseudo-radical stance against power or hegemonic discourse effectively involves the gradual disappearance of direct and actual political engagements outside the narrow confines of academia, as well as the increasing self-enclosure in an elitist jargon that precludes the very possibility of functioning as an intellectual engaged in public debates. So, the choice, according to Žižek, comes down to either dealing with a too rapid or metaphoric transposition of certain biological-evolutionist concepts to the study of the history of human civilisation, or – in the case of cultural studies – sharing the stance of cognitive suspension, characteristic of postmodern relativism. But, as Žižek concludes, 'prohibited' ontological issues seem to have returned (with a vengeance) in the former case. In clear contrast to the strict prohibition against direct ontological issues in cultural studies, the proponents of the third culture unabashedly approach the most fundamental pre-Kantian metaphysical issues, such as the ultimate constituents of reality, time, space, the origins and the end of universe, what consciousness is, how life emerged and so on.

PoPoMo Correlationism

The struggle has been rekindled with the speculative turn triggered by Quentin Meillassoux's *After Finitude* (2008).[4] It is also worth pointing out that we have by now drifted out of all-too-structuralist postmodernity. In the words of Claire Colebrook: 'It is [the] equivocity that engenders postmodernism, for it establishes the signifier, system, subject on the one hand, and the real or the retroactively constituted world on the other.'[5] What binds an otherwise heterogeneous group of speculative realists is their shared antipathy towards correlationism.[6] A correlationist accepts that we only ever have access to the correlation between thinking and being – epistemology and ontology – and never to either of the terms in isolation.[7] In other words, correlationism marks a self-reflexive loop (marked by finitude) where nothing can be independent of thought. The familiar flavour of cognitive suspension or plain agnosticism vis-à-vis the 'outside' (noumenon) is shared by most post-Kantians.[8] Kant, himself a 'weak correlationist', did in fact allow for the possibility of the 'in-itself', albeit unknowable.[9] But if the idea of the world independent of our access seems unintelligible, as another speculative realist Ray Brassier cautions, perhaps the fault lies more with our notion of intelligibility than with the world:

> The phenomenological radicalization of transcendentalism, initiated by Heidegger, found itself excavating deeper and deeper into the 'primordial' . . . uncovering the conditions for the conditions of the conditions. Yet, the deeper it digs towards the pre-originary the more impoverished its resources become and the greater its remove from things themselves. Heidegger and his successors end up striving for the pre-reflexive through increasingly reflexive means; exacerbating abstraction until it becomes reduced to . . . playing its own exuberant vacuity. This meta-transcendental problematic reaches some sort of apogee in Derrida who introduces both a healthy measure of scepticism and a fatal dose of irony into the proceedings by revealing how the immediacy of access was always already contaminated by mediation or *différance*. . . . Once the problematic of access and of the access to access has reached its ironic *dénouement* in this terminally self-enclosed spiral of reflexivity it is no surprise to see the very notion of a world indifferent to our access to it dismissed as unintelligible. Phenomenology begins with the things themselves, and ends up

pouring over words, nothing but words. Perhaps, this is the inevitable *dénoue-ment* of the philosophy of access [correlationism].[10]

Realism

Denying realism amounts to megalomania, according to Karl Popper. But we need to bear in mind that not so long ago a realist 'coming out' and embracing a mind-independent reality would be met with ridicule. It would have been considered, at the very least, naïve. Still, the (new) materialism in general, and the (empiricist) affective turn in particular, seem to be gaining momentum to such an extent that even some of the scholars of this affiliation urge caution.[11] As it happens, many a logocentric thinker has been unjustly turned into a straw person. As Charles T. Wolfe cautions, 'the trick is to not go all the way with embodiment, so as not to end up in what Deleuze, speaking of Maurice Merleau-Ponty, called the "mysticism of the flesh"'.[12] However, as far as the discipline of architecture is concerned, this otherwise healthy dose of scepticism is not only utterly premature but also counterproductive, and quite literally so. Somewhat paradoxically, architecture has historically undergone a gradual disassociation from the material realm and become an ultimate white-collar profession. The consequent withdrawal from reality ('into itself') has been seen either as (bad) escapism or as a (good) strategy of resistance: 'The withdrawal is into an idealist realm, a realm secluded from everyday life and from contamination by the unacceptable new order.'[13] The urge to ward off the givens and to continue to contemplate alternatives is most worthy, especially in the face of architects' jumping on the band wagon of the ¥€$ (is more) 'pragmatic yet utopian third way'.[14] Architects seem desperate in their effort to catch up with the media. The non-normative has become the norm, writes Terry Eagleton.[15] The spearhead of critical theory in architecture Michael Hays laments how the most theoretically aware contemporary architects have unfortunately rejected what he sees as the most important operative concept of the theory of architecture at the moment of its refoundation in the 1970s, namely autonomy.[16] But idealist bracketing also comes at a price. Architects might end up painting themselves into a corner of impotence by depriving themselves of the means to intervene, which, after all, has always been the main trait of (any) materialism.[17] As Eugene Holland admits, 'any postmodern Marxism worthy of the name will want to abandon teleology and adopt contingency and emergence as better paradigms for under-standing history'.[18] This is how architects Reiser and Umemoto proclaim the new materialist position:

We assert the primacy of material and formal specificity over myth and inter-pretation. In fact, *while all myth and interpretation derives from the immedi-acy of material phenomena, this equation is not reversible.* When you try to make fact out of myth language only begets more language, with architecture assuming the role of illustration or allegory. This is true not only of the initial condition of architecture but actually plays out during the design process in a similar way. Material practice is the shift from asking 'what does this mean?' to 'what does this do?'[19]

We cannot afford to throw out the baby of toolkit with the bathwater of ideology 'precisely because it is not a matter of ideology, but of a machination'.[20] The best strategy of resistance seems to lie not in opposition but in (strategic) affirmation. To embrace naturalism is to see cognition as belonging to the same world as that of its 'objects'.[21] There is no need to postulate the existence of a more fun-damental realm (transcendental 'skyhooks'). *Natura naturans* (naturing nature/creator) and *natura naturata* (natured nature/created) are inseparable. There is no ultimate foundation, but the immanence of powers, relations and bodily compositions: 'power is not homogeneous, but can be defined only by the par-ticular points through which it passes'.[22] The first step to break out of the per-nicious self-reflexive loop is to acknowledge that – with or without us – matter does matter. This is what Charles Sanders Peirce refers to as 'firstness'. Then there are relations or 'secondness'. Crudely put, the dyad marks the difference between the (intrinsic) properties and (extrinsic) capacities. Lastly, there is also the 'centre of indetermination' or 'thirdness' where an interval between percep-tion and action is inserted (the mind). It is crucial not to dismiss the 'pedagogy of the senses', where secondness presupposes firstness, and thirdness incorporates both firstness and secondness.[23] This is another way of saying that everything starts with the sensible or, as Whitehead's disciple Susanne K. Langer put it: 'All thinking begins with seeing.'[24] It is neither about the appearance of essence, nor about the conditions of apparition. Rather, it is about the mutual presupposition of the virtual – the modality with the real-yet-not-actual ontological status – and the actual, where the virtual would be utterly sterile without the actual.[25] The reciprocity of the two is crucial, as the cultural studies scholar Lawrence Grossberg explains in an interview:

The distinction between possibility and virtuality is crucial, and I think that most theories of imagination have been theories of possibility. Of which, the utopian is the most obvious example. The result has been a politics that is almost never rooted in the present. But I think one must look to the present because

it is in the present that you find the virtual, that you find the contingency. . . .
I think it is rooted in the possibility (if one can use that word) of reconceiving
the imagination as intimately connected with the analytics of the empirical.
Imagination is not separate from science, analysis, or description of the actual.
Imagination has to be rethought as a rediscovering of the contingent, the
virtual in the actual . . . and that it seems to me is a very different notion of the
imagination than what the Left has ever had.[26]

The world, after all, 'does not exist outside of its expression'.[27] Deleuze
and Guattari were explicit about this often misunderstood maxim.
Transcendence is always a product of immanence. One could argue that
reification is necessary for the expression to start migrating, a major pre-
condition for the creation of an artistic style.[28] It has become somewhat
common for their epigones to favour the virtual over its expression.[29] But the
fact of the matter is that you cannot have one without the other. Expression
is not the meaning but the torsion of both the expressor and the expressed. If
'non-organic vitality' is the content, argues Zourabichvili, then expression is
its 'agrammatical syntax'.[30] Their determination is absolutely reciprocal. In
any event, it is useless to seek a more substantial truth behind the phantasm
(essence of appearance). Furthermore, seeking such a truth via a confused
sign leads to mere symptomatologising.[31] It is equally futile to contain the
truth within stable figures (sense of apparition): 'to construct solid cores of
convergence where we might include, on the basis of their identical properties, all its angles, flashes, membranes, and vapors'.[32] Hence there is no
possibility of phenomenalisation either, because every form, conversely, is a
compound of the relationship between forces. This is how Michel Foucault
sees Deleuze's counter-effectuating strategy as a way of overcoming both
'bad habits', namely, symptomatologising and phenomenalisation:

> Phantasms [incorporeal events] do not extend organisms into the imaginary;
> they topologize the materiality of the body. They should consequently be freed
> from the restrictions we impose upon them, freed from the dilemmas of truth
> and falsehood and of being and nonbeing (the essential difference between
> simulacrum and copy carried to its logical conclusion); they must be allowed
> to conduct their dance, to act out their mime, as 'extrabeings'.[33]

Traditionally, the truth was defined as adequation and non-contradiction but,
as I will argue, both claims can be challenged from the perspective of a genea-
logical method. If there is no referent, the former loses all meaning, while the

requirement for the latter is shown to depend on the illusion of the potential mastery of a wholly self-transparent discourse, namely phenomenology.[34]

Non-Discursive

A lot of lip service has been paid to bridging the gap between theory and practice, but the true imperative should be to stop regarding transdisciplinarity, with its nomadic structure, and disciplinary specificity as mutually exclusive. It should not come as a surprise that some of the most prominent beacons of contemporary architectural theory are happily trespassing.[35] What binds them is zero-degree tolerance for narrow-mindedness. Another imperative is to exclude – once and for all – the law of the excluded middle. We need to get rid of this Occamite tendency, because not all the potentialities are an already accrued value. In this way architecture will be able to reclaim the medium specificity from a genuine realist/materialist position and be treated rightfully as a non-discursive practice.[36] This will certainly not be easy, as the hegemonic binary system knows no such logic. Its inherent dualism brings together the most unlikely of allies: the Cartesians and informationists (ex-cyberneticists).[37] Regrettably, the media theorist Friedrich Kittler is right to credit the father of the information theory Claude Shannon with writing the most influential Master's thesis ever.[38] By Kittler's account, Shannon even 'thought digitally', which is plausible and, for that, all the more dangerous, just as any other approach which distinguishes between meaning and information. Opposing 'the static Aristotelian duality' of form and matter with the meta-theoretical trinity of processing (executing commands), transmitting (requiring an address) and storing (memory as database) is not helpful.[39] The analogy between needing an address to retrieve computer data and an address to locate a house in a city (or even to recall memories) is as popular as it is misleading. It all seems to boil down to the following 'dilemma', as posited by Gibson:

> The issue between the two kinds of theory [primacy of language vs. primacy of perception] can be illustrated by the following question. Does a child distinguish between two physically different things only after he has learned to make different responses to each, names, for example; or does he first learn to distinguish them and then (sometimes) attach names? On the former alternative he must learn to respond to things; *on the latter he must learn to respond to the difference*. . . . The issue is deep and far-reaching.[40]

Ecosophy

Indeed, what motivates the author's research is the architect's habit of taking for granted the homology between representation and presentation. There is widespread consensus on this fallacy among laymen and professionals alike. As Robin Evans diagnosed, 'we are landed not only with a picture theory of vision, but with a pervasive picture method of construction for manufactured objects as well'.[41] We are also landed with the hypothesis of the five senses, the proof of Aristotle's enduring authority. The number five relates to the supposed channels of sensation running from the periphery to the centre. In the case of vision, the sequence is all too familiar: object > retinal image > image in the brain > various operations on the sensory image > full consciousness of the object and its meaning.[42] Such an approach to perception – as the conscious experience of sensory input – remains in its essence Aristotelian through and through. The philosopher of mind Susan Hurley named the implicit model of the mind behind such an approach 'the classical sandwich', with perception as input, action as output, and cognition as in-between.[43] We see with our eyes, don't we? No, Gibson was resolute, we see with saccading eyes in the mobile head on the locomotive body supported by the ground, the brain being only the central organ of an entire visual system.[44] According to Gibson, the brain may produce sensations, hallucinations, dreams, illusions and after-images, but never perceptions. You are not your brain.[45] The perceptual system is synaesthetic, that is, cross-modal and supported by proprioception, which refers to the body's ability to sense movement within joints and their position. It is therefore also kinaesthetic and, as such, inseparable from action.[46] Kinaesthesia is not *like* something, explains the proponent of the corporeal turn Maxine Sheets-Johnstone, it is what it is.[47] Neither thingness, nor essentiality.[48] Seeing is a matter of skill and participation, and not contemplation. Perception and action are not propositions, nor are they based on a proposition, and cannot, therefore, be either correct or incorrect.[49] The ecological approach to perception knows no such thing as 'sense data'. Ecological, it must be qualified, stands for reciprocity between the life form and its environment.[50] Their mutual relation is not one of computing but of resonance. It is no coincidence that the school of ecological perception describes perceiving as tuning in – as in radio frequency – as opposed to the computational metaphor (with the brain as a computer, eye as a camera and so on).[51] Perception cannot be considered independently of the environment, since it is defined as an evolved adaptive and constructive relation between the organism and the environment. Unfortunately, experimental psychology research has relied overwhelmingly on object perception, rather than environment perception, with the findings of the former providing the basis for understanding the latter.[52] Architecture continues to suffer from this fallacy. Arguably the greatest feat of contemporary psychology has been to include the environment of life forms in the study of the psyche.[53] To separate the cultural from the natural environment – as if there were a world of mental and a world of material products – is a fatal mistake. There is only one world.[54] Only recently have biologists considered the (feed-back/feed-forward) effect of niche construction on the inheritance system.[55] The theory of niche construction proposes that an organism does not passively submit to the pressures of a pre-existing environment, but that it actively constructs its niche (genetically, epigenetically, behaviourally and symbolically). Implications for the discipline of architecture are obvious: perception is an important area of study because it provides information about the environment, which is in turn intimately related to the life of life forms. Architecture ought to reclaim its vanguard position within the epigenetic turn, which embraces technology in general terms (*technē*) as constitutive of humanity, and not merely the other way around.[56] It is high time to complement the passive principle of natural selection (logical argument) with the active principle of self-organisation (natural argument).[57] The principle of exteriorisation – the city as an exoskeleton is a good example – is evolution continued by other means. This is beautifully illustrated in the opening scene of *2001: A Space Odyssey* (1968) by Stanley Kubrick, compressing 4.4 million years of tool evolution from the bone to the spaceship.[58] The epigenetic structure of inheritance and transmission is, as the very term suggests, external and non-biological. As such it transcends our particular existence. It extends beyond our biological finitude. Moreover, as Guattari claims, 'man and the tool *are already* components of a machine constituted by a full body [socius] acting as an engineering agency, and by men and tools that are engineered (*machinés*) insofar as they are distributed on this body'.[59] The long-lasting legacy of privileging *epistēmē* over *technē* needs to be rethought, as the philosopher of technology Bernard Stiegler urges.[60] The 'what' (*technē*) and the 'who' (the human) are co-constitutive. Strictly speaking, architecture, as a sedimented epigenetic (mnemonic) device, has an even higher order of autonomy which makes it epi-phylo-genetic.[61] If epigenetics is the concept of non-genetic heritability (such as language acquisition), then epiphylogenetic means that the rhetoric of 'we build our cities and in return they build us' is to be taken literally.[62] Stiegler explains:

> Epiphylogenetics, a recapitulating, dynamic and morphogenetic (*phylogenetic*) accumulation of individual experience (*epi*), designates the appearance of a

new relation between the organism and its environment, which is also a new state of matter. If the individual is organic organized matter, then its relation to its environment (to matter in general, organic or inorganic), when it is a question of a *who*, is mediated by the organized but inorganic matter of the *organon*, the tool with its instructive role (its role *qua* instrument), the *what*. It is in this sense that the *what* invents the *who* just as much as it is invented by it.[63]

It is time for the discipline to awaken from the slumber of anthropocentrism and shake off the baggage of old dualisms. Deleuze and Guattari propose that we drop anthropomorphism for geomorphism, which defies (all-too-human) interpretation.[64] In the same vein, Keith Ansell-Pearson calls for a major reconfiguration of ethology: 'Behaviour can no longer be localised in individuals conceived as preformed homunculi, but has to be treated epigenetically as a function of complex network systems which cut across individuals and which traverse phyletic lineages and organismic boundaries.'[65] Relation comes before that which it places in relation.[66] In Heideggerian parlance, it is dwelling that precedes both building and abstract or subjective thought.[67] In contrast to binary logic, one should always proceed from the middle – *par le milieu* – both conceptually and literally.[68] As explained by the philosopher of science Isabelle Stengers, Deleuze deliberately plays on the double meaning of this French term, which stands for both the middle and the surroundings.[69] Proceeding from the middle is arguably the best way to undo the habit of thinking in terms of formal essences and sensible formed things. As the philosopher Gilbert Simondon was well aware, the tradition tends to forget a sort of middle, an intermediary. And it is at the level of this intermediary that everything gets done.[70]

The complementarity between the animal and its environment was a life-long project of the psychologist J. J. Gibson. His (unwitting) affiliation with Deleuze and contribution to radical empiricism in general is still underappreciated.[71] The most notable point of convergence between the two thinkers is their more or less overt theory of passive synthesis, with which they vehemently oppose, or better yet, complement, the active synthesis of representation.[72] Passive syntheses fall outside of the jurisdiction of an ego whereby a living present is a multiplicity of 'contemplations'.[73] Deleuze describes passive synthesis as one which 'is not carried out by the mind, but occurs in the mind'.[74] As a discipline, architecture has more often than not sought legitimacy from without. The irony is that it felt embarrassingly inadequate because of its heuristic, that is, anexact (yet rigorous) modus operandi.[75] The two thinkers stress distinctness and obscurity in opposition to scientism based on Cartesian distinctness

and clarity. No less than a genuine change of heart – triggered by the realist/
materialist impetus – is required for the architecture of conjecture to (continue
to) resist becoming the architecture of canons. The modernist divide between
materiality on the one hand and design on the other is vanishing, according to
the sociologist Bruno Latour: 'The more objects are turned into things – that
is, the more matters of fact are turned into matters of concern – the more they
are rendered into objects of design through and through.'[76] This is to say that
one can no longer indulge in the idea that there are, on the one hand, objective
material constraints and, on the other, symbolic human subjective values. As
the philosopher Henk Oosterling puts it, 'Dasein ist design.'[77] When a society
modulates its matter it is not a reflection *of* culture, it *is* culture.[78] Therefore, the
discipline should regain self-confidence and do what it does best, in the words
of the architectural theorist Mark Wigley: 'Architecture neither houses nor
represents culture, neither precedes nor follows culture. Rather it is the mechanism of culture.'[79] What distinguishes architecture from simple handicraft and
makes it a 'material practice', according to Stan Allen, is the interplay between
abstract tools and concrete ends.[80] It requires both the intellectual and practical
tools to work effectively in this paradoxical environment, 'at once immersed in
the world of images and abstract notations, yet intimately connected to the hard
logics of matter and forces'.[81] However, if taken separately, both perspectives
continue to embody correlationist conceits.[82] Practice is to be considered neither as an application of theory nor as its inspiration, but as action. In the words
of Foucault and Deleuze, 'there's only action – theoretical action and practical
action'.[83] To appropriate this battle cry is to have done with representation.

Notes

This essay first appeared in *Footprint* 6, no. 10/11, *Architecture Culture and the Question
of Knowledge: Doctoral Research Today*, edited by Deborah Hauptmann and Lara
Schrijver (Delft: DSD in partnership with Stichting Footprint and Techne Press, 2012),
129–41.

1. Žižek, 'Lacan between Cultural Studies and Cognitivism'.
2. In 'The Third Culture' (1995) John Brockman challenged the supposed incommen-
    surability between humanities and sciences – C. P. Snow's 'Two Cultures' – and has
    continued to do so in his work since.
3. Chaos theory works from the simple to the complex, while complexity theory works
    from the complex towards the simple. Two highly readable, non-mathematical
    treatments which capture the paradigm-breaking nature of dynamic systems are
    Prigogine and Stengers's *Order out of Chaos* and Gleick's *Chaos*.

4. Meillassoux, *After Finitude*. See also: Bryant, Srnicek and Harman, *The Speculative Turn*.

5. Colebrook, 'Postmodernism Is a Humanism', 288, 292.

6. By the proponents' own account, speculative realism does not really exist; rather, it is a generic term for a group of thinkers that advocate very different ontologies and epistemologies that are often opposed to one another. The two features that unite them are (1) a commitment to some variant of realism and (2) a refusal to privilege the world–human correlate.

7. Gregory Bateson, 'The Cybernetics of "Self"'.

8. DeLanda, 'Materialism and Politics', 29.

9. Schrödinger, *What is Life?*

10. Brassier, 'The Pure and Empty Form of Death'.

11. Colebrook, 'Sexuality and the Politics of Vitalism'.

12. Wolfe, 'De-Ontologizing the Brain'.

13. Kaminer, *The Idealist Refuge*, 9.

14. Ingels, *Yes Is More*.

15. Eagleton, *After Theory*, 16–17.

16. Hays, 'Ideologies of Media', 263. 'The aspiration to an autonomy of disciplinary forms and techniques as a way of creating and measuring the distance between a critical practice and the degraded status quo of consumer culture.' Hays sincerely admits that he is not yet fully able to account for this new attitude but wants to reflect on it and on 'the ideologies it has replaced'. The ideologies he is referring to were written almost in manifesto form and were issued by coincidence ('or perhaps not') in 1966: Rossi's *The Architecture of the City* and Venturi's *Complexity and Contradiction in Architecture*.

17. 'Fit for the boudoir, and not for the street.' Graafland, 'On Criticality', 698. Cf. Tafuri, 'L'architecture dans le boudoir'.

18. Holland, 'Nonlinear Historical Materialism', 184. For an overview of the range of topics that new materialism concerns itself with, see: Coole and Frost, *New Materialisms*.

19. Reiser and Umemoto, *Atlas of Novel Tectonics*, 23; emphasis added. See also: Scott, *The Architecture of Humanism*, 168.

20. Guattari, *Chaosophy*, 115.

21. Heft, *Ecological Psychology in Context*, 73.

22. Deleuze, *Foucault*, 25.

23. Peirce, *Philosophical Writings of Peirce*, 74–97.

24. Langer, *Philosophy in a New Key*, 95. See also: Gibson, *The Ecological Approach to Visual Perception*, 250.

25. 'Virtuality' – derived from the Latin *virtualis*, and having come to mean that which

exists potentially but not actually – is a form of physical modality, distinct from possibility and necessity to account for the double status of singularities which are real in their effects but incapable of ever being actual. See: DeLanda, 'Deleuze in Phase Space', 150. See also: Smith, 'Deleuze's Concept of the Virtual'.

26. Grossberg, 'Affect's Future', 320.

27. Deleuze, *The Fold*, 152.

28. I refer here to the 'specialised lines of expression' such as (one-dimensional) genes or (epigenetic) words. See: DeLanda, 'Deleuze, Materialism and Politics', 165. 'While before the rise of living creatures all expression was three-dimensional – the geometry of a crystal, for example, was what expressed its identity – genes are a one-dimensional form of expression, a linear chain of nucleotides, and this linearization allows material expressivity to specialise.' Ibid., 164.

29. As Bernard Cache cautions, the key is not to repeat the mistake of the avant-garde at the beginning of the twentieth century who, with the onset of new technologies, immediately dismissed the older techniques and ideas as outmoded and anachronistic: 'listening to architects describing how we were living in a non-Euclidean, virtual space. I just couldn't stand it any longer and had to respond'. Cache, 'George L. Legendre in Conversation with Bernard Cache'.

30. Zourabichvili, 'Six Notes on the Percept', 202.

31. A near synonym of symptomatology is 'interpretosis', 'the "despotic" legacy of any discourse whose primary pivot is the signifier'. Nealon, 'Beyond Hermeneutics', 160.

32. Foucault's review of Deleuze's *The Logic of Sense* (1969) and *Difference and Repetition* (1968), 'Theatrum Philosophicum'.

33. 'The *Logic of Sense* can be read as the most alien book imaginable from *The Phenomenology of Perception* [by Merleau-Ponty].' Foucault, 'Theatrum Philosophicum'.

34. Ferry and Renault consider phenomenology as that 'which the hypothesis of an unconscious, or more generally of an exterior that motivates all discourse without the speaker's knowledge, specifically excludes'. Ferry and Renault, *French Philosophy of the Sixties*, 9.

35. For example, 'street philosopher' DeLanda, 'physicist' Kipnis and 'literary theorist' Kwinter. Kwinter firmly believes that the question of space 'can no longer be thought fruitfully within the domain of language or even within its broader analytical paradigm, but only through the minute study of our physical, material and technical milieus – of which language is little more than a subset'. Kwinter, 'On Vitalism and the Virtual', 185.

36. The insistence on medium-specificity arose in the era of modernism and has become associated with the art critic Clement Greenberg. The concept, however, can be traced back to Gotthold Ephraim Lessing's 1766 essay *Laocoon*. Lessing dismantles

Horace's famous claim *ut pictura poesis* ('as is painting, so is poetry'), arguing that these media are inherently different. While poetry unfolds in time, painting exists in space. By contrast, architecture, I would suggest, exists in space-time. In this I side with McLuhan in that the medium is specific through its effect and not its content. As Henry Moore wrote: 'Rodin of course knew what sculpture is: he once said that sculpture is the science of the bump and the hollow.' James, *Henry Moore on Sculpture*.

37. Hayles discusses the regime of computation (complexity to complexity) as an alternative to classical metaphysics (simplicity to complexity). Hayles, *My Mother Was a Computer*, 15.

38. Kittler represents a stream of media theory which came out as an alternative to the Marxist and hermeneutic theories dominating German discourse in the latter part of the twentieth century. Shannon's paper, drawn from his 1937 Master's thesis, 'A Symbolic Analysis of Relay and Switching Circuits', was published in the 1938 issue of the *Transactions of the American Institute of Electrical Engineers*.

39. Also known as the triad of making, storing and transmitting. The attempt to 'fix' dialectics by introducing a third term is a well-known yet futile exercise.

40. Gibson, *The Senses Considered as Perceptual Systems*, 282; emphasis added.

41. Evans, *The Projective Cast*, 359, 370.

42. This fallacy has become commonplace. See: Gibson, *The Ecological Approach to Visual Perception*, 252.

43. Hurley, *Consciousness in Action*.

44. Gibson rejects a snapshot/aperture conception of vision in favour of the ambient/ambulatory one. See: Gibson, *The Ecological Approach to Visual Perception*, 1.

45. The substitution of the brain for the Cartesian spirit is known as the 'Francis Crick Fallacy'. As Crick wrote in the journal *Nature*: 'Scientists need no longer stand by listening to the tedious arguments of philosophers perpetually disagreeing with each other. The problem of consciousness is now a scientific problem.' Alva Nöe, interview by Gordy Slack, 'You Are Not Your Brain'.

46. The 'perceptual system' thesis was set out by Gibson in an earlier book, *The Senses Considered as Perceptual Systems*. For a contemporary account of proprioception, see: Massumi, *Parables for the Virtual*.

47. Sheets-Johnstone, *The Primacy of Movement*, 139, 146–50. See also: Sheets-Johnstone, *The Corporeal Turn*.

48. 'Essentiality is the property of formal, fixed essences, the circle. Thingness is the property of sensible, perceived, formed things, for example the plate or the sun or the wheel.' Deleuze, *Cours Vincennes*, 'Anti-Oedipe et Mille Plateaux' (27 February 1979).

49. Michaels and Carello, *Direct Perception*, 109.

50. The word ecology comes from the Greek *oikos*, a house. But it can also mean household, family, milieu, vicinity, habitat or environment.

51. The animal may change as a consequence of experience, but we view that change not as an accumulation of knowledge, but as a keener ability to detect the affordances of the environment. According to Gibson, learning becomes the education of attention. See: Gibson, *The Senses Considered as Perceptual Systems*, 270.

52. Ittelson, 'Environment Perception and Contemporary Perceptual Theory'.

53. Chemero and Silberstein provide a comprehensive taxonomy of the two most important debates in the philosophy of the cognitive and neural sciences. The first debate is over methodological individualism: is the object of the cognitive and neural sciences the brain, the whole animal or the animal–environment system? The second is over explanatory style: should explanation in cognitive and neural science be reductionist-mechanistic, inter-level mechanistic or dynamic? Our thesis unequivocally sides with the dynamic animal–environment system approach, which I name 'Gibsonism'. See: Chemero and Silberstein, 'After the Philosophy of Mind'.

54. Gibson, *The Ecological Approach to Visual Perception*, 130.

55. Odling-Smee, 'Niche Inheritance'. The epigenetic turn calls for a re-examination of the status of Lamarckism. In contrast to Darwinism, Lamarckian inheritance is the idea that an organism can pass on to its offspring characteristics that it acquired during its lifetime.

56. Epigenesis is the term used to describe the relatively mysterious process of how form emerges gradually but dynamically out of a formless or homogeneous environment or substrate. See: Kwinter, 'Soft Systems', 214.

57. Against the second law of thermodynamics: negentropy (negative entropy).

58. It is a difference in degree before it is a difference in kind.

59. Guattari, *Chaosophy*, 110; emphasis in the original.

60. Stiegler, *Technics and Time, 1*.

61. Ibid., 134–79. Biologist Conrad Waddington (1905–75) is often credited with coining the term epigenetics in 1942 as 'the branch of biology which studies the causal interactions between genes and their products, which bring the phenotype into being'. The extent to which we are preprogrammed versus environmentally shaped awaits universal consensus. The field of epigenetics has emerged to bridge the gap between nature and nurture.

62. A socialist realist slogan also attributed to Churchill. Ontogeny: development (developmental and organismic scales). Phylogeny: descent and branching (reproductive and evolutionary scales).

63. Stiegler, *Technics and Time, 1*, 177.

64. Deleuze and Guattari, *A Thousand Plateaus*, 318–19.

65. These developments call for a major reconfiguration of ethology. See: Ansell-Pearson, *Germinal Life*, 171. For Gibson the formula is neither mentalism nor conditioned-response behaviourism, but environmentalism. See: Gibson, *The Ecological Approach to Visual Perception*, 2.

66. Deleuze and Guattari, *A Thousand Plateaus*, 350.

67. Heidegger, 'Building Dwelling Thinking'.

68. This is in contrast to the deconstructivist Jacques Derrida, who does not start from the middle but rather 'from the limits'. The mathematician Arkady Plotnitsky offers a comparative analysis between the two contemporaries Deleuze/Derrida as follows: Middle/Limits, Geometry/Algebra, Thinking/Writing. See: Plotnitsky, 'Algebras, Geometries and Topologies of the Fold'.

69. The former means without grounding definitions or an ideal horizon, while the latter is meant to indicate that no theory gives you the power to disentangle something from its particular surroundings. See: Stengers, 'An Ecology of Practices'.

70. Simondon, 'Genesis of the Individual'. See also: Adkins, 'A Short List of Gilbert Simondon's Vocabulary'.

71. His major works are: *The Ecological Approach to Visual Perception* (1979); *The Senses Considered as Perceptual Systems* (1966); *The Perception of the Visual World* (1950).

72. Beneath active syntheses of thought there are passive syntheses of perception, and beneath them still there are passive organic syntheses of metabolism. See: Protevi, 'Deleuze, Jonas, and Thompson'.

73. As used by Franz Brentano and then Husserl, 'intentionality' means that mental states like perceiving are always about something, that is, directed towards something. By contrast, for Deleuze intentionality does exist, but it is always multiple. In other words, there is never a single originator of the intention. Desire itself is a multiplicity of competing drives. See: Deleuze and Guattari, *Anti-Oedipus*.

74. Deleuze, *Difference and Repetition*, 71. The distinction between passive and active syntheses is not dissimilar to the one made by the Nobel laureate Kahneman between the 'automatic System 1 and effortful System 2'. See: Kahneman, *Thinking: Fast and Slow*.

75. Gibson draws on Polanyi's notion of tacit knowledge. See: Gibson, *The Ecological Approach to Visual Perception*, 22. 'Everything . . . has long been known implicitly by practical men – the surveyors of the earth, the builders, and the designers of the environment. It is *tacit* knowledge.' Cf. Polanyi, *The Tacit Dimension*.

76. Latour, 'A Cautious Prometheus?', 2. 'Humanists are concerned only about humans; the rest, for them, is mere materiality, or cold objectivity. But by treating their life supports as matters of concern, we pile concerns over concerns, we fold, we envelop, we embed humans into more and more elements that have been carefully

explicitated, protected, conserved and maintained . . . This little shift in the definition of matter modifies everything: it allows practitioners to reuse all of the notions of materiality and artificiality, but freed from the restrictions the older style of modernist matters of fact had imposed on their use.' Ibid., 10.

77. Oosterling, 'Dasein as Design'.

78. 'From representation to things' is the core thesis of Lash and Lury, *Global Culture Industry*, 7. 'For Horkheimer and Adorno, culture . . . was still in the superstructure. . . . our concern was with how things actually move, how they "transition" between many states, how they are (self-)organised as temporal, rhythmic morphologies or coherent behaviours.' Ibid., 19.

79. Wigley and Kipnis, 'The Architectural Displacement of Philosophy', 7.

80. Allen, 'Pragmatism in Practice'.

81. Allen, commentary in 'Stocktaking 2004: Nine Questions about the Present and Future of Design', 44.

82. Boogst, *Alien Phenomenology*, 14. 'The scientist believes in reality apart from human life, but it is a reality excavated for human exploitation. The scientific process cares less for reality itself than it does for the discoverability of reality through human ingenuity. Likewise, the humanist doesn't believe in the world *except* as a structure erected in the interest of human culture.'

83. Foucault and Deleuze, 'Intellectuals and Power', 205–7.

3   Northern Line

Introduction

THIS CHAPTER TAKES as a point of departure the Deleuzian concept of the Northern Line. Scholarly accounts of the Dutch Baroque suggest that, in contrast to the organic force of their Italian counterparts, the Dutch painters set themselves apart with a genuinely new haptic painterly tradition, effectively creating an abstract machine with its power of repetition. It is with the seventeenth-century Dutch painter Johannes Vermeer that the unleashing of affect is first seen; to our mind this grants him the status of the bearer of the Deleuzian Northern Line.[1] However, the most important 'Dutchman' in the eyes of Deleuze remains Spinoza, the prince of immanence. Thus, our argument requires laying the pre-philosophical plane of immanence, creating a Northern Line concept and inventing the conceptual personae, or aesthetic figures, of the architects we see as the heirs of this tradition: UNStudio (UNS), NOX and OMA. This triad will be utilised to situate contemporary Dutch architecture within an aesthetic position that argues for a reciprocal determination of the abstract and concrete, or, with Deleuze, the virtual and the actual. We will draw on Deleuze and Guattari's reading of the Northern Line as a theoretical disposition towards the differential difference in contrast to the dialectical difference. The latter operates in terms of opposition, negation and, *ipso facto*, resistance correlative to a molar notion of power (*pouvoir*) and not, as with the former, the (molecular) level of 'desiring assemblages'.[2] Our argument will show that the Northern Line provides an aesthetic reading – neither distributed nor organised around the mind, nor oriented towards cognition – that is capable of escaping architecture's long-standing dependence on representationalism.

In *What Is Philosophy?* Deleuze and Guattari develop the conceptual persona; with this concept we will work through a process of decoding, of decomposing the architect and the work into apersonal and pre-subjective levels.[3] Put otherwise, we will engage Deleuze–Guattari where, working from desiring assemblages, they circumvent the phenomenon of ideology, treating it as an epiphenomenon; we similarly propose to treat architecture in terms of what they refer to as passive syntheses, which undermine the active synthesis of representation.[4] Of course, this extra-propositional and sub-representative level of thought-events requires a mode of analysis that cannot rely on the fully actual, for this would inevitably lead to conflating the material cause with the incorporeal effect. By this we mean to say that things themselves are bearers of ideal events, which do not coincide with their properties. Any (actual) incarnation may in fact be seen as a (provisional) solution to the problem posed by the virtual, which is consequently not ideal but problematic. The concept prevents regression into simple reductionism since there is no homology between the actual and virtual.

This chapter will present an analysis or, more in keeping with Deleuze–Guattari, a schizoanalysis of the working methods of the Dutch architects mentioned above. We will further suggest that it is not the architect who invents the conceptual persona, but rather the persona itself that provides the architectural body of work with a certain (endo)consistency formerly known as style. Finally, with this work we hope to develop a reading of several Deleuzian thought models which we believe have been somewhat overlooked in contemporary discourse on Deleuze and the impact of his philosophy on architecture. This will include the three syntheses of the connective, the disjunctive and the conjunctive in relation to the paranoiac, miraculating and celibate machines respectively.

Distribution of the Sensible

The idea of the 'idea behind architecture' is the Platonic idealism we wish to repudiate. With this, it is important to understand that Deleuze and Guattari see absolutely no distinction between a desiring-production and social production. As they argue in *Anti-Oedipus*, desire is objective and immanent: 'There is no particular form of existence that can be labelled "psychic reality".'[5] And a few paragraphs later: 'There is no such thing as the social production of reality on the one hand, and a desiring-production that is mere fantasy on the other.'[6] Further, and in clear terms, 'desiring-production is one and the same thing as social production'.[7] This in turn means that there is no individual fantasy; there are only social fantasies, a revelation that effectively turns psychoanalysis on its head. Deleuze and Guattari refer to such 'material psychiatry' as schizoanalysis where the connections and disjunctions operate ad infinitum. As Smith and Ballantyne have argued, although

> Freud begins to take us to a field where we can enter a discourse of flow – of novel and intense material connections with that which is non-habitual, non-genital, non-human – unfortunately for Freud there is a 'natural' connection and investment; a personalising of desire that ties the ebbs and tides of the libido to the self and the familiar/familial'.[8]

The unleashing of desire is essential for our approach, given that we take the conditions of genesis (production) as the basis of experience to be the very medium of architecture. What distinguishes immanent architecture is that it does not merely fulfil the (pre-given) expectation, it also produces its audience: a people yet to come. In contrast to *Anti-Oedipus* – the first volume of *Capitalism and Schizophrenia* – the second volume, *A Thousand Plateaus*, has a much wider range of registers: cosmic, geological, evolutionary, developmental, ethological, anthropological, mythological, historical, economic, political, literary, musical and many more (a thousand plateaus), where every plane is matter unfolding, where relations are effected by specific expressions which, in turn, are events of specific powers to relate.

Despite the introduction of ever more new terms, the abstract machine stays virtually the same: together the passive syntheses at all these levels form a differential field within which stratification takes place as an integration or resolution of that field. As a matter of fact, this machinism dates back to Deleuze's *Difference and Repetition*, originally published in 1968. We find this especially pertinent given that throughout history there has been a prejudicial tendency to set the realm of sensibility against that of reason or understanding. Deleuze was among the first to propose a transformation of transcendental idealism into transcendental empiricism, with far-reaching consequences in both metaphysical and epistemological registers:

> If [transcendental] aesthetic appears more profound to us than that of Kant, it is for the following reasons: Kant defines the passive self in terms of simple receptivity, thereby assuming sensations already formed, then merely relating these to the a priori forms of their representation which are determined as space and time. In this manner, not only does he unify the passive self by ruling out the possibility of composing space step by step, not only does he deprive this passive self of all power of synthesis (synthesis being reserved for activity),

but moreover he cuts the Aesthetic into two parts: the objective element of sensation guaranteed by space and the subjective element which is incarnate in pleasure and pain. The aim of the preceding analyses, on the contrary, has been to show that receptivity must be defined in terms of the formation of local selves or egos, in terms of the passive syntheses of contemplation or contraction, thereby accounting simultaneously for the possibility of experiencing sensations, the power of reproducing them and the value that pleasure assumes as a principle.[9]

Sensibility itself becomes a field of (artistic/architectural) creation and experimentation. Such a thesis invites us, *pace* Jacques Rancière, to examine 'the distribution of the sensible'[10] in the social field as an issue of social and political individuation.[11] The question is no longer that of the ultimate nature of reality; rather it is the distribution of the sensible and insensible within which we find ourselves immersed. We ought to start by distinguishing diagrams from signs, be they vectorial – augmentative powers and diminutive servitudes – or scalar (Table 3.1).

Defined diagrammatically . . . an abstract machine is neither an infrastructure that is determining in the last instance nor a transcendental Idea that is determining in the supreme instance. Rather, it plays a piloting role. The diagrammatic or abstract machine does not function to represent, even something real,

Table 3.1 Four scalar signs of affection: although a sign, according to Spinoza qua Deleuze, can have several meanings, it is always an effect of one body upon another. In 'Spinoza and the Three "Ethics"', Deleuze distinguishes between vectorial and scalar signs. The former are signs of increase and decrease – continuous variations of power – while the latter express one's state at a moment in time, 'a slice of duration'. Affects are irreducible to affections, sensations or perceptions. The figure compares the four principal types of scalar signs that vary according to the contingent nature of assemblage. Based on Deleuze, *Essays Critical and Clinical*.

INDICATIVE	ABSTRACTIVE	IMPERATIVE	HERMENEUTIC
sensory perceptive	retaining selected affective characteristic	effect as end	
physical effect		moral effect	imaginary effect
SENSIBLE INDICES	LOGICAL ICONS	MORAL SYMBOLS	METAPHYSICAL IDOLS
TE sign	*RE sign*	*DE sign*	Deleuze
index	*icon*	*symbol*	Peirce

Source: author.

but rather constructs a real that is yet to come, a new type of reality. Thus when it constitutes points of creation or potentiality it does not stand outside history but is instead always 'prior to' history.[12]

The significance of the Northern Line is that it binds the undetermined, determinable and (mutually) determined. It is not a given, as Deleuze writes in *Difference and Repetition*, but that by which a given is given.[13] With respect to architecture, as we hope to show, Cartesian foundationalism does not hold; instead we find the necessity of foundation can only exist for determinable ground, not the final complete determination that remains only ever reciprocally determined. In other words, the system cannot be deterministic and the nature of this circle is to remain radically open, hence diagrammatic.[14]

For Deleuze and Guattari the machine does not conflict with either culture or nature. The machine is not reducible to the mechanics conceived as the protocol of some technical machines or the particular organisation of an organism. Machinism therefore designates every system that cuts off fluxes going beyond both mechanicism and vitalism: 'The unconscious is a factory and not a stage.'[15] We will next try to distinguish between the respective desiring machines: the working parts of UNS, the immobile motor of NOX and the adjacent part of OMA and their three forms of energy: 'Libido, Numen, and Voluptas; and their three syntheses: the connective syntheses of partial objects and flows, the disjunctive syntheses of singularities and chains, and the conjunctive syntheses of intensities and becomings'[16] – see Table 3.2, which we have borrowed and adapted from *Anti-Oedipus*.

Manimal: Paranoiac Machine

At the first level of synthesis, the body without organs stands opposed to its desiring machines, repelling them in the manner of a 'paranoiac machine'.[17] This can be regarded as analogous to what Deleuze called the 'pure present' in *Difference and Repetition*, since the paranoiac machine immediately erases whatever appears on its surface in order to allow for something new to appear. The passive perceptual syntheses of imagination are preceded by a myriad of passive syntheses at the organic level, making the organism 'the primary habit it *is*'.[18] Habit (*habitus*) is therefore a contraction of habitual contractions that occur on multiple levels. The synthesis of habit, in turn, precedes the memory and recollection of conscious thought. The contraction is not a reflection.[19] It provides a 'rule' in the form of sensorimotor responses to present stimuli that anticipate the future on the basis of the past.[20] At this

Table 3.2 Three cuts: an abstract machine is defined by Deleuze and Guattari as a system of cuts. The figure shows three different kinds of cuts which pertain to the three components of desiring-production: (i) flow, or the portioning-cut of desiring machines; (ii) code, or the detachment-cut from which issues the BwO; and (iii) stock, or the remainder-cut that produces the nomadic subject. Based on Bogue, *Deleuze on Literature*.

need to be controlled e.g. water, social, traffic, immigrants, sewage, somatic (blood, urine, milk) *bêtise* (stupidity)	controlling of flow (primarily from economics)	
correlative: no flow w/o code and vice versa		
transmission or exchange from one pole to another input/output	correlative of flow inscription, recording keeping track of the flows	
uncoded flow: nightmare		
capital/money	code/existence	possession related
	(does NOT pre-exist) e.g. DNA; biological = social it changes, molecular passing along information	as material or juridical (mine = me)

Source: author.

level a (physical) organism could be said to be ruled by instinctual response. The 'connective syntheses of production', through which linear sequences of the 'and then' form are constituted, remains undetermined. However, as Deleuze and Guattari point out, it captures an aspect of the intensive, the machinic assemblage, by connecting or coupling heterogeneous 'partial objects' through the emission of 'energy flows'.[21]

If there is a plane of composition that has marked the oeuvre of UNS, then it is the Manimal, a computer-generated image of the hybridisation of a lion, a snake and a human. To be clear, the Manimal is neither figural nor structural but machinic: 'As a technique, it excites because it has been produced in a manner radically different from all pictorial techniques that have been previously employed by artists.'[22] We can formulate this equation as: Manimal = lion AND snake AND human. According to Ben van Berkel and Caroline Bos, there are three main aspects that make the hybridising technique of the Manimal architecturally interesting; these concern the relations of the technique with the author, time and mereology. The first concerns the ambiguity of authorship, given the plurality of 'sometimes invisible' participants (not excluding the software programmers). The relation to time is one of continuous variation or 'a sequence that could, in principle, run indefinitely'. Accordingly, UNS openly express anxiety over 'freezing architecture in time' given that, according to them, only change exists. Most importantly, with regard to the part-to-whole relation, the unity of the Manimal as an image is not disrupted by the diversity of its ingredients, which is what most distinguishes the technique from the traditional technique of collage:

> This is the most radical choice for architecture to face. The totalising, decontextualising, dehistoricising combination of discordant systems of information can be instrumentalised architecturally into one gesture. . . .
>
> The architecture of hybridization, the fluent merging of constituent parts into an endlessly variable whole, amounts to organisation of continuous difference, resulting in structures that are scale-less, subject to evolution, expansion, inversion and other contortions and manipulations. Free to assume different identities, architecture becomes endless.[23]

Ever since its appearance, the Manimal has been the *spiritus movens* of UNS and continues to feature prominently in their discourse. Its genealogy is well known by now: from the 'fragmented organisation of disconnected parts' to the 'displaced organisation of connected parts' to the 'seamless organisation of disconnected parts' or the 'portrait of becoming', where Van Berkel and Bos express that they 'have never had a lot of faith in interpretation'.[24] The first 'fragmenting' paradigm is illustrated by the exploded view of Le Corbusier's Villa Savoye, accompanied by the Bauhausian mannequin head adorned in the technique of collage as a seam: stitching together separate parts that retain their respective identities. By contrast, the second displacing paradigm is exemplified by the formal analogy between Francis Bacon's figural (neither figurative nor abstract) portrait and a piece of architectural metabolist megastructure (architecture cum urbanism). It is presented as a transition phase towards the endless (and, and, and so on), best illustrated by the Möbius strip as well as the Manimal itself. The fascination with the 'production of production' ranks UNS among the leading architects of the flow in the very precise sense of the libidinal form of energy. Aaron Betsky points out in 'Unfolding the Forms of UNStudio'[25] that, from the beginning, UNS have used the body as a model (and metaphor):

> Up to this point, the architects had argued for the emergence of form out of the manipulation of physical material. They proposed what they called the 'invisible detail'. They articulated this detail in opposition to either the articulated meeting of materials that structural expressionism would champion, or the smooth making of enclosed forms that would seek to deny the physicality of the object. Instead, they thought that details should drink in the difference

between materials, make possible their meeting, allow the form to be folded, and then disappear.[26]

Their *Move* opens up not only with kaleidoscopic images but also chains of seemingly unrelated terms.[27] However, this uncompromising decontextualising and dehistoricising strategy comes at a price. When asked how to negotiate the difference between (anthropocentric) scale-dependency and (geocentric) scale-lessness, the conceptual persona remains utterly consistent in failing to give an answer.[28] This is simply not an issue for UNS given their theoretical and practical agenda. The Manimal, as we see it, stands not for keeping track of the flow, but for the flow itself, any flow; UNS refer to such a 'non-reductionist' approach as 'deep planning'.[29] The ease with which a myriad of partial objects is handled by this 'paranoiac machine' proves the point: '*Move* introduces inclusiveness in the design approach ... Inclusiveness allows fragmentation and difference to be absorbed into a coherent, continuous approach, abandoning the strategies of fragmentation and collage'.[30] They later conclude: 'The inclusive model is anti nothing.'[31] What UNS also unapologetically abandon is history: 'We have already forgotten history, shaken off the metaphors belonging to wood, bricks and steel. We have already seen emptiness. Now it is time to redefine materiality.'[32] And redefine it they did. Not according to its chemical composition, or vis-à-vis sensibility, but on the basis of performativity in the emergence of the project. For UNS, 'between art and airports', only the present matters, and entire processes are rendered visible.[33] Their favourite colour is blue, the colour which, according to the trend forecaster Li Edelkoort, 'dissolves contrasts and wipes out details ... and undoes form'.[34]

D-Tower: Miraculating Machine

Corresponding to the constitution of a 'pure past' are the disjunctive syntheses by which whatever is produced through the connective syntheses is recorded on the surface of the body without organs. BwO therefore functions as a gigantic memory or pure past (Mnemosyne). This past is pure in the sense that it does not contain entities open to representation; it also makes the present pass, as it were.[35] Deleuze and Guattari show that this 'miraculating machine', which attracts rather than repels the desiring machines that populate it, becomes determinable (although not determined).[36] The 'disjunctive syntheses of recording' have the form of 'either ... or ... or'. At this level a life form can engage in signifiance – a term that indicates the signifying capacity as the primary effect of a regime of signs within the semiotic register.

In *Creative Evolution*, Bergson claims that what distinguishes the instinctual response from a free response of a thinking organism is that there is a gap between the stimulus and response of the latter.[37] The disjunctive synthesis involves the creation of divergent relations among the series that occur on the body without organs.[38] It therefore refers to the virtual continuum, 'a pure fluid in a free state, flowing without interruption, streaming over the surface of a full body'.[39]

In *Anti-Oedipus*, Deleuze and Guattari present the flow and the code as correlative notions. There is no code without the flow and vice versa. It comes as no surprise that uncoded flow represents a true nightmare from the point of view of any society, for it is quite literally elusive and fleeting. The code, as opposed to the flow, introduces a measure of attraction and zones of convergence. The coding process is therefore not inclusive, but exclusive, which is to say that it is not a matter of the production of production but rather the production of recording. It is no coincidence that Lars Spuybroek, the founder of NOX, is not only well versed in history but also openly critical of the atemporality associated with mainstream modernism.[40] His D-Tower from 2003, created in collaboration with the artist Q. S. Serafijn, is a paradigmatic example of the production of recording. The tower is 12 metres tall and made of epoxy. During the daytime, it is white-greyish, while at night, from 8 p.m., the tower is lit up by LEDs. It has four colours. The colour of the day is fed by a website where a group of Doetinchem volunteers keep a diary. Each day over the course of six months they answer fifty questions about fear, hate, love and happiness. The computer measures the day's emotions based on the answers. At night, it shows the city's emotion of the day: red stands for love, blue for happiness, yellow for fear, green for hate. In the words of Brian Massumi:

> The tower changes color according to the results, becoming a beacon of the collective mood. Affect has been given visual expression. The predominant affective quality of people's interactions becomes visible. This can undoubtedly reflect back on the interactions taking place in the town by making something that was private and imperceptible public and perceptible. A kind of feedback loop has been created between private mood and public image that has never existed in quite this way before.[41]

Whereas UNS seem to be oblivious to the issues of signifi(c)ance, it is quite the opposite in the case of NOX. The mood of Doetinchem is not red *and* blue (love and happiness), but *either* red *or* blue (love or happiness). It is not the tower that is the body without organs, but the whole of Doetinchem. If anything, the tower is an ad hoc organ (without the body). While UNS are concerned with the problem (of endlessness), NOX seem to be more interested in the solution (or convergence, that is singularities), hence the title of *The Architecture of Continuity*.[42] The polar opposite of this continuity, with a noumenal form of energy – which refers to the coming together of action-perception-construction (relation) – is not discontinuity but endlessness itself (infinite). Of the three conceptual personae, it is NOX that most explicitly embrace the Northern Line, although, in this particular case, 'gothic' can be read as a synonym for Northern Line.[43] In an interview entitled 'The Aesthetics of Variation', Spuybroek cites liberally from Worringer:

> 'The Ceaseless Melody of the Northern Line' is one of the chapters in [Worringer's] book *Formprobleme der Gotik* (1911) – in English, *Form in Gothic*. Let's just start off with: 'in Northern ornament repetition does not bear this restful character of addition' – and with this he means classicist symmetry – 'but has, so to speak, a character of multiplication. The intervention of any desire for organic moderation and serenity here is lacking.' A shot right between the eyes of Alberti. Symmetry replaced by repetition, by serial rhythms of multiplication. Nobody really understood at the time how Worringer could have done this book on the gothic three years after his famous *Abstraction and Empathy* (1908), which became the bible of early abstract painters. But it's the same expressionism: 'the Northern Line does not get its life from any impress which we willingly give it, but appears to have an expression of its own, which is stronger than life.'[44]

What sets NOX apart is the attention to what is going on (genealogy) in what happened (archaeology) or the attention to the distribution of singularities on the body without organs: 'Life Constructs. Agency builds.'[45] The vagueness of BwO is not to be taken as a lack of logic, but quite the opposite. According to Lars Spuybroek, it is precisely that which constitutes relations. Most importantly, these relations are exterior to their terms. It is the relations that create the whole, and not the part or finalities, as Spuybroek calls them. Finality, in turn, is the polar opposite of generality: 'things are necessarily vague [not ambiguous], since they are one and many at the same time'.[46] It is for this reason that diagramming is still the most important innovation in architecture, claims Spuybroek in 'Motor Geometry'. On a techno-cultural level, diagramming signifies a move towards metadesign or 'designing the way of designing itself'.[47]

Naked Boxer Eating Oysters: Celibate Machine

Finally, the conjunctive syntheses give rise to the 'celibate machine', which, as the practical equivalent of the 'pure future' (Nietzschean eternal return), unites the repulsive tendency of the paranoiac machine and the attractive tendency of the miraculating machine.[48] The eternal return is defined by Deleuze in a very formal manner, as summed up by James Williams in the following proposition: only difference returns and never the same.[49] This, in turn, means that novelty is always an expression of pure differences in new events. The three machines – paranoiac, miraculating and celibate – are strictly non-sequential. The last one is the locus of *jouissance* and affirmation: *sentio ergo sum.* The 'conjunctive syntheses of consumption' take the form of a reciprocally determined mode of existence by (retroactively) concluding 'so it's . . .'.[50] This is a 'larval subject', beyond the human, who affirms life by evolving with (rather than within) an unrepresentable time, 'a strange subject with no fixed identity, wandering about over the body without organs . . . being born of the states that it consumes'.[51] The conjunctive synthesis therefore involves the creation of convergent relations among series, an operation which forms 'individuation fields' that already prefigure the intensive pre-actualisation.

If the interest of UNS lies in the physiological register and that of NOX in the register of significance, then OMA could be said to have an ongoing interest in the psychological, with Voluptas as its form of energy.[52] The Downtown Athletic Club discussed in Koolhaas's *Delirious New York*[53] provides for (metropolitan) conditions that engender (larval) subjects that consume them. According to the architectural historian Hans van Dijk, Koolhaas does not use the club's section only as a corrective intervention in order to resist the banality of the high-rise, or for mere programme distribution, as that would amount to the ordinary and reductive use of a diagram. Rather, the club's section becomes a deliberate design device to employ the abstract machine, which produces the skyscraper and makes it susceptible to the unforeseen.[54]

We have located the 'Naked Boxer Eating Oysters – Celibate Machine' in *Delirious New York*. Here Koolhaas studied how the programmes of the thirty-eight-storey Downtown Athletic Club subverted the usual uniformity of the blank-faced tower to become the 'apotheosis of the Skyscraper as instrument of the Culture of Congestion'. The club harbours a sometimes surreal collection of activities – squash courts, a swimming pool, a colonic centre and an indoor golf course – united only by the circulatory core of thirteen elevators that unite and feed all the floors. The ninth combines a room full of punching bags with an oyster bar. 'Eating oysters with boxing gloves, naked,' says Koolhaas, 'such is the "plot" of the ninth story, or, the twentieth century in action'. According to Jeff Kipnis, the free section is the necessary invention:

> A recasting of the metropolis's vertical infrastructure into a building device to achieve the unregulated anonymities – and thus stage the unfettered behaviors – that are not possible in free-plan [in order to] detach the subject in a building from the regime of immediate experience, with its emphasis on satisfied expectations and phenomenological, haptic, aesthetic, and symbolic pleasures, in order to place them elsewhere as subjects of a different spatial regime, one with other pleasures, other expectations, other politics.[55]

This makes OMA an expert in the 'production of consumption or consummation', both libidinal and political, which is virtually the same.[56] However, by no means does the (quasi) subject come ready-made only to be detached; rather, it is reciprocally determined.[57] It can therefore only declare (in retrospect) 'so that's what it was'. It is a 'celibate machine'. As Arie Graafland writes in *Architectural Bodies*:

> Koolhaas describes The Downtown Athletic Club in Manhattan (DAC) as a [bachelor] machine where the New York 'bachelor' brings his body into peak condition. To find that original idea which was ultimately realized in America, we must turn to a second machine ['the culture of congestion' aka Ginzburg's 'social condenser' being the first], that of Marcel Duchamp, who a few years previous to DAC had realized his *La Mariée mise à nu par ses célibataires, même* [The Bride Stripped Bare by Her Bachelors, Even]. . . . Indeed, from Beckett to Duchamp, this is an important impulse in the thinking of a number of intellectuals at the beginning of this [twentieth] century.[58]

As we have seen, Deleuze rejects the Kantian restriction of synthesis to the active 'I think' and the relegation of the passive self to receptivity. That is to say that the bachelor or celibate machine is not the same thing as the willing machine. The bachelor is a playful suitor, as with Duchamp, hovering on the border between the respectable and the unknown, and hence suspect: that is, forever produced as a new alliance between the paranoid and the miraculating, between desiring machines and the body without organs. The celibate machine consequently creates the nomadic subject as a residue, something left over. This subject can be an individual, text, practice, architecture or an institution. It is an offshoot of a particular constellation of forces. The opposition between the forces of attraction (continuum) and repulsion (endlessness) produces an open series of intensive positive elements that are never to reach the state of equilibrium of a system. Instead, they express a variety of metastable states, which a (larval) subject undergoes. It is worth repeating that – contrary to popular belief – nomads do not move but stay put. Instead of changing their habitat, like migrants or sedentaries, nomads change their habit. The nomadic subject 'consumes and consummates each of the states through which it passes, and is born of each of them anew'.[59] As Fadi Abou-Rihan suggests, the conjunctive synthesis is 'quasi traumatic' in that it acts as the 'signpost of a radical shift in the subject's thought, perception, and experience'; in other words, a shift in the very manner in which the subject deploys 'itself for itself and for others'.[60] He further explains the significance of this ontogenetic imbroglio:

> Through the conjunctive (it's me and so it's mine . . .) synthesis, Deleuze and Guattari are effectively redefining insight and in the process rearranging the terms if not the relevance of the debate here. The synthesis in question is ostensibly a 'so that's what it is!' moment of insight and a clarity identified by its effect to reorganize radically not only delirium (thought) but hallucination (perception) and intensity (experience) as well. The 'so that's what it is!' is not so much a revelation or an uncovering of the subject to itself but the making of a subject.[61]

While the subject does depend on the interaction between I experience, I think and I see, Abou-Rihan continues, 'it is not the sum total of all three moments or modes [intensity, delirium and hallucination]; it is an offshoot and a side-effect rather than a unity precisely because it is constantly disrupted by its nature as a subject in *jouissance*'.[62] In this way Deleuze and Guattari manage to rebut a long tradition in both philosophy and psychoanalysis that has insisted on inscribing the subject as primarily grounded in thought (Descartes) or language (Lacan). Such fetishistic subjects have deluded themselves into thinking in the mode of the ready-made that is at the centre of its various experiences and understandings, *separate* from the constellation of intensities that it undergoes.

This revelation sheds a new light on the critique of Koolhaas's alleged regressive strategy of frequent reference to retroactivity. Take, for example, his report on a student field trip to Berlin in the early 1970s. Under the subtitle *Reverse Epiphanies*, Koolhaas admits to the following 'negative revelation': 'The [Berlin] wall also, in my eyes, made a total mockery of any of the emerging attempts to link form to meaning in a regressive chain-and-ball relationship.'[63] The wall's meaning, according to him, appeared to change almost daily or even hourly, often depending on remote events and decisions. 'So, that's what it was.' It turned out that its significance, as a piece of architecture, was in fact marginal. Koolhaas, by his own admission, would never again believe in form as the primary vessel of meaning. How could he, given the ubiquitous capitalist machine that decodes flows and deterritorialises the socius, only to conjoin them anew on its immanent field in order to extract a surplus value? The question arises whether the energy released via production (of consumption) can be reclaimed as Voluptas, that is to say not in the sense of regressing to the wall (any wall – metonym for architecture) as a territorial sign (coding), and not by overcoding: enter the celibate machine. While conscious investment generates subjugated groups who privilege power over desiring-production in their attempt to change the socius, unconscious or libidinal investment generates subject groups whose programmeless politics subordinates the socius to pure desire with no interest, cause or teleology.[64] At their most experimental, art and architecture have the capacity to escape their historical moment. This is the *sine qua non* of the project of defatalisation. Upon receiving the Pritzker Prize in 2000, Koolhaas was interviewed by one of the editors of *S, M, L, XL*, Jennifer Siegler. In some of his answers we find an almost uncanny resonance with the 'production of production, recording and consummation' thesis that we put forward:

Jen: That must be why you make people nervous. You take in everything. People feel that.

Rem: I can't ever be oblivious. I wrote a sentence today: 'The tyranny of the oblivious . . .' My whole life has been about envying the tyranny of the oblivious. And feeling the vulnerability of the . . . recorder.

Jen: Of the what?

Rem: Of those who record.

Jen: You call yourself a recorder.

Rem: The thing is that I have a really intense, almost compulsive need to record. But it doesn't end there, because what I record is somehow transformed into a creative thing. There is a continuity. Recording is the beginning of a conceptual production. *I am somehow collapsing the two – recording and producing – into a single event.*[65]

A People Is Missing

It goes without saying that our triad appears too neat.[66] However, it bears repeating that it is never exclusive. Each of the respective conceptual personae/ aesthetic figures discussed above is a product of a specific machinism and the (desiring) machines are part of the same continuum. This means that the three syntheses are irreducible. It is also impossible to circumvent any of them. Yet, according to our (schizo)analysis, a difference of emphasis appears nevertheless.[67] We will refer to it as style. This style is not an effect, but a quasi-cause. It may be argued that Dutch architects such as Claus and Kaan and MVRDV have an exquisite style. By contrast, we would argue that UNS, NOX and OMA have no style. Rather, thanks to the abstract machine or the Northern Line, it is style that has them. Let us reiterate that the schizophrenia Deleuze and Guattari embrace is not a pathological condition. For them, as Massumi explains, 'the clinical schizophrenic's debilitating detachment from the world is a quelled attempt to engage it in unimagined ways. Schizophrenia as a positive process is inventive connection, expansion rather than withdrawal.'[68] What sets our triad apart – as potential proponents of immanent architecture – is the ambition not to fulfil the desire of a ready-made audience but to produce its own audience and quite literally so. Thus, we emphasise passive syntheses with the clear architectural agenda of forcing the shift from the design of form to the design of experience. We proceed from the premise that the individual is not form but power.[69] What we refer to as the 'mapping of agency', which is complementary but antecedent to the well-known agency of mapping, is best explained by Deleuze qua Klee in *A Thousand Plateaus*:

> The artist opens up to the Cosmos in order to harness forces in a 'work' (without which the opening onto the Cosmos would only be a reverie incapable of enlarging the limits of the earth); this work requires very simple, pure, almost childish means, but also the forces of a *people*, which is what is still lacking.[70]

Consider the juxtaposition with the architecture theorist Robert Somol's 'active', that is representational (social constructivist), historical triad, where he starts by questioning the stability of form (Table 3.3). By contrast to our 'passive' triad, this *logocentric* triad found that form was not neutral, but constructed by linguistic and institutional relations. According to Somol, the agenda was first broached in Robert Venturi's deployment of collage as a deviation of form to become information or sign, which was not merely compositional but would include both text and low-brow references. By contrast, Peter Eisenman's deviation would move to the trace, the missing index of formal processes, stressing absence and the conceptual. Finally, John Hejduk would investigate the theatrical construction of form through highly orchestrated relations and instructions, both linguistic and contractual. Somol's three-pronged critique variously foregrounds: context with Venturi (framing mechanisms outside form); process with Eisenman (active procedures within formation); and usage with Hejduk (form's relation

Table 3.3 Three architectural triads: a comparative analysis between the (i) authors' passive, (ii) Robert Somol's 'active' and (iii) Michael Hays's Lacanian systematisation. The difference that marks the first is the dissolution of the self-identical subject: first, in the contraption of habit by the paranoiac machine; second, in the memory of the pure past by the miraculating machine; and finally, in the third synthesis, by the celibate machine, time is witnessed as pure form without content, demented, 'out of joint'. In contrast to the model of recognition adhered to by Somol and Hays, the encounter is captured only on the basis of the involuntary thought. It emits signs and intensities that are (empirically) imperceptible, sub-representational yet affective.

(i) Author	PARANOIAC	MIRACULATING	CELIBATE
	machine / *libido*	machine / *numen*	machine / *voluptas*
	UNS	NOX	OMS
	partial objects (p.o.)	resonance b/w p.o.	pure intensities
	percept / hallucination	thought / delirium	experience / intensity

(ii) Somol	IN-FORMING	TRANS-FORMING	PER-FORMING
	Venturi	Eisenman	Hejduk
	context / icon	process / index	usage / symbol

(iii) Hays	IMAGINARY (I)	SYMBOLIC (S)	REAL (R)
	Rossi	Eisenman	Hejduk (IR)
			Tschumi (SR)
	analogy	repetition	encounter / spacing (*différance*)
	arch. big Other signif.	impossibility of signif.	absence / code

Source: author.

to a subject). For Somol, with the neo-avant-garde, 'form would be precisely subjected to the functions of its linguistic descendants: in*form*ing, trans*form*ing, and per*form*ing'.[71] But as Somol professes, yet fails to live up to, working diagrammatically is not to be confused with simply working with diagrams. That is to say, the (non-formal/sub-representational) mapping of agency is not to be conflated with the agency of mapping (in-/trans-/per-forming). Abstract machines do operate within concrete assemblages, but they make the territorial assemblage open on to assemblages of another type (molecular, cosmic) that constitute becomings.

By contrast, Koolhaas in his seminal 'Generic City' suggests that 'molar 'Identity is like a mousetrap in which more and more mice have to share the original bait, and which, on closer inspection, may have been empty for centuries.'[72] In other words, what makes abstract machines abstract is that they know nothing of forms and substances. Form is never subjected to anything.[73] Nor is it representation of the real as in Michael Hays's Lacanian systematisation (third triad: imaginary – symbolic – real). Despite their apparent opposition – projective Somol and critical Hays – they share a correlationist stance: philosophy of access and access to access.[74] For schizoanalysis, as opposed to psychoanalysis, the real

= desiring-production.[75] In *Anti-Oedipus* Deleuze and Guattari consider that 'the machines of desire ... no longer allow themselves to be reduced to the structure any more than to persons[. They thus] constitute the Real in itself, beyond or beneath the Symbolic as well as the Imaginary.'[76] Every abstract machine is nothing but a consolidated aggregate of (unformed) matters and (non-formal) functions, that is phylum and diagram. It is singular and creative, real yet non-concrete, actual yet non-effectuated. That is precisely why abstract machines can be dated and named: UNS's paranoiac machine, NOX's miraculating machine and OMA's celibate machine. Not that they refer to architects or to architecture (effectuating moments). On the contrary, it is the names and dates that refer to the singularities of the machines, and to what they effectuate.

Notes

This essay, co-authored with Deborah Hauptmann, first appeared in *Deleuze and Architecture*, edited by Hélène Frichot and Stephen Loo (Edinburgh: Edinburgh University Press, 2013), 40–60.

1. Deleuze, *Essays Critical and Clinical*, 143.
2. Deleuze and Guattari, *A Thousand Plateaus*, 496–7.
3. Deleuze and Guattari, *What Is Philosophy?* If we make an analogy with Deleuze and Guattari's conceptual persona, who is not the thinker's representative but rather the reverse, we could say that the architect is only the envelope of her principal aesthetic figure. Deleuze and Guattari explain the reversal as follows: 'Aesthetic figures and the style that creates them have nothing to do with rhetoric. They are sensations: percepts and affects, landscapes and faces, visions and becomings.' Ibid., 177.
4. Deleuze describes passive synthesis as one which 'is not carried out by the mind, but occurs in the mind'. They are passive as they do not presuppose an active agency on the part of the self-identical subject governed by a principle of common sense. Beneath active syntheses of thought there are passive syntheses of perception, and farther beneath them still there are passive organic syntheses of metabolism; see: Protevi, 'Deleuze, Jonas, and Thompson'. See also: Deleuze, *Difference and Repetition*, 71, 73.
5. Deleuze and Guattari, *Anti-Oedipus*, 27.
6. Ibid., 28.
7. Ibid., 30.
8. Smith and Ballantyne, 'Flow', 24.
9. Deleuze, *Difference and Repetition*, 98.
10. Rancière, *The Politics of Aesthetics*.

11. According to Rancière, aesthetics is central to politics as the social and political systems are founded on the distribution of the sensible (aesthetic regimes): 'forms of visibility, ways of doing and making and ways of conceptualizing'. Ibid., 91. We agree with Katharine Wolfe's assertion that – despite Rancière's denunciation of Deleuze's philosophy in general and his theory of imperceptibility in particular – he is much closer to Deleuze than generally thought; see: Wolfe, 'From Aesthetics to Politics'.

12. Deleuze and Guattari, *A Thousand Plateaus*, 141–2.

13. Deleuze, *Difference and Repetition*, 222.

14. 'What holds an assemblage together [what gives it consistency] is not the play of framing forms or linear causalities but, actually or potentially, its most deterritorialised component.' Deleuze and Guattari, *A Thousand Plateaus*, 374. See also: Williams, 'Deleuze's Ontology and Creativity'.

15. Guattari, *Chaosophy*, 73–4.

16. Deleuze and Guattari, *Anti-Oedipus*, 338.

17. Ibid., 9.

18. Deleuze, *Difference and Repetition*, 74.

19. Ibid., 91.

20. Lorraine, 'Living a Time Out of Joint'. 'Deleuze derives a notion of the living present as a contraction or synthesis of time from Hume: two moments (for example the tick-tock of a clock) are impressed upon the imagination which acts as a kind of sensitive plate that retains one moment (or one case of two moments) as the next appears. This results in a living present that is a synthesis of the past (the retention of preceding moments or cases, say two tick-tocks) and the future (anticipation that the next moment or case will be like the past, the expectation that yet another tick-tock will follow).' Ibid., 34.

21. Deleuze and Guattari, *Anti-Oedipus*, 309, 323.

22. Van Berkel and Bos, eds, *Move: (2)*, 80.

23. Ibid., 83.

24. Daniel Birnbaum and Greg Lynn, 'In Conversation with Ben van Berkel and Caroline Bos, "Digital Conversation"', 15.

25. Betsky, 'Unfolding the Forms of UNStudio', 9, 11.

26. Van Berkel and Bos, 'Corporal Compactness'.

27. Van Berkel and Bos, eds, *Move: (1)*. 'Sex, Warhol, Television, Disney, Fellini, Resonance, God, Pornography, Therapy, Tarkowski, Politic, XTC, Money, . . .', Ibid., 10–11.

28. Van Berkel, 'The New Understanding'.

29. Van Berkel and Bos, 'Deep Planning'. The 'Midtown (NY) cross-section' diagram is illustrative of the approach: flow of passengers into Manhattan, flow of passengers

(subway), flow of goods into Manhattan, actual building horizon, building height permitted by zoning.

30. Van Berkel and Bos, eds, *Move: (1)*, 15.

31. Ibid., 221.

32. Ibid., 156–7.

33. 'Such is our inconsistency and impatience, which you could also say is an irrepressible belief in the imagination. This is why the unlikely coupling of art and airports to us represents a new statement, a figment, an appeal to an imagination that is both public and private and that cannot be ignored.' Birnbaum and Lynn, 'Digital Conversation', 21.

34. Edelkoort, 'In Free Fall', 96–7.

35. 'When the present is a dimension of the past the process relating the two is different from when the past is a dimension of the present. With the past as prior, processes of making pass and changing relations in the pure past come to complement the process of contraction in the living present. There is therefore an extraordinary richness and potential for experimentation and applications in Deleuze's philosophy of time.' Williams, *Gilles Deleuze's Philosophy of Time*, 14.

36. Deleuze and Guattari, *Anti-Oedipus*, 11. See also: Deleuze, *Two Regimes of Madness*. 'The organless body attracts the organs, appropriates them for itself, and makes them function in a regime other than the one imposed by the organism, in such a way that each organ is the whole body – all the more so, given that the organ functions for itself and includes the functions of all the others. The organs are thus "miraculously" born on the organless body, obeying a machinic regime that should not be confused either with organic mechanism or with the organization of the organism.' Ibid., 20.

37. 'Instinct perfected is a faculty of using and even of constructing organized instruments; intelligence perfected is the faculty of making and using unorganized instruments.' Bergson, *Creative Evolution*, 140.

38. Deleuze and Guattari, *Anti-Oedipus*, 13.

39. Ibid., 8.

40. 'The new doesn't come from the future, it comes from the past. That's what potentiality is: a mating of old existing events patterning into tendencies, an unfolding of events.' Spuybroek, 'Sensograms at Work', in *The Architecture of Continuity*, 164.

41. Massumi, 'Transforming Digital Architecture from Virtual to Neuro'.

42. Spuybroek, *The Architecture of Continuity*.

43. Spuybroek, *The Sympathy of Things*, 46–7.

44. Spuybroek in an interview by Arjen Mulder, 'The Aesthetics of Variation', 142–3.

45. Spuybroek, *The Architecture of Continuity*, 19.

46. Ibid., 23–4.

47. Spuybroek, 'Motor Geometry', 50.

48. In Nietzsche's notion of the eternal return, all events communicate and no predicate is excluded in the event of events. This is a synthetic affirmative disjunction which spells death to the self, the world and God 'to the advantage of divergent series as such, overflowing now every exclusion, every conjunction, and every connection'. See: Deleuze, *The Logic of Sense*, 176.

49. Williams, *Gilles Deleuze's Philosophy of Time*, 16.

50. Deleuze and Guattari, *Anti-Oedipus*, 12.

51. Ibid., 16.

52. In Roman mythology, Voluptas or Volupta was the beautiful daughter born from the union of Cupid and Psyche. She is one of the Charites, or three Graces, and is known as the goddess of sensual pleasures whose Latin name means pleasure or bliss.

53. Koolhaas, *Delirious New York*.

54. Van Dijk, 'Critical Project or the Project of Criticism?', 72.

55. Kipnis, 'Moneo's Anxiety', 103.

56. See Arie Graafland's introduction to *Architectural Bodies*, 'Artificiality in the Work of Rem Koolhaas', 8–9. See also the statement by Deleuze and Guattari: 'Our view presupposes only one economy [political *and* libidinal], and hence the problem . . . is to show how unconscious desire sexually invests the forms of this economy as a whole.' *Anti-Oedipus*, 88.

57. 'If there is to be a "new urbanism" . . . it will no longer aim for stable configurations but for the creation of enabling fields that accommodate processes that refuse to be crystallized into definitive form; it will no longer be about meticulous definition, the imposition of limits, but about expanding notions, denying boundaries, not about separating any identifying entities, but about discovering unnamable hybrids; it will no longer be obsessed with the city but with the manipulation of infrastructure for endless intensifications and diversifications, shortcuts and redistributions – *the reinvention of psychological space.*' Koolhaas, *S, M, L, XL*, 961–9; emphasis added.

58. Graafland, 'Artificiality in the Work of Rem Koolhaas', 44. 'Deleuze and Guattari characterized the bachelor machine as a machine of consumption, a gratification that could be called auto-erotic [auto-affective]. This mechanical eroticism proclaims a new connection. A new power [Voluptas] is liberated.' Ibid., 64.

59. Deleuze and Guattari, *Anti-Oedipus*, 20. It is also important to recognise that for Deleuze and Guattari, 'the lived state [comes] first, in relation to the subject that lives it'. Ibid., 40.

60. Abou-Rihan, *Deleuze and Guattari*, 73.

61. Ibid., 72–3.

62. Ibid., 71.

63. Koolhaas, *S, M, L, XL*, 214–33.
64. Whereas the socius is used to indicate social organisation at the level of the social-libidinal mode of production in *Anti-Oedipus*, in *A Thousand Plateaus* it is further refined to indicate a set of analytic tools that include strata, instruments of capture, war-machines and regimes of signs. For an account of the socius situated in a critique of Koolhaas, see Graafland, *The Socius of Architecture*, Part One.
65. Koolhaas, 'Interview by Jennifer Sigler'; emphasis added.
66. Peirce coined the term triadomany for such an over-reliance on trichotomies; see Peirce, *Collected Papers of Charles Sanders Peirce*, CP 1.569 Cross-Ref: ††.
67. It may be said that what distinguishes these approaches – connective, disjunctive and conjunctive – is at once their strength and weakness in respect of each other. That is to say that they become more susceptible to potential co-option by the dominant regime and fetishisation: the first via the physical, the second via the semiotic and the third via the psychic.
68. Massumi, *A User's Guide to Capitalism and Schizophrenia*, 1.
69. The logic of relations is founded on this premise – the individual as power (*puissance*) – as well as on the independence of relation in relation to its terms; see Deleuze, *Cours Vincennes*, 'Sur Spinoza' (17 February 1981).
70. Deleuze and Guattari, *A Thousand Plateaus*, 337.
71. Somol, 'Dummy Text'.
72. Koolhaas, *S, M, L, XL*, 1248.
73. 'Abstract machines are always at work upon stratified territories, constantly "setting things loose", but at the same time, that which is deterritorialised, the "new" which is invented from the diagram, is constantly being put back to work, productively employed and "enveloped" again by the strata that surround it. Hence there is in fact, contra Somol and Whiting, no absolute opposition between the indexical/territorial and the diagrammatic/abstract.' Spencer, 'The Critical Matter of the Diagram', 13.
74. Radman, 'Architecture's Awaking from Correlationist Slumber' (Chapter 2 in this volume).
75. While psychoanalysis settles on the imaginary and structural representatives of reterritorialisation, schizoanalysis follows the machinic indices of deterritorialisation; see Smith, 'The Inverse Side of the Structure'.
76. Deleuze and Guattari, *Anti-Oedipus*, 52.

4   Sensibility is Ground Zero:
    On Inclusive Disjunction and Politics of
    Defatalisation

THIS CHAPTER ENDEAVOURS to rebut a long-standing philosophical and psychoanalytic tradition of inscribing the subject as primarily grounded in thought or language. As such, the fetishist self-identical subject is deluded into being the epicentre of various experiences and understandings, separate from the constellation of intensities that it undergoes. Yet, as the philosopher Claire Colebrook explains: once we try to think the origin of all that is, the very ground of being, then we arrive properly not at the origin of sensibility, but sensibility as origin. Sensibility is ground zero. A special agility of mind is required once we find ourselves on the metastable ground where things are not logically necessary but merely contingently obligatory. The claim is not that anything goes, for that would constitute a regression to postmodernism. Architecture as a discipline does not represent culture but is a mechanism of culture. It is flush with matter. The architect's ethos rests on the premise that what is there could have been otherwise and that there is no simple correlation between urban and social form. The ecological attitude entails no preference for either the tendency of the components to couple together or their intrinsic independent behaviour. Rather, the processes of both territorialisation and deterritorialisation, both striation and smoothing, are to be taken as reciprocally constitutive.

Transcendental Empiricism

Even materialism has to come to terms with the real-yet-incorporeal. Gilles Deleuze's answer is transcendental empiricism, which on the face of it might appear to be an oxymoron. However, there is nothing inconsistent about thinking immanence this way, for it is transcendental in its refusal of any 'image of thought', and it is empirical in its openness to affective encounters.[1] The key is not to model the transcendental after the empirical as Kant did.[2] Instead of elevating the empirical to the transcendental, Deleuze describes the real structure of the latter without reference to the former. The emerging and the emerged pertain to two modes of one reality (monism). Everything starts from the sensible but is subsequently extended into the intelligible. Put otherwise, the intelligible is the occlusion of the sensible and not the other way around. Moreover, sensations mobilise the differential forces that make thinking possible. This is what Deleuze means by 'pedagogy of the senses'.

The convergence of matter and thought is diagrammed in *The Fold: Leibniz and the Baroque* as two floors of a baroque house connected by 'draperies'. The vertical upper floor is described as a closed private room decorated with 'a drapery diversified by folds'. The lower horizontal floor contains common rooms, with 'several small openings': the five senses.[3] It is indicative that there is no structural homology between the two floors. The form of expression and the form of content do not share a form. There is no meta-form. What connects the two is a process of progressive different/ciation. The architecture theorist Hélène Frichot offers the following interpretation of the allegory:

> We can observe in the upstairs apartment of Deleuze's Baroque house, the folds of soul, and below, on the ground floor, the pleats of matter. Upstairs the voluminous space of the house is entirely dark, it has no windows to the outside . . . Downstairs there are windows, a door, and a . . . set of steps . . . This is the realm of the five senses. . . . The event, restless inhabitant of this house, is that which neither the material nor the immaterial, neither ground nor upper apartment, can entirely account for.[4]

As it turns out, Deleuze's philosophical adversary is not Plato, but the great systemiser Aristotle, who *subsumes particulars under* the appropriate *generality* on the basis of resemblance or representation.[5] By contrast, Deleuze finds less resemblance between a racehorse and a workhorse than between a racehorse and a racing car.[6] Universality never explains anything, it begs an explanation. In the flat ontology, genera are as contingent as the particular species. There is no logical relationship between the individual singular and the universal singular that engenders it. The Aristotelian syllogism, whose prestige has not been dented in the slightest over the past two millennia, is still indispensable for discrete (binary) logic. So is Euclidean mathematics for metric (striated) space, as well as Newtonian physics for isotropic (absolute) space. But when it comes to the logic of continuity (smoothness) it is Leibniz who provides the much-needed conceptual tools. More recently, Deleuze recognised the creative potential of science in general, and differential calculus in particular, to deal with becoming. This 300-year-old mathematical convention allows for the treatment of relations independently of their terms. Differential relations as linked rates of change shift the emphasis from signification to significance, or to the distribution of singularities structuring the manifold.

As the philosopher of technology Bernard Stiegler repeatedly advocates, we ought to stop privileging *epistēmē* over *technē*. The same plea applies to the discipline of architecture, which continues to privilege 'archi' over 'tecture'. It is unfortunate that the self-appointed guardians of disciplinary boundaries are working hard to keep the two realms separate. It is equally damaging to privilege linguistic theories on account of their academic prestige given the limitations of the representational approach. The humanities are simply bankrupt in dealing with the real, that is, with dynamic far-from-equilibrium systems.[7] They cannot but commit the fallacy of conflating the process with the product, a practice known as 'tracing'.[8] According to the speculative realist Ray Brassier, Deleuze's alternative is to conceive of Being itself as neither/nor. This is how he spells out the Deleuzian concept of inclusive disjunction of actual equivocity and virtual univocity:

> The inclusive disjunction is characterized by a unilateral asymmetry: the actual distinguishes itself from the virtual without the virtual distinguishing itself from the actual in return. . . . Being must always be said *both* as virtual and actual; as deterritorialization and as reterritorialization; as smooth space and as striated space; as anorganic life and as strata; as nomadic distribution and as sedentary hierarchy.[9]

Instead of relying on the 'agency of mapping', thinking needs to go in the opposite direction (counter-effectuation), towards the virtual and 'mapping of agency' (line of flight).[10] Despite the temporary decision (effectuation), inclusive disjunction never excludes a potential. The crucial question is: how can we unhook ourselves from the points of subjectification that secure us, nail us down to the dominant reality?[11] *Pace* Fukuyama-inspired libertarian fantasies, the end of history was announced prematurely. What is required as an antidote is the politics of defatalisation. We have to remain wary of any determinism.[12] Famously, Nietzsche was critical of Darwin's all-too-adaptive paradigm. After all, it is thanks to the leeway between the level of genes and the level of organism (epistrata) on the one hand, and the elbow room between the organism and the cosmos (parastrata) on the other, that the new is produced.[13] That is why we will never conclusively know what a body can do and why we are destined to perpetual experimenting. And this is to be done neither by submission nor by willing, but by meeting the universe halfway.[14] In the words of the non-standard architect François Roche, 'the stuttering between Resilience (recognizing vitalism as a force of life) and Resistance ("creating is resisting") seems, in a schizophrenic logic, a plausible hypothesis'.[15]

Vital Asymmetry

Back to sensibility as the ground zero.[16] The father of pragmatism, Charles Sanders Peirce, proposes the following thought experiment. Imagine a pitch-black cave with no gravity, where one relies exclusively upon one's own proprioception (joint sense), sense of smell (olfactory) and temperature-sensing (skin), the three orders of differentiation.[17] Note that these senses only operate locally through an interval of change with no reference to extrinsic space. In other words, each of them is initially self-referenced. As one navigates the Peircean cave, one starts to distinguish between zones in the gradient field and their thresholds (there are no clear-cut boundaries). What this means is that the movement starts to make the connection. Eventually one is able to identify invariants as the three heterogeneous series – proprioceptive, olfactory and thermal – start to relate. We gradually witness the concrescence of extensive and therefore surveyable space, which is born out of topological intensive space of sensation. Smooth space has turned into striated. A surveyable space has emerged as a composition from an overlap of vague qualitative voluminousness, singular points and pure unextended interval. In the words of Peirce:

> The evolution of forms begins, or at any rate, has for an early stage of it, a vague potentiality; and that either is or is followed by a continuum of forms having a multitude of dimensions too great for the individual dimensions to be distinct. It must be by a contraction of the vagueness of that potentiality of everything in general but of nothing in particular that the world of forms comes about.[18]

The speculative pragmatist Brian Massumi stresses that the striated Euclidean geometry in no way contradicts the smooth topological one. They are enfolded, as are a territory and an earth. The nesting of geometries according to their level of generality has been revealed by the mathematician Felix Klein, after whom the famous two-dimensional manifold is named.[19] We shall deal with the order of resilience to transformation qua his Erlangen Programme in more detail below. The mutual dependence or reciprocal determination of the smooth and the striated is often overlooked by eager proponents of the topological turn in architecture who loathe the non-non-Euclidean geometries.

The world is self-generating from potential. According to Massumi, the primitives of the system are lived abstractions that have a nature of the qualitative continuum, and not bits of information (informationist fallacy). What is truly remarkable is that the order of movement and space is reversed. Points in space do not pre-exist their connection. The logic of sensation leads to the logic of relation. Movement does not happen *in* space. Rather, space is a derivative of movement: 'it is the movement of mapping that makes its own territory and territory is made entirely out of sensation; out of experience, out of qualities and differential experience: literal world of sensation'.[20]

The logic of coexistence (relation) is radically different from the logic of separation (discreteness). Massumi emphasises the stark contrast between Peirce's cave and the most famous cave parable, that of Plato (Table 4.1). Curiously enough, in Plato's version the beholders are immobilised by chains and there-

Table 4.1 Two cave parables. Based on Massumi, 'The Virtual'.

PLATO	PEIRCE
IMMOBILISATION (chained down)	Starts from pure MOVEMENT
Forced DISTANCING	PROXIMITY
World MEDIATED (thinkable)	ENCOUNTER (events)
World populated (by pre-existing DISCRETE forms)	Vague qualitative CONTINUUM
Space geometrically PRESTRUCTURED	Form, position, structure EMERGE (virtual continuum; something out of almost nothing; no theology)
COGNITIVE relations (form seen in a distance)	PARTICIPATIVE (emergence precedes knowing; one does not critique, one does; creative: world out of movement)
MORALISTIC	INVENTIVE (appearance emerged)
ENSLAVEMENT	FREEDOM (chance, spontaneity)
TRANSCENDENT (one reaches knowledge only by leaving the cave and ascending to a higher level)	IMMANENT (there are no higher planes, just another twist)
DOUBT	NO DOUBT (it all happens through one's movement; no distance as in visually structured world)

Source: author.

fore compelled to rely on their vision alone, wondering whether (mediated) appearances might be but illusions. In the Peircean version there is no room for doubt, since everything results from one's unmediated interaction (contemplative vs participative space). In the short essay 'Factory', the media philosopher Vilém Flusser makes a similar assertion: *'homo faber* becomes *homo sapiens sapiens* because he has realised that manufacturing means the same thing as learning – i.e. acquiring, producing and passing on information'.[21] No wonder that the *sine qua non* of most optical illusions is the stillness of the beholder. By contrast, seeing is an activity.[22] No sensation is truly passive.

Furthermore, positing discreteness as a derivative of the continuum is even more fundamental in the eternal issue of which takes ontological primacy, permanence or change (being or becoming), usually associated with the two opposed Presocratics, namely, Parmenides and Heraclitus. We ought to move beyond the simple opposition between the two, which seems to imply a kind of symmetry between the striated and the smooth (actual and virtual). The issue is often wrongly presented as a matter of perspective, disregarding a crucial difference between extracting permanence from change and, conversely, inducing movement to stasis. The cofounder of Objectile, architect Bernard Cache, explains the conundrum by reference to the ancient Greek practice of optical correction whereby the artist/architect often deliberately distorted the artefact in order that it might appear correct. Although Plato recognised the validity of such corrections, he objected to the result. In his eyes, to compensate for the foreshortening of the statue that is placed atop a column one would need to alter the proportions of the original and produce an (inferior) simulacrum.[23] According to Cache, this is because, in comparison with the mathematics of his time, Plato lacked the means to cogitate ideas that, due to projective deformation, remain invariant:

> In order to see something other than corruption in [an optically corrected artefact], it would have been necessary for Plato to have projective invariants available to him, and in particular the relationship of relationships, that second-degree logos Spanish mathematicians rightly call *razón doble*, which expresses the number of that which is conserved in projective deformations.[24]

Cache offers a short genealogy of invariants: isometric, homothetic, projective and topological.[25] Simply put, the respective invariants map various degrees of permanence despite the change. The question is what kind of relationship gets preserved or remains unaffected by the transformation. The most primitive invariant is the relationship of identity, an isometric relationship of sameness. It is followed by the second variable invariant which articulates Greek rationality, the homothetic relationship. Two figures are homothetic if they are related by an expansion or geometric contraction. Prior to the invention of the numerical bi-ratio, Desargues and consequently Pascal created the first geometrical projective invariants, namely, alignment and intersection. Finally, in 1736, Euler produces the first topological invariants that are preserved through surface deformations of any kind insofar as their continuity is maintained. The most frequently used example is the topological sameness between the doughnut and the mug, both with a single hole, irrespective of its position or size. Euler's famous formula, which establishes the invariability of the sum of vertices (v) and faces (f), reduced by the number of edges (e) for any polyhedron, constitutes the first topological invariant.[26] This opened up an area of investigation which is far from exhausted and without which there would certainly be no concept of the body without organs (BwO) as we know it.[27]

In 1872 Felix Klein grasped this movement of geometric reason which progresses by inventing increasingly sophisticated invariants as a means of manipulating ever greater variations.[28] Thanks to him we can now define the whole of geometry as the study of invariants of a particular transformation group.[29] As we have seen, an invariant is exactly what it sounds like, a magnitude that does not change under the action of the transformation group, or a set that gets mapped on to itself by the same group.[30] Klein went on to classify all geometries known to him and realised that they formed a hierarchy in which, as we progress from Euclidean geometry in the direction of topology, fewer and fewer properties remain invariant and groups include more and more transformations. Conversely, as we regress, the geometric spaces become increasingly less bland or more detailed or striated (Figure 4.1). The Erlangen Programme, named after the homonymous city in Germany, allowed us to see that all geometry could be treated in the same way and that geometries which at first glance looked disparate were in fact expressions of the same underlying principles. Without succumbing to either unities and totalities, or nominalism, the above sequence of symmetry-breaking fits the Deluzian one = all formula of multiplicities. The nesting of geometries is thus quintessential for the project of transcendental empiricism as a process ontology which is at cross purposes both with the transcendental idealism and naïve empiricism (positivism). The essential thing, from the point of view of empiricism, is the noun multiplicity, which designates a set of lines or dimensions which are irreducible to one another, as Deleuze explains. 'Every "thing" is made up in this way.'[31] The new materialist philosopher Manuel DeLanda offers the following genealogy of what is perhaps the most important Deleuzian concept:

GEOMETRY	Euclidean	Affine	Projective	Topology
TRANSFORMATION	Size	Skewing	Perspective	Stretching
INVARIANT	Angle	Parallels	Straight Line	Sequence

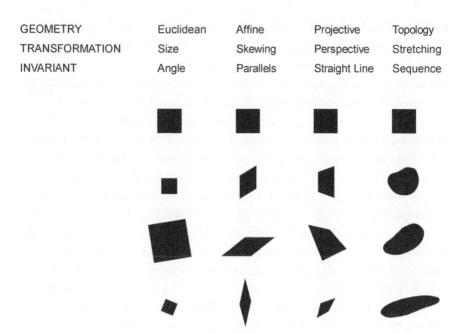

Figure 4.1 Klein's Erlangen Programme: different geometries as subgroups, classified by invariants under transformations, with topological geometry included.

Source: author.

Although the creators of these classifications saw in them a purely logical construction . . . Deleuze views them as morphogenetic, as if metric spaces were literally *born* from non-metric ones through a loss of symmetry . . . While in cardinal series judgments of exact numerical identity of two series can be made, in ordinal series only rigorous judgments of greater or lesser *differences* can be made. Deleuze, whose ambition was always to create the first philosophical system based exclusively on positive differences, made a great deal out of this link. (The concept of 'positive difference' must be contrasted with the idea of difference as mere lack of similarity, an idea which introduces difference in a negative way, as an absence or deficit of resemblance.)[32]

Topologising

Where does all this leave us in terms of architecture? To adopt a topological approach to architecture and urbanism, I would suggest, is to think in terms of capacities (to affect and be affected), rather than mere (intrinsic) properties. As the anthropologist and cyberneticist Gregory Bateson maintained, capacity is always relational: it makes no sense whatsoever to try to understand the

anatomy of half a chicken.[33] Sadly, architectural thinking has always had a preference for proportional invariants. But a preference for simplicity, as Cache
concludes, has less to do with the elimination of redundant features (legitimate
use of simplicity arguments known as Occam's razor) and more with familiarity.

The architecture theorist Jeffrey Kipnis concurs. As has been shown, if we
trace the evolution of geometry from the descriptive via analytic and projective
to topology, we get a different notion of mathematical sameness. Sameness is
Kipnis's synonym for invariance. At the opposite end of the spectrum from
the familiar sameness of Euclidean geometry there lies the topological sameness in dynamic terms. Kipnis cannot resist an all-too-homological analogy:
'Descriptive geometry, like [the postmodern architect] Krier, sought to establish
categories and to construct membership and equivalence tests in order to control difference.'[34] While projective geometry gives rise to a dynamic rather than
categorical theory of the same, with topology we can finally arrive at the following conclusion, as Kipnis indeed does: 'Look at the faces and figures around you:
all variations, no original theme.'[35] The architects who allegedly operate under
this regime of different sameness are the usual suspects: Greg Lynn, Karl Chu,
FOA, Asymptote and so on. What we get from Kipnis's analysis is a graphic
depiction of what the champion of critical architecture Michael K. Hays refers
to as the 'smoothing of architecture'.[36] It brings to mind the canonical hand-
drawn sketch by the British maverick architect Cedric Price captioned *The City
as an Egg*, featuring boiled, fried and scrambled eggs depicting cities of antiquity,
the nineteenth century and modern times, respectively.[37] Kipnis is careful to
draw the line between the 'good' smooth, and the 'bad' semiotic-process, architects. The champion of the latter is Peter Eisenman, who 'must posit an initial
primitive [which is] then transformed in steps so that the result stands like an
indexical record of the transformation, that is, as a text; in other words, the
train wreck is always read from the train'.[38] Conversely, the non-standard architects avoid both formal typologies and train wrecks to launch variation without origin. Kipnis concludes how, despite a common misunderstanding, this
approach draws deeper impetus from the dynamic premises of mathematical
topology than from the aesthetics of shapes. But therein lies the rub. By disen-
gaging the aesthetic from the mathematical, Kipnis effectively sides with those
who relegate it to an autonomous realm whose criteria of value are supposedly
nonrational, amoral and apolitical matters of beauty and style.[39] What I want to
suggest instead is that topologising needs to be extended to the aesthetic. The
space of experience or *spatium*, which is antecedent to the experience of space,
is topological.

The continuous variation is first and foremost an effect of movement. And it is not buildings that move; rather, a variation operates in the relation that precedes both the object and the subject. On this point Deleuze cites Spinoza: 'variation of my force of existing, or . . . *vis existendi*, . . . or *potentia agendi*, the power of acting, and these variations are perpetual'.[40] For Spinoza there is a continuous variation, as Deleuze explains, and this is what it means to exist. In this light, the Greek *entasis* for example – the application of a convex curve to a surface for aesthetic purposes – is not an optical but rather affective 'correction'.[41] The same could be said of Michelangelo's Campidoglio, whose trapezoidal shape draws the city closer to the square, as it were.[42] This would be inconceivable to their Egyptian and medieval predecessors, albeit for different reasons. In the words of Erwin Panofsky:

> The Egyptian theory of proportions, identifying the 'technical' with the 'objec-
> tive' dimensions, had been able to combine the characteristics of anthropom-
> etry with those of a system of construction; the Greek theory of proportions,
> abolishing this identity, had been forced to renounce the ambition to determine
> the 'technical' dimensions; the medieval system renounced the ambition to
> determine the 'objective' ones.[43]

Panofsky thus characterises the Egyptian method as constructional, the classical as anthropometric and the medieval as schematic. I would like to suggest that the leeway between the technical and objective goes beyond mere anthropo-metrics and points to a dynamic relationship.[44] The leeway between the optical (phenomenal) and affective (virtual) seems also to have lost its currency today, with some notable exceptions.[45] The widely accepted change of terminology from the Greek mereological 'proportion' to the modern autonomous 'fraction' is telling. Nonetheless, the dynamic of the assemblage conceived as multiplicity cannot exclude the relation of sensory appreciation (for that would be akin to the anatomy of half a chicken).[46] How could it? If it did, we would operate under a veiled modernist (subject/object) framework, despite (or because of) all the rhetoric. The plane of composition is not to be conflated with the plane of reference, or – *cum grano salis* – production (object) is not to be conflated with its reception (effect). It is even conceivable that the absolute topologising would shed a different light on what appears to be the most rigid of geometries (phenomenologically).

Let us propose an alternative smoothing cascade which depends on the degree to which the construction as a part contributes to the whole: (1) construction is ignored as irrelevant, (2) construction is not emphasised, (3) building is the construction, (4) construction is the building, (5) construction is central and to be expressed as a style.[47] We shall tentatively presume that the gradual increase in the degree of performative contribution to the whole is inevitably achieved at the expense of some other criteria. To put it naïvely, the less the criteria stem from the quasi-objective consideration (construction), the more they become quasi-subjective (aesthetic), with a caveat that such clear-cut oppositions are purely methodological and not ontological.

We begin with irrelevant construction (1). They are buildings designed as graphic or sculptural compositions which often reveal little of the actual construction. In such architecture, the construction itself need not emphasise the expression, and the designer is more concerned with the image than with tectonics. The prime aesthetic figure of this approach is (the latter-day) Frank Gehry. In *What Is Philosophy?*, Deleuze and Guattari define an aesthetic figure as sensory becoming or otherness caught in a matter of expression. Architecture, in this sense, does not actualise the virtual event but incorporates it: 'it gives it a body, a life, a universe'.[48]

The second embodiment is the one where the construction is not emphasised (2). The construction, which is undeniably the supporting structure of any building, may not always be visible. However, thanks to the spatial arrangement it is possible to sense the presence of the construction without being directly confronted by it. The construction can also be less pronounced when it is part of architecture rather than proclaiming itself as a construction. An anonymous family house will suffice as an example of a construction that is not emphasised, a default position of sorts.

When the building is small in scale and built of natural materials, the actual construction need not draw attention to itself. In this case other material qualities dominate: the method of assembly, size and dimension, function of space, illumination, details, colours, and so on. This applies to the building that is the construction (3). An aesthetic figure of this category is (early) Zaha Hadid.

The Industrial Revolution helped to discover and develop new materials. Some designers choose to emphasise new, frequently large-scale materials in such a way that the construction is not only dominant but is also the essential aspect of the building. Not only does the construction make the building possible, it is the building itself (4). Functionalism in general, and high-tech in particular, are two twentieth-century styles that emphasise the construction in this way, the aesthetic figures being the two British Sirs: Richard Rogers and Norman Foster.

At the beginning of the twenty-first century there emerged a style which drew inspiration from nature and emphasised the inseparability of material from structure. Architects who favour this style examine natural dynamic systems, material behaviour and their application in architecture and engineering. The style came to be known as biomimetic architecture (5). Its aesthetic figure is Greg Lynn.[49] Its most prominent predecessor, however, remains the Catalan Antoni Gaudí.[50] As for the latest, mainly digitally driven, addition to the construction spectrum, I subscribe to Peter Sloterdijk's view on its (as yet) unfulfilled promise:

> Of course biomorphism in architecture is a remarkable thing. But it's mainly an expression of the fact that modern mathematics has caught up with organic forms. So we should avoid drawing false conclusions from this phenomenon. . . . From the perspective of a coming politics of nature, architectural biomorphism should be interpreted as a symbol of the fact that technique has attained the necessary *savoir-faire* to declare its responsibility over organic forms.[51]

It bears noting that, according to the prominent advocate of biomorphism Neil Leach, we are entering a new phase, as the application of parametric (associative) tools is shifting up the scale to the level of the urban.[52] In any case, the spacing of this construction spectrum (1–5) is meant to challenge Hays's excessively phenomenological 'smoothing of architecture', referred to above as the fallacy of isomorphism, given that the polar opposites of (1) and (5) happen to bear the greatest (formal) resemblance. In other words, the logic behind such a classification is still one of typologisation rather than topologisation. It suffers from what Michel Foucault identified as phenomenalisation.[53] Cuvier's legacy seems to have evaporated.

On the level of structure, it is possible to lay out a fitness landscape with four basins of attraction or four typical mechanisms. They can be referred to as species which deal with acting forces in terms of their redirection: (a) form-active structure systems, (b) vector-active structure systems, (c) section-active structure systems and (d) surface-active structure systems.[54] Form-active structures, such as the dome, are systems in single stress condition bearing compressive (or tensile) forces. Vector-active structures mark systems in coactive stress condition: compressive and tensile forces. The most representative example of this species is the truss. Section-active systems tame sectional forces (beams) through bending stress condition. Finally, surface-active structures are systems in surface stress condition. The representative of the species is the tent, with its membrane forces.

It is perfectly conceivable that each of the structures (a)–(d) can be incarnated in any of the constructions (1)–(5) (Table 4.2). There are simply no grounds for judging any of the above as superior, if not aesthetically or in terms of their affective power. Once again we turn to the basic Spinozian definition of affect, which is an ability to affect or be affected. In the words of Massumi:

Table 4.2 Construction spectrum and structure state space.

CONSTRUCTION (C)	STRUCTURATION	
(1) C Irrelevant		
	(a) Form Active	(naturalising)
(2) C Not Emphasised	*performative*	
	(b) Vector Active	(abstracting)
(3) Building = C		
	(c) Section Active	(substantial)
(4) C = Building	*aesthetic*	
	(d) Surface Active	(ephemeral)
(5) C = Style		

Source: author.

Right off the bat, this cuts transversally across a persistent division, probably the most persistent division. Because the ability to affect and the ability to be affected are two facets of the same event. One face is turned towards what you might be tempted to isolate as an object, the other towards what you might isolate as a subject. Here, they are two sides of the same coin. . . . No need to detour through well-rehearsed questions of philosophical foundations in order to cobble together a unity. You start in the middle, as Deleuze always taught, with the dynamic unity of an event.[55]

This tectonic digression is meant to illustrate the potency of the concept of inclusive disjunction. My plea for topologising as genuine smoothing has no other purpose but to adequately conceptualise the event. It is not about what happened, but about what is going on in what happens. Foucault lists three major attempts at conceptualisation of the untimely in the recent past: neo-positivism, phenomenology and the philosophy of history.[56] Needless to say, they all failed miserably:

Neopositivism failed to grasp the distinctive level of the event; because of its logical error, the confusion of an event with a state of things . . . Phenomenology, on the other hand, reoriented the event with respect to meaning . . . from this evolves a logic of signification, a grammar of the first person, and a metaphysics of consciousness. As for the philosophy of history, it encloses the event in a cyclical pattern of time. Its error is grammatical; it treats the present as framed by the past and future. . . . Thus, three philosophies that fail to grasp the event.

Foucault continues by laying down the respective fallacies:

The first, on the pretext that nothing can be said about those things which lie 'outside' the world, rejects the pure surface of the event and attempts to enclose it forcibly . . . The second, on the pretext that signification only exists for consciousness, places the event outside and beforehand, or inside and after . . . The third, on the pretext that events can only exist in time.[57]

It should be noted that Deleuze and Guattari do not recognise abstraction in the cascading of invariants in the sense of the principle of parsimony or finding the common denominator. In this they resist the geometric abstraction of the art historian Wilhelm Worringer, only to embrace 'a line of variable direction that describes no contour and delimits no form'.[58] The nesting – with different orders of abstraction (relationship of relationship) – offers the basis for the (posthuman) leap of imagination. It is a way to perceive the relation exterior to its terms, or the realm of the virtual.[59] Unlike a transcendent heaven inhabited by pure beings without becoming (unchanging essences or laws with permanent identities), the virtual could be said to be populated exclusively by pure becomings without being.[60] This, of course, is an asymptotic (unattainable) condition. In other words, once we arrive at this ultimate level of pure relationality through counter-actualisation, we are not just rid of the contingent actuality (trains and train wrecks), but can begin to ponder the alternative processes of individuation, in terms of pre-actualisation. Counter-actualisation, in fact, always complements pre-actualisation, as DeLanda explains. While the former extracts multiplicities from actually occurring events, the latter takes these and allows them to progressively unfold and differentiate (again, without fully actualising them). The operation of pre-actualisation would not only give multiplicities a certain autonomy from the intensive processes acting on their real causes, it would also endow these impassive and sterile effects with whatever morphogenetic power they enjoy.[61]

Most importantly, in view of our declared anti-essentialist, anti-foundationist and defatalising position, granting consistency to virtual multiplicities (as well-posed problems) endows them in turn with a degree of autonomy from their particular solutions. In stark contrast to positivist sciences, the focus is on the singularities (invariants of invariants) rather than the forces themselves. But to abandon the conventional axiomatic approach in favour of the problematic, one needs to dare to leave the familiar behind. After all, laws are not necessary. They are facts, and facts are contingent because they can change without an apparent reason. Fortunately, there are ways of extracting information from a complex topological shape in order to display it in a comprehensible way, courtesy of the French mathematician Henri Poincaré. DeLanda explains how the 'Poincaré section' works:

An actual system may be 'sampled' or 'sliced through' to obtain its full quasi-causal component, the entire set of attractors defining each flow pattern and the bifurcations which mediate between patterns. In other words, a Deleuzian section would not consist in a mere reduction of the original dimensionality, but in an elimination of every detail of the actual event except its topological invariants: the distribution of its singularities, as well as the full dimensionality of its state space.[62]

Consider the rabbit–fox (prey–predator) mutual dependence. It cannot be grasped by isolating too narrow a sample (in terms of the temporal/spatial scale), for that would be merely accidental and, as such, overdetermining. Zooming out to the all-encompassing level would result in the opposite: underdetermination, which would miss the specificity of the assemblage. By contrast, the Poincaré section reveals the long-term tendency of the coupling or a way of determining a problem without reference to potential solutions. The truth is neither a matter of legality as in Kant, nor intersubjectivity as in Husserl, nor a matter of interpretation as with hermeneutics. In contrast to the immanent patterns of becoming, all of the above are hylomorphic, as they import the guiding principle from the outside. The alternative is to become isomorphic, with the quasi-causal operator which ensures the irreducibility of problems to their solutions. It is only in this way that one can identify specific tendencies and capacities, or what Deleuze calls singularities and affects. The effort to open up multiple paths of differentiation – lines of flight – prevents one from succumbing to the covertly teleological argument of the liberal agenda where all that is required is to fine-tune the status quo.[63]

Molecular Revolution

The question of metaphysics has always been that of the ground. According to the architecture theorist Mark Wigley, its history is that of a succession of different names for the ground – *logos*, *ratio*, *archē*, and so on. Each of them designates being, understood as supporting presence for whatever stands like an edifice.[64] Consequently, before the enquiry even begins, the subject is always already determined as enduring above and beyond its transitory predicates. As such, it is prevented from affirming the movement of affection. As I have tried to argue, the cure is to bracket natural perception, in which every single body, quality or action appears as already constituted. In the words of Deleuze: 'To make the body a power which is not reducible to the organism, to make thought a power which is not reducible to consciousness.'[65] To embrace such a constructivist stance is to embark on the project of defatalisation.[66] The proposal is not to be taken lightly in the era of privatising profits and socialising losses.[67]

Another name for this intensive thinking, which keeps both fatalism and instrumental rationality at bay, is ecology. It rejects the law of parsimony (Occam's razor) in favour of the logic of the included middle. As we have seen, this logic of continuity must not be collapsed with the logic of discreteness. This remains a latent danger and a symptom of the hylomorphic attitude defined as the imposition of form upon supposedly inert matter. The warning issued almost a century ago by the Russian painter Wassily Kandinsky is as timely as ever: 'There is ... the danger that mathematical expression will lag behind emotional experience and limit it. Formulas are like glue, or like a "fly paper" to which the careless fall prey.'[68] Before we list the virtues of non-linear thinking as the watershed of the politics of defatalisation, let us briefly enumerate the five cardinal fallacies of linear thinking:[69]

1. *Closure*: once established, systems are not open to outside influences or sources of energy or information.
2. *Determinism*: the laws of linear systems function universally and cannot be broken. Effects are proportionate to, and can be accurately predicted from, their causes.
3. *Reversibility*: the laws governing linear systems apply in both temporal directions, so that time appears to be inconsequential to them.
4. *Equilibrium*: forces and counter-forces, as well as actions and reactions, tend to balance each other out.
5. *Reductionism*: the whole is the sum of its parts. Since the parts are not changed by their place in the whole, the whole can be reduced to the parts that comprise it.

To supersede the engrained culture of law, with its imperative to control and predict, is to make way for creative thinking which does not take contingency as the mere opposite of necessity. In the words of the godfather of speculative realism, Robin Mackay, 'the thought of contingency stands as a kind of ultimate consummation of the puncturing of human conceit ... It is the bitterest pill to swallow, a distillate of everything indigestible that thinking has served up to us.'[70] The task of transcendental empiricism is to carry out the ambitious project of desubstantialisation of the subject for the process (subjectification). It was the radical empiricist William James who already taught us that crying causes sadness and not the other way around. Similarly, flight is not the result of fright. We are afraid precisely because we are fleeing.[71] In the same vein, the process ontologist Alfred North Whitehead proposed that the sub-ject ought to have been the super-ject all along.[72] A derivative status for the subject shifts the conceptual coordinates entirely from the a priori (axiomatic) means-to-ends logic to the (empirical) attunement to structural coupling (milieu). The linearity of problem-solving becomes almost trivial in comparison to what Deleuze and Guattari call dramatisation.[73] Put simply, the solution's worth is measured by the pertinence of the problem. In *Difference and Repetition*, Deleuze posited that problems/ideas were extra-propositional and sub-representative. These are the virtues of non-linear thinking:

1. *Openness*: systems cannot but be open to outside influences or sources of energy or information. The point debunks essentialism, which privileges intrinsic properties over and above the exteriority of relations.

2. *Singularity*: there are no universal laws, for they too evolve. Effects are not always proportionate to, and cannot be accurately predicted from, their causes. The general lesson of the logic of relation – eco-logic as opposed to ego-logic – is that the stable regularities we observe in actuality do not have specific causes which can be demarcated and isolated. They can only be understood as a dynamic cascade of many processes operating over time (topologisation).

3. *Irreversibility*: time is real. By real we mean irreversible and having real effects or consequences. Each thing perfectly expresses not only the state of one of the universe's neighbourhoods during a specific time interval, but also its own particular historical trajectory within it.[74]

4. *Metastability*: the finite (extensive and engendered) conceals the intensive engendering processes of becoming. The proverbial homeostatic fixation is responsible for the normalising and thus normative tendency. Moreover, the structuralist fantasy of a variably deformable object in a complex vector field as the main principle of design must be challenged. By contrast, only force can be related to another force. Action on action, and not action on object is the formula.

5. *Irreductionism*: event and novelty cannot be subsumed under some general order, because they are emergent properties. Hence, the whole is not of the parts, but alongside them and in addition to them. The sciences have the tendency to reduce downward to the constitutive elements (atoms, quarks, strings), whereas the humanities have the tendency to reduce upward (ideology, politics, culture). Both micro and macro reductionism are pernicious.[75]

To recapitulate, in the linear system there is a correlation between input and output. The greater the force, the greater the change. By contrast, non-linear systems have no such simple 1:1 correlation. A small cause can produce a great effect, or no effect, or variable effect, and so on. In the words of Guattari: 'While the logic of discursive sets endeavours to completely delimit its objects, the logic of intensities, or eco-logic is concerned only with the movement and intensity of evolutive processes.'[76] Process, which Guattari counterposes to system and structure, seeks to grasp existence in the very act of its constitution, definition and deterritorialisation.

The ethico-political lesson of the logic of relation is that everything is contingently obligatory or ontotopological, and not logically necessary or onto-theological.[77] A life form never pre-exists an event. The exteriority of relations is not a principle, Deleuze underlines, it is a vital protest against principles.[78] Resetting ourselves in a metaphysical perspective, as the author of *After Finitude*, Meillassoux, suggests, permits us to reconstruct our existence beyond faith alone or the sole opportunism of interest.[79] Therein lies a possibility of pursuing a genuine politics of defatalisation.

We have seen that the attribute 'non-linear' is as meaningful as its counterpart in the term non-elephant zoology.[80] In other words, linearity is very rare, except in a (flawed) theory that is more often than not obsessed with mastery.[81] Whereas the generic entails subsumption of an occurrence under an a priori rule (form of judgement), the genetic always seeks the rule anew (ethico-aesthetics)[82] (Table 4.3). As Einstein put it: 'So far as the theories ... are about reality, they are not certain; so far as they are certain, they are not about reality.'[83] Not only do we need to adopt non-linearity as a major principle, we must also develop cartographies of power which do not take shortcuts through complexities.[84] The lack of exactitude compensated by the rigour of their modus operandi places

Table 4.3 Features of Linear and Nonlinear Thinking.

EGOLOGY	ECOLOGY
Closure	Openness
Determinism	Singularity
Reversibility	Irreversibility
Equilibrium	Metastability
Reductionism	Irreductionism

Source: author.

those in charge of cultural production at the forefront of the molecular revolu-tion.[85] Molecular, as in always already collective or social; and revolution, as in (inclusive) disjunction or the machinism of singularisation.[86]

Notes

This essay first appeared in *This Deleuzian Century: Art, Activism, Society*, edited by Rosi Braidotti and Rick Dolphijn (Leiden & Boston: Brill/Rodopi, 2014), 57–86.

1. 'The image of thought concerns the problem of presupposition in philosophy – that is, the presupposition of an image that serves as a fundamental ground for what is called thinking to appear.' Lambert, *In Search of a New Image of Thought*, 1.
2. De Beistegui, *Immanence*, 6. See also: Deleuze, *Two Regimes of Madness*, 362–3.
3. Deleuze, *The Fold*, 5.
4. For architectural appropriation of the concept, see: Frichot, 'Stealing into Gilles Deleuze's Baroque House'.
5. Deleuze's hostility towards the greatest of systemisers, Hegel, is well known.
6. 'You will not define a body (or a mind) by its form, nor by its organs or functions [but by its] capacity for affecting or being affected.' Deleuze, *Spinoza*, 124.
7. Classical thermodynamics is fixated on equilibrium with a teleological single opti-mum. By contrast, the metastability of the far-from-equilibrium systems presup-poses a pseudo-equilibrium (over time). For a superb textbook on dynamic systems theories, see: Thelen and Smith, *A Dynamic Systems Approach to the Development of Cognition and Action*.
8. In stark contrast to the creative practice of cartography or mapping (immanent evaluation).
9. Brassier, 'Stellar Void or Cosmic Animal?', 205; emphasis in the original.
10. Corner, 'The Agency of Mapping'.
11. Deleuze and Guattari, *A Thousand Plateaus*, 160.
12. The sociologist Richard Sennett consequently warns against the 'brittle city', the result of overdetermination and systemic closure. See: Sennett, 'The Open City'.
13. Deleuze and Guattari, *A Thousand Plateaus*, 322. The ideally continuous belt or ring of the stratum – the ecumenon defined by the identity of molecular materials, substantial elements and formal relations – exists only as shattered, fragmented into epistrata and parastrata that imply concrete machines and their respective indexes, and constitute different molecules, specific substances and irreducible forms.
14. Barad, *Meeting the Universe Halfway*.
15. Roche, 'Reclaim Resi[lience]stance//......R²', 2.

16. Colebrook, 'Derrida, Deleuze and Haptic Aesthetics', 29. Once we try to think the origin of all that is, the very ground of being, then we arrive properly not at the origin of sensibility, but sensibility as origin.

17. Peirce, *Reasoning and the Logic of Things*, brought to my attention by Brian Massumi's superb interpretation at the Experimental Digital Arts lecture 'The Virtual'.

18. Peirce, *Reasoning and the Logic of Things*, 258.

19. The Klein bottle is a 3D version of the Möbius strip.

20. Massumi, 'The Virtual'.

21. Flusser, *The Shape of Things*, 50.

22. Evans, *The Projective Cast*, 352.

23. Panofsky, *Meaning in the Visual Arts*. 'In contrast to [the Egyptian sculptor], the Greek artist could not immediately apply the canon to his block, but must, from case to case, consult with the "visual percept" that takes into account the organic flexibility of the body to be represented, the diversity of foreshortenings that present themselves to the artist's eye, and possibly, even the particular circumstances under which the finished work may be seen.' Ibid., 100.

24. Beaucé and Cache, 'Objectile', 121.

25. Cache, 'Geometries of Phàntasma'.

26. The formula is: $v - e + f = 2$; e.g. Cube: $8 - 12 + 6 = 2$.

27. Deleuze introduced the notion of the 'body without organs' (BwO) in *The Logic of Sense* (1969); but it was not until his collaborative work with Félix Guattari – particularly *Anti-Oedipus* (1972) and *A Thousand Plateaus* (1980) – that the BwO came to prominence.

28. Klein published an influential research programme and a manifesto under the title *Vergleichende Betrachtungen über neuere geometrische Forschungen*.

29. Michaels and Carello, *Direct Perception*, 31–6.

30. For some concrete examples of invariants, we can list the structural ones, such as gravity and horizon; or transformational invariants, such as seasons, diurnal cycle etc.

31. Deleuze and Parnet, *Dialogues*, xii. Multiplicities are made up of becoming without history, of individuation without subject. It is a being-multiple, instead of a being-one, a being-whole or being as subject.

32. DeLanda, 'Materiality', 373.

33. Bateson, 'Lecture on Epistemology'.

34. Kipnis, 'Form's Second Coming', 59.

35. Ibid.

36. Hays, 'Ideologies of Media'.

37. It also brings to mind Kevin Lynch's three normative models: the city of faith, the

city as a machine and the organic city. See: Lynch, *Good City Form*. See also: Vidler, 'The B-B-B-Body'.

38. Kipnis, 'Form's Second Coming', 59.

39. Bennett, 'How Is It, Then, That We Still Remain Barbarians?', 658.

40. Deleuze, *Cours Vincennes*, 'Sur Spinoza' (24 January 1978).

41. A slight convexity or swelling, as in the shaft of a column, intended to compensate for the illusion of concavity resulting from straight sides. Latin, from Greek, tension, from *enteinein*, to stretch tight.

42. The existing design of the Piazza del Campidoglio and the surrounding palazzi was created by Michelangelo Buonarroti in 1536–46.

43. Panofsky, *Meaning in the Visual Arts*, 102.

44. Wilson, 'Classical Theory and the Aesthetic Fallacy'. 'The most crucial [issue] is the lamentable separation of the roles of "art" and "function" as if they were in opposition to each other, whereas the very essence of Classical thought insisted on their fusion.' Ibid., 39.

45. DeLanda, 'Nonorganic Life'. 'If a simple liquid solution can harden into crystal or glass, ice or snowflake depending upon the multiplicities of nonlinearities shaping the solidification process, human societies – which have a larger range of attractor types – have far more leeway in how they develop stable configurations ... there is much to be learned from analyzing in detail the actual processes of stratification and destratification that have occurred in different societies at different times.' Ibid., 154.

46. It is not at all a matter of bringing things together under one and the same concept, but rather of relating each concept to the variables that determine its mutations. See: Deleuze, *Negotiations*, 31.

47. The construction spectrum, based on the lecture by P. M. C. Scheers, 'Structure, Supporting Structure and Dimensioning', TU Delft (2002).

48. Deleuze and Guattari, *What Is Philosophy?*, 177.

49. Lynn, *Animate Form*. 'Animation is a term that differs from ... motion. While motion implies movement and action, animation implies the evolution of a form and its shaping forces; it suggests animalism, growth, actuation, vitality and virtuality [where] the term virtual here refers to an abstract scheme that has the possibility of becoming actualized, often in a variety of possible configurations.' Ibid., 99.

50. Gaudí calculated the exact curves of the Sagrada Familia in Barcelona by hanging small sandbags from chains. In his studies, the floor plan of the church was attached to the ceiling of his studio. By suspending chains from that floor plan and interconnecting them he was not just calculating the form of their curves, but also the form that could be implemented in masonry (compressive and not tensile stress). This makes Gaudí the first form-finding rather than form-making architect.

51. Sloterdijk, 'Foreword to the Theory of Spheres', 238.

52. For a critique of the mechanistic fallacy at an urban level, see: Graafland, 'An Afterthought on Urban Design'. '"Ground" is in *perception* and *community*.' Ibid., 278.

53. Foucault, 'Theatrum Philosophicum'. Treated as a means to an end, affect becomes reified. For a case of phenomenalisation, see: Zaera-Polo, 'Politics of the Envelope'.

54. The structure spectrum, based on: Engel, *Structure Systems*, 20.

55. Massumi, interviewed by Joel McKim, 'Of Microperception and Micropolitics', 183.

56. Deleuze, *Two Regimes of Madness*. 'The Thinking has an essential relation to history, but it is no more historical than it is eternal. It is closer to what Nietzsche calls the Untimely: to think the past *against* the present – which would be nothing more than a common place, pure nostalgia, some kind of return, if he did not immediately add: "*in favor*, I hope, of a time to come".' Ibid., 241; emphasis in the original.

57. Foucault, 'Theatrum Philosophicum'.

58. Deleuze and Guattari, *A Thousand Plateaus*, 499. Cf. Worringer, *Abstraction and Empathy*.

59. Deleuze credits Hume with discovering the exteriority of relations. Deleuze, *Empiricism and Subjectivity*.

60. The antidote to pure becoming is in the actual body.

61. DeLanda, *Intensive Science and Virtual Philosophy*, 74.

62. Ibid., 131. Cf. Deleuze and Guattari, *A Thousand Plateaus*, 251.

63. The prominent advocate of such an approach is Fukuyama, who argues that the progression of human history as a struggle between ideologies is largely at an end, with the world settling on liberal democracy after the end of the Cold War and the fall of the Berlin Wall in 1989. Fukuyama, *The End of History and the Last Man*.

64. Wigley, *The Architecture of Deconstruction*, 7–8.

65. Deleuze and Parnet, *Dialogues*, 62.

66. Hage, 'The Open Mind and Its Enemies'.

67. Slavoj Žižek, in a talk delivered to Occupy Wall Street protestors in New York's Liberty Plaza on 9 October 2011: 'Look at the movies that we see all the time. It's easy to imagine the end of the world. An asteroid destroying all life and so on. But you cannot imagine the end of capitalism.' Žižek, 'Remarks on Occupy Wall Street', 118.

68. Kandinsky, *Point and Line to Plane*, 30.

69. For an overview of the fallacies of linear thinking, see: Taylor, 'Coevolutionary Disequilibrium', 80–1. That anyone should find the 2008 economic downturn surprising can only be the consequence of precisely this sort of linear thinking.

70. Mackay, 'Introduction', 2. 'Freud remarked that modern man had undergone three

deep "narcissistic wounds". Copernicus had demonstrated that the earth is not the centre of the universe; Darwin, that the human being is a product of natural selection, emerging through the same blind material processes as every other creature; finally, psychoanalysis was to undermine our impression that we are master of our own consciousness and destiny, for unconscious processes beyond our perception and control steer our relation to the world and to ourselves.' Ibid., 2–3.

71. James, *The Principles of Psychology*.

72. Whitehead's replacement of the subject by the superject resonates with Hume's theory of subjectification. In opposition to the psychologisms that start from an entity of 'myself', Hume sees the subject as coagulation in the field of sensation. See: Deleuze, *Two Regimes of Madness*, 349. Hume marked a decisive moment in the philosophy of the subject, because he referred to acts that went beyond the given (what happens when I say 'always' or 'necessary'?). Cf. Whitehead, *Process and Reality*, 29. It is fundamental to the metaphysical doctrine of the philosophy of organism, that the notion of an actual entity as the unchanging subject of change is completely abandoned. An actual entity is at once the subject of experiencing and the superject of its experiences.

73. Deleuze proposes to consider structure as a concrete universal, such that actual things can be viewed as local solutions that explicate the ideal and asignifying connections implicated in the former's virtual constitution. This is why the 'accompaniment' in thought of these processes of realization or individuation is what defines Deleuze's practice as a method of dramatization. See: Toscano, *The Theatre of Production*, 169.

74. Kwinter, *Architectures of Time*, 26–8.

75. Graham Harman, a proponent of object-oriented ontology (a version of speculative realism), has raised the problem of what he calls overmining and undermining objects. In the former case, objects are seen as passive vehicles for signification, whereas, in the latter, they are subdued by the supposedly more fundamental level. Harman, 'On the Undermining of Objects', 21–40. It was Bruno Latour who coined the term irreductionism in his book *The Pasteurization of France*.

76. Guattari, *The Three Ecologies*, 44, 52. Unlike Hegelian and Marxist dialectics, ecologic no longer imposes a resolution of opposites.

77. Ontotopology means that experience is not an event 'in' the mind, separate from the environment. Rather, the mind emerges from the interaction with the environment. Ontotheology is attributed to Heidegger's view that all Western metaphysical systems make foundational claims, or, as Morton puts it, ontotheology proclaims that some things are more real than others. See: Morton, 'Objects as Temporary Autonomous Zones', 154.

78. 'Indeed if one sees in it something which runs through life, but which is repugnant

to thought, then thought must be forced to think it, one must make relations the hallucination point of thought.' Deleuze and Parnet, *Dialogues*, 55.

79. Interview with Meillassoux at 'After Nature' blog. See also: Quentin Meillasoux, *After Finitude*.

80. Mathematician Stanislaw Ulam remarked that to call the study of chaos 'nonlinear science' was like calling zoology 'the study of non-elephant animals'. Gleick, *Chaos*, 60.

81. Even if thought had not arrived at this urgency out of internal necessity, the economic situation, the technological situation, the political situation, the ecological situation and so on, in an increasingly interconnected, shrinking world, cannot but forcibly bring to our attention the corrosion of the illusions of autonomy, sovereignty, control and planning, and make more urgent the call for the new modes of thought that are needed once we attempt to think events outside any predetermined matrix of possibility or probability, and once we accept that we ourselves, our culture and our common sense, are the products of a contingent history. See: Mackay, 'Introduction', 1–9. Cf. Ayache, *Blank Swan*.

82. Deleuze and Parnet, *Dialogues*. 'The abstract does not explain, but must itself be explained; and the aim is not to rediscover the eternal or the universal, but to find the conditions under which something new is produced (*creativeness*).' Ibid., vii.

83. Ontological indeterminacy, radical openness and infinity of possibilities are at the core of mattering. See: Adam Kleinman's interview with Karen Barad, 'Intra-Actions'.

84. Braidotti, *Transpositions*, 31.

85. Political economy and libidinal economy are one and the same. See: Guattari, *Molecular Revolution*, 87.

86. Alliez, Colebrook et al., 'Deleuzian Politics? A Roundtable Discussion'. Colebrook: 'The key thing about Deleuzian politics is that it's less about the conscious will, the decision, the rational, the calculation, . . . As long as we deal with the domain of cognition, we'll never know at what point a body's pleasures or powers [affects] become diminished or mobilised.' Ibid., 178–9.

5   Architecture of Immanence

It's purely abstract, says Deleuze, these 'rights of man', purely abstract, completely empty. It's like what he was trying to say about desire: desire does not consist of erecting an object, of saying I desire this . . . we don't desire an object, it's zero; rather, we find ourselves in situations [that are evolving].[1]

ARCHITECTURE HAS MASTERED metric space – lengths, areas and volumes – all too well. The discipline has yet to come to grips with the intensive space or *spatium*. The problem is that, while it drives fluxes of matter and energy, the difference in intensity tends to cancel itself out spontaneously.[2] An intensive quantity is best understood by contrast with its opposite. An extensive quantity refers to magnitudes which can be spatially subdivided.[3] Conversely, if we split a volume of water at 60°C we do not get two halves of 30°C. The same holds true for elasticity, pressure, duration, density and colour, not to mention joy, suffering, love and hate. In other words, the part-to-whole relationship – which remains perfectly suitable for the register of the extensive – needs to be radically rethought in order to capture the whole, which is not *of* the parts, but alongside them and in addition to them.[4] However, this is not a plea for a (royal) parametricist modus operandi. Quite the contrary: technological (or any other) determinism needs to be kept at bay in favour of a (minor) heuristic practice.[5]

Consider the following precedent from the realm of art. In 1913 Marcel Duchamp produced what he considered to be his most important (anti-retinalist) work: *Three Standard Stoppages*. Duchamp cut three lengths of thread of one metre each, dropped them in free-fall from the same height and reified their contingently acquired shapes into three respective 'yardsticks'. The relation among the three thread events, as he called them, diminished the authority

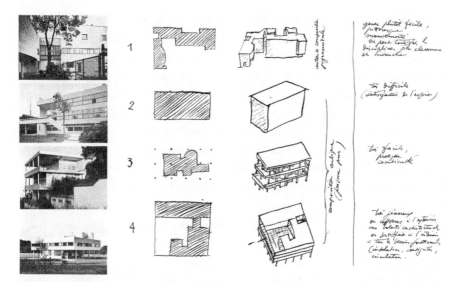

Figure 5.1 Le Corbusier, The Four Compositions (*Les quatres compositions*) (1931): (1) La Roche-Jeanneret Houses in Paris (1923); (2) Villa at Garches (1927); (3) Villa at Carthage (1929); and (4) Villa Savoye at Poissy (1929–31).

Source: © FLC/ADAGP c/o Pictoright Amsterdam 2020.

of the (conventional) metre. His new measurement scheme was a qualitative system which took as measure the approximate relation among events (contingently obligatory situation), instead of the quantitative method of the metre (logical necessity): 'That was really when I tapped the mainstream of my future. In itself it was not an important work of art, but for me it opened the way – the way to escape from those traditional methods of [representation] long associated with art.'[6]

Le Corbusier's famous sketch *The Four Compositions*, accompanied by marginal notes, is quite revealing in this respect (Figure 5.1). It depicts an evolutionary chart of the container-to-content relationship, with the La Roche-Jeanneret House in Paris (1) and the Villa at Garches (2) as the polar opposites.[7] The spectrum (1-3-4-2) spans the vernacularesque inside-out on the one hand, and the boxlike interior (content) subordinate to the exterior (container) on the other. It can be read as an attempt to navigate between the Scylla of mechanicism and the Charybdis of organicism,[8] that is to say, between two respective constructivisms: the additive principle of the small form and the subtractive principle (hollowing out) of the large form.[9] The distinction is appropriated from *Cinema 1: The Movement-Image* (1983), where Gilles Deleuze associates the large form with the SAS' formula: from situation (S) to transformed situation (S') via intermediary of action (A). The small form moves from action to situation, towards new action (ASA'). In the former, action is induced by situation, while the latter operates according to a reversed sensorimotor schema. In Deleuze's words, this is to 'contrast the univocal large organism which embraces the organs and functions to the actions and organs which are gradually formed in an equivocal organisation'.[10] It is important to note that the two conceptions – global and local – are not opposed, but rather express different ways of constituting the mereological relationship: 'The limit of the first would be empty space, but that of the second would be disconnected space'.[11]

There are also conditions under which one can move from one space to the other. The two limits are themselves reunited in the notion of 'any-space-whatever', or what can be referred to as the phase space.[12] In the world of cinema, according to Deleuze, Chaplin's genius lies precisely in mastering both forms simultaneously (3). The example of the Four Compositions is meant to demonstrate that Le Corbusier was aware of the issue: a piece of architecture is not to be defined either by its elements (too easy) or by a centre of unification or comprehension (too difficult), but by its invariants in the face of transformation (tendency/virtuality). There is nothing dialectical about this procedure (difference as opposition/negation). It is a matter of the relations of speed and slowness; it is a situation (differential).[13] Forces have different speeds and economies, explains Claire Colebrook, and a tendency is just a specific relation between expenditure and conservation.[14] Despite Le Corbusier's (high modernist) rhetoric, this could only be achieved in the process of experience/experimentation (ethico-aesthetics/affect). Prescriptions such as the (in)famous Five Points are *ipso facto* always retroactive.[15] So is, or ought to be, any manifesto.

Scott Lash argues that, in fact, there have always been (at least) two modernisms: 'on the one hand, American and French modernism that has been largely aestheticist in character, and British and German modernism that is social-critical in character. The Franco-American tradition is more likely to be formalist and stereotomic, while the Anglo-German tradition is more likely to be structuralist and tectonic.'[16] Seemingly, little has changed since the Middle Ages, with Romanesque architecture on the one hand and Gothic on the other.[17] However, one ought to be suspicious of any attempt to describe history from a transcendental perspective, for it inevitably leads to an empty categorisation and periodisation of events. In the words of John Rajchman: 'In his noo-ology Deleuze thus tried to free philosophy and the "time" of philosophizing from the whole idea of epoch, and so from portentous images like the self-realization of Spirit or "Destining" of the West.'[18] It is always a question of concrete and evolving situations (assemblages).[19]

As for the current architectural state of affairs, organicist stereotomy in the guise of biomimetics seems to be gaining the upper hand.[20] Perhaps it was to be expected as a reaction to the hegemony of high-tech tectonics from the last quarter of the elapsed century. The choice seems to boil down to either the naïveté of techno-utopian neo-scientism on the one hand, or the solipsism of 'poetic' neo-phenomenology on the other.[21] Labyrinth and sphere. No wonder that the claimants of the title of the current architectural avant-garde should be split along precisely this line: Zahaesque topological parametricism vs Sejimaesque Euclidean minimalism.[22] Empathy and abstraction? What we expect from the machinic or eco-logical alternative is not a reactive and thus reactionary attitude, but a positive determination beyond ex-futurism and neo-archaism. It might just hold the secret of how to go beyond the totality derived from the parts and the totality from which the parts emanate, to produce an architecture of immanence.

Notes

This essay first appeared in *Architecture & Situation* Vol. 4, edited by Ella Chmielewska, Tahl Kaminer and Dorian Wiszniewski (Edinburgh: Architecture, University of Edinburgh, 2014), 18–19.

1. A quote from 'G as in "Gauche" (Left)', in Deleuze and Parnet, *ABC Primer*.
2. DeLanda, 'Deleuze and the Use of Genetic Algorithms in Architecture'.
3. DeLanda, *Intensive Science and Virtual Philosophy*, 69.
4. Massumi, 'The Thinking-Feeling of What Happens'.
5. For an example of functional determinism, see: Alexander, *Notes on the Synthesis of Form*.
6. Moure, *Duchamp*, 232.
7. The Four Compositions include: La Roche-Jeanneret House in Paris (1923), Villa at Garches (1927), Villa at Carthage (1929) and Villa Savoye at Poissy (1929–31). See: Besset, *Le Corbusier*, 98–9.
8. For similar reading – framed around the polar opposites of contingency/picturesque vs order/classical – see: Spuybroek in an interview by Arjen Mulder, 'The Aesthetics of Variation', 133–4.
9. Graafland, 'Artificiality in the Work of Rem Koolhaas', 42.
10. Deleuze, *Cinema 1*, 163.
11. Ibid., 187. 'Matter that has no empty spaces, is profoundly schizoid.' See also: Deleuze and Guattari, *Anti-Oedipus*, 19.
12. Kwinter's term for the phase space is the Waddingtonian Chreod. Kwinter, 'A Discourse on Method', 40–5.
13. Bodies are not differentiated on the basis of formal class (genera), but rather on kinetic and kinematic terms, that is, by the capacities to affect and be affected.

14. Colebrook, 'Creative Evolution and the Creation of Man', 113.

15. Koolhaas proposes that the European avant-garde manifestos always fell short in their realisation, whereas the Americans – due to their undeniably pragmatic culture – realised new worlds and ideas without having any actual manifesto proclaimed. Koolhaas, *Delirious New York*. Le Corbusier elucidated his five points of architecture in the journal *L'Esprit Nouveau* and his book *Vers une architecture*: *pilotis*, free facade, open floor plan, ribbon windows and the roof garden.

16. Lash, *Another Modernity*, 29–30.

17. For a distinction between the static relation of form/matter vs the dynamic relation of material/forces, see: Deleuze and Guattari, *A Thousand Plateaus*, 364.

18. Rajchman, *The Deleuze Connections*, 40.

19. For Deleuze all that history does is translate a coexistence of becomings into a succession. See: Deleuze and Guattari, *A Thousand Plateaus*, 430.

20. For an account of mixing subtractive and additive processes, see: Eisenman, 'From Object to Relationship II'. 'Subtractive space implies a center and is centripetal in conception; additive space is concerned more with the periphery, with edges and corners, and is centrifugal in conception.' Ibid., 41.

21. A distinction that is all-too-readily compared with McLuhan's hot media of high definition/low participation, and its opposite, cool media of low definition/high participation. See: chapter 2 in McLuhan, *Understanding Media*.

22. A reference to the two Pritzker laureates, Zaha Hadid (2004) and Kazuyo Sejima (with Ruye Nishizava, 2010). For an account of parametricism, see Hadid's partner: Schumacher, 'Architecture's Next Ontological Innovation'. By contrast, Sejima has been described by Toyo Ito as 'an architect who uses the maximum simplicity to link the material and the abstract.' <www.labiennale.org/en/architecture/director/> (accessed 25 May 2011).

6   The Impredicative City:
        or What Can a Boston Square Do?

It is necessary first to see the machine at work before attempting to deduce the function from the structure. (Canguilhem, 1992)[1]

The . . . City is sociology, happening. (Koolhaas, 1995)[2]

A system is simple if all its models are simulable. A system that is not simple, and that accordingly must have a nonsimulable model, is complex. (Rosen, 2000)[3]

Introduction

IN HIS PHOTOGRAPHIC series *Selected People*, the American photographer Pelle Cass displays a remarkable space-time axis reversal, the striking simplicity of which exemplifies the schizoanalysis of the city.[4] The prefix 'schizo' is used to designate resistance to the paranoiac fixation on a *single* (and supreme) source of all significa-tion.[5] The subject matter of his experiments takes us to a square in Boston. Yet, in terms of our investigation, the choice is purely contingent. Our ambition is to map the becoming of a specific place by way of non-correlationist hetero-poietic mat-tering, irremovable impredicative (autocatalytic) looping and non-local causing.[6] In simple terms, it is the movement that determines the space, not the other way around. As Deleuze put it in his theses on movement, 'the production of singular-ities (the qualitative leap) is achieved by the accumulation of banalities (quantita-tive process), so that the singular is taken from the any-whatever, and is itself an any-whatever which is simply non-ordinary and non-regular'.[7] We will follow his call to renounce any order of preference, any teleology.

Our chapter will draw upon schizoanalytic cartography to concentrate on perception which occurs not on the level at which actions are decided but on the level at which the very capacity for action forms. If representation is a means to an end (tracing), cartography is a means to a means (intervention). The goal-oriented human action cannot be used as the design criterion because the freedom of action is never a de facto established condition, it is always a virtuality.[8] This antecedent level of potentialisation is proto-epistemological and already ontological. It concerns change in the degree to which a life form is enabled vis-à-vis its (built) environment.[9] It is precisely the reciprocal determination of the life form and its environment (mode of existence) that makes perception a pertinent area of study. After all, living has interests that do not (always) coincide with those of thinking and it is for this reason that one perceives invariants, not forms.[10] To depict, one has to learn to perceive form. To design (built environment), one has to unlearn to perceive form, as we will attempt to demonstrate with the help of Cass.

The life form never pre-exists an event, hence the prefix 'life' or, more to the point, the city-life-form. Simpler still, action, perception and environment are located on a continuum. Only recently have biologists conceded the effect that niche construction has on the inheritance system, whereby a life form does not passively submit to the pressures of a pre-existing environment, but actively constructs its existential niche – the city as a case in point.[11] Baldwinian Evolution, or evolution by epigenetic means, is achieved through accumulation and improvement of cultural artefacts and practices. The quote 'we shape our cities; thereafter they shape us' is to be taken literally.[12] This is to say that, under the onto-topological commitment, experience is not an event in the mind. Rather, the mind emerges from an interaction with the environment. The implications for the discipline of architecture and urbanism, considering its role in the 'evolution by other means',[13] remain significant and binding. It is from this perspective that we will challenge the predominant homeostatic fixation on structure in architectural thinking in favour of the event-centred ontology of relations.[14] Moreover, we will insist that relations are irreducible to their terms.[15] The process – counterposed to the metaphysics of substance – seeks to grasp existence in the very act of its becoming.[16] Architects cannot take geometric ideologies as their starting point. Instead, as Guattari would have it, they need to think in terms of ecologies, that is, transversally cutting across the scales of the socius, the psyche and the environment.

Urban Schizoanalyses

The city as the 'noumenon closest to the phenomenon' has to be theorised by keeping both mechanistic reductionism and vitalist essentialism at bay.[17] This is the lesson of Deleuzian machinism, which maintains a strict distinction between virtual singularities as irreducible emergent properties of systems (the problem) and the actual system itself (the solution). To put it bluntly, let scientists focus on problem-solving. No one does it better. However, a problem always gets the solution it deserves. What we want to claim for art and architecture is the domain of problem-making (counter-effectuation). Human beings might be excellent at passive adaptation, but in the Anthropocene they must become better at active existential niche-construction. Instead of changing habitats as migrants do, they are forced to change habits as nomads do.[18] Paradoxically, nomads stay put. They take intensive travels, rather than extensive. In the first part of this chapter we will embark on one such intensive journey, at the end of which four lessons will be drawn. In the second part we will change the speed of delivery and style of argumentation in order to speculate on a new image of thought. This image of thought reconstrued as 'thought without an image' is not restricted to the representation, correspondence or adequation of a self-identical object to a self-identical subject, but foregrounds the reciprocal determination of the knower and the known. As Claire Colebrook put it:

> Not only could there not be a subject as some fully self-present substance that subsisted and persisted before and beyond all relation, for the very self as identity must refer back to (and therefore be different from itself); but also, any supposed ground from which relations would unfold must itself be effected from relations. . . . the actualized world of constituted terms does not exhaust what can be said to be: actuality emerges from virtual tendencies, and those tendencies could always create new systems and new terms.[19]

First, a few caveats and one concrete example are in order. Architects are proverbially good at primary or predicative properties such as lengths, heights and depths. Take a ruler, take an object and juxtapose them. What the discipline needs to unlock are relational properties. An example of such an impredicative property is a walk-on-able surface where the conditions and the conditioned are determined at one and the same time. Affordance is expressed by one's relation with another object (like a primary property) and actualised in one's relation with another object (unlike a primary property). This neologism was coined by the founder of the ecological approach to perception, J. J. Gibson:

An affordance is neither an objective nor a subjective property; or it is both if you like. An affordance cuts across the dichotomy of subjective–objective and helps us to understand its inadequacy. It is both physical and psychical, yet neither. An affordance points both ways, to the environment and to the observer.[20]

This puzzle has eluded us across three centuries. Primary and relational properties are two different yet complementary concepts sustaining two different yet complementary causalities, related to the dynamic and static geneses respectively.[21] The impredicative loop is built by interacting (actual) parts that cause an incorporeal (virtual) effect, which in turn becomes a (non-dynamic) quasi-cause by determining the degrees of freedom for the very interacting parts.[22] Proscription: the a priori. Prescription: cartography.

Any Square Whatever

In this part we will address the issue of how the urban milieu defies analysis based on primary properties, description and intentionality or phenomenological surveillance. We propose to regard the municipal or metropolitan fabric solely as a conjunction of flow, as an actual, physical and virtual aggregate which stretches along several temporal and spatial axes. We will map this relational space by examining a single image by Pelle Cass. To that end, it will be imperative to switch recursively from the mode of analysis, to the analysis of image, to the image itself and back again. With the mode of analysis we indicate a static type of visual examination of a digital reproduction of the digital file, now located in the printed environment of a book, or even as an electronic book. The analysis of the image itself provides more difficulty, because we cannot speak of the image as such. It is not only the continuous change of milieu (field or plane) which modulates the experience of the image, but also the continuous change of the beholder which changes the image. The temporal consequences of recognition in re-seeing cause the image to become its own context. After all, the image can never be unseen. Even the very anticipation of the image creates a pretext for seeing the image for the first time – not to mention the cultural, gender, age and other backgrounds which have already charged each viewer with a completely different set of perceptual sensitivities. Then there is the image itself, which can never be understood as anything other than what it does with the viewer at the specific moment that it is viewed. An image is immanent, it is not a representation of something else, just as every depiction is already a selection of all there is to a certain situation.

Figure 6.1 Source: Pelle Cass, *Shoppers 2, Quincy Market, Boston*, 2013.

In his photo series *Selected People*, Cass exemplifies a fitness landscape which itself resists reification. In the image called *Shoppers 2, Quincy Market, Boston* (Figure 6.1), we can see a pedestrian surface which appears to be a square filled with a blend of North American people walking in a multitude of directions. Although the image reveals no information about the connecting streets or places, all present on the image seem to have a vague sense of bearing and seem to strive to stay on a specific track, albeit in a very casual way. There seems to be a balanced selection of persons in terms of gender, race and age, and there is no hint of violence, threat or misbehaviour. The picture was taken on a warm day, most of the 'inhabitants' of the image wear summery outfits, yet there are no distinct shadows, suggesting that the square was overcast during the time the photograph was taken. At first glance the image appears to be a natural depiction of a mild afternoon in a leisurely environment – presumably an area near the Quincy Market in Boston, as the title suggests. The photo was not taken from an exceptional angle, but perhaps out of the window of an adjacent building. The artistic style does not seem to have an urge to draw attention to itself, nor is there any trace of complicated procedure in terms of production or any specific technical requirements in order to make this image. The only anomaly that is at first detected is a seemingly predominant penchant for orangey-yellow colours in this city. Then there is the crowdedness of the place, which does not seem to bother any of the actors in the frame. Yet this first impression is deceptive.

On second inspection, the number of inhabitants of the image is much smaller than at first appears to be the case. We observe that most of them are duplicated, triplicated or multiplied many times over. This immediately explains the previously detected anomalies. The colour dominancy is caused by the multiplication of a handful of people wearing outfits in the same hue. Secondly, it is clear that the deceptive mutual unawareness is caused by the fact that they were never in a crowd to begin with. They simply could not see each other at the moment they were there. Note that for many it would be possible to see the other(s) from their position, but not at that particular moment, procuring a first step in what we have called space-time axis conversion. The method used here must consist of layering several images taken from the exact same angle and position, in which only a few of all the possible postures are actually used in the final product. This tells us that what we see is already a selection of possibilities and cannot be mistaken for a non-constructed depiction. Even the colour scheme comes into question again. It could well be that the author of the post-production of the photograph chose only those with a certain tint of yellow for the image.

The author must also have made a second choice, to do with the credibility of the image. If any of the people were superimposed, creating multiplications of themselves, or blending with others, that would immediately alarm us. Despite the fact that the image is already highly manipulated and heavily hyperrealistic, having people blend into each other would make it worse, which is a nice indication of the elasticity of our imagination. The author must have invested much care in giving everyone their own niche, and thus limiting all potential options dramatically. Once the woman with the trolley was featured more or less in the middle of the image, most subsequent options were already rendered impossible. As soon as all the photographer's 'free gifts' were placed (such as the girl with the ponytail facing herself or the woman with the sarong), the rest had to follow automatically. Note that we have not even begun to address the content of the image itself, or its meaning and connotations, and we will not do this either, as it is completely gratuitous. It does not matter if it was winter, or if the people were Polish, or if the woman with the trolley was placed in the image first. The image is industrially produced, only following the drift of its inhabitants based on very pragmatic rules and principles. The image is not an image about subjects. Rather, it goes straight to the heart of the matter: the urban flow. And this is what makes this image so strong.

The (photo-)camera has often been seen as an extension of the eye, an artificial medium in the way McLuhan would describe an 'extension of man'.[23] The tool is used as a hylomorphic instrument to carve a soul out of the optical sensation. It enables us to witness the *vivre* and style of the artist in charge of the production. Cass, however, uses the instrument in a different and, we would claim, constructionist way. The obvious quality of photography is to instantly freeze time, and the quality of cinema is to bring us the movement-image. Bodies are not described in movement, but instead the continuity of movement describes the object. In fact we could not even describe Cass as a photographer, not only because he manipulates his products in the way an editor of a film would do, but because he photographs literally everything. Yet it is the selection he makes and the intervals he chooses to put in between each section that defines what he does. We could call him the intervalist. The strength of this mix lies in the fact that Cass specifically uses some weaknesses of both photography and film. Photography does not excel in sequencing (at least not in one picture) and film does not shine in arresting time or in creating time out of space (but it does excel in the creation of space out of time). Thus, Cass draws upon the weakest points of both these media to create this new world, the existing-yet-never-directly-visible momentum 'no longer recomposed from formal transcendental elements (poses), but from immanent material elements (sections)'.[24]

Lesson One: Haptic Space

There are four good reasons for this lengthy exposure of the image. Firstly, the image shows us all the basic principles that drive and create the city in all its appearances. And the abstraction imposed upon it helps us to see different patterns and grids, attractors and repellers, drives and affects. We see the futurity, which holds the potential of multiple actualisations. Of all the physical, mental, economic, affective and physiologic flows, we see only a few highlighted. The selection is already made; that is why we are in no need of a narrative, for it does not matter why someone is moving from this spot to the next, or why some paths are more often chosen than others. What matters is the mere fact that it occurs and that we can witness it, following a single basic rule: no person can create the same space at the same time as someone else. Paths can be slightly diverted or temporally disrupted, affective encounters may cause slowings-down or speedings-up or path changes, but on a meta-modelling level all will remain the same.[25] We are witnessing a metastable system in progress, spatially compressed to enable temporal expansion. It is the description of space being produced by time. Time is the third dimension, not the fourth. Any shape of *chronos* stands to *kairos* as a Euclidean optical space stands to a haptic topological space. This means that the first movement creates a space that is forever occupied. This first space will set the agenda for the emergence of the next and so on. And even long after the first space has been vacated it will never be non-space again, it will always be charged by its own quasi-causality. It has dictated the next step and the next. The square has never been empty. And that shows itself most clearly in the editing of Pelle's image; once the first person is placed, the whole grid snaps into place, a mild grid, but a grid nevertheless. The established relations are only ever contingently obligatory. Unlike those that are logically necessary, these relations are not conceptual but immanently causal.[26]

Lesson Two: Absolute Survey

Secondly, there is the most pragmatic level. It is about the place itself: the square, which allows for a multitude of engagements. In our case this place is used primarily for transit, and the variety of destinations of the inhabitants of the image suggest that there are several options to connect different points. We can also see that there is a tendency towards the vertical crossing of the square, but because of heavy manipulation we cannot be sure of that. Or can we? The applied abstraction serves as a filter, a stroboscopic filter. It only illuminates the situation with a certain interval, rendering deeper layers and patterns of flow visible by way of absolute survey, or the capacity to surpass the given.[27] This Spinozian 'third kind of knowledge' precedes the emergence of the phenomenological 'aboutness' and its finite movement from one discrete part to another. The survey is absolute by virtue of its infinite speed, which reveals a consistency of the heterogeneous whole without reducing it to the parts.[28] It shows the chatoyancy of the city.[29] In the image we can see two market stalls at the edge of the compass card. They were probably not allowed to be located in the middle of the place, as that would excessively disrupt flows. This type of intervention by municipal regulations is often mistakenly thought to be contributing to city-making, while we all know that laws are always constructed *ex post facto*. A beautiful example of (a comment on) phallic thinking is the short film by John Smith, *The Girl Chewing Gum*, from 1976. As with our Boston image, it takes a while to realise that the instructions given in the film are in fact descriptions of the scene that immediately follows. The film is edited in such a way that the sound precedes the image and the tone of the voice is set in an instructive mode, rather than a descriptive tone.

Lesson Three: Energetics

Thirdly, the image addresses flows as a two-step sling. Let us assume for a moment that life forms are driven by two forces and not dispute or discuss the nature or origin of these forces. The first layer could be called desire (aka aspiration, aka agency) and the second one affect. To be clear, this is not an attempt to classify affect as a secondary force, or to mimic Silvan Tomkins's classification of putting affect into nine categories.[30] But could we regard autonomous drives (such as the need for food, sex, shelter, warmth etc.) as being the deep attractors in Waddington's epigenetic landscape (Chreod) and name them desires, and could we take connected drives (such as interactions, stimuli, preferences) as specified forms of drives and call them affects?[31] In that case – in relation to Waddington – affects can be seen as accelerators, the differences that make a difference, and the desires can be seen as the strength of the attractions.[32] The depth of the attractor is to desire what the (up- and downward) tangent is to affect. In this image we can see that some inhabitants have clear goals, they walk with a pragmatic purpose, coming from one place to go to another. Yet the exact path is never completely predictable; along the way there can be diversions, obstacles, interactions (positive or negative), attractions, collisions (or the avoidance thereof) and so forth. In other cases we can see people being driven by the need for interaction; they meander around the place in search of interaction (shopping, inspiration, *das Mittendrin sein*, flirtation, perversion and so on). The need for interaction can be seen as a meta-drive, as it provides us with the potential to resolve the myriad of specific drives (molecular perspectivism of drives, not of molar egos). Perhaps it is more precise to refer to it as an intra-action. In contrast to inter-action, which presupposes molar individuals that precede their interaction, Karen Barad's neologism signifies the mutual constitution of entangled agencies that remain antecedent and exterior to the *relata*.[33]

Lesson Four: Posthumanism

We come to the fourth and final lesson that we can learn from the image: debunking a system of vanity and the megalomania of correlationism, or how to break through the anthropocentric frame of reference. The market had been there before the marketplace as such existed. This square is just an expression of the infra-action which resonates transindividually.[34] The wound was always here, we just lived to embody it.[35] The flow dictates its causes; roadside-restaurant as the ultimate new city, completely attuned to modern flows, converters, hubs, the parking lot. Post-surveillance, auto-surveillance, engendering, emplacement. Meta-narrative, sub-narrative. Religiosity, despairing, clairvoyance, abiogenesis. The voyeur, the *flâneur*. They all belong to this world. In *Difference and Repetition* Deleuze gives due credit to his nemesis's achievement: 'Kant is the one who discovers the prodigious domain of the transcendental. He is the analogue of a great explorer – not of another world, but of the upper or lower reaches of this one.'[36] The transcendental, it must be underscored, is not transcendent but always a product of immanence or 'thisworldlyness'.[37] For our purposes, it is worth remembering that Deleuze and Guattari tether transcendence to the state, while making a strong connection between immanence and the city: '[cities] develop a particular mode of deterritorialization that proceeds by immanence; they form a *milieu of immanence*'.[38] The irony of Pelle's image about flows is that it shows so clearly that the days of pilgrimage are over. The image comes to you, you don't need to go to the image.

Grades of Sense

There is arguably no greater influence upon architectural thinking than René Descartes and his metaphor of the ghost in the machine. The ecological psychologist Michael Turvey provides an updated version of this metaphor.[39] Nowadays, to establish a link to the outside world, the ghost has all the digital media at his disposal. Let us briefly revisit the three Cartesian grades of sense as spelled out by Turvey. The first is strictly physical and accessible through science in general and mechanics in particular. The second grade of sense is more challenging, as it concerns qualia, or secondary qualities. It is hybrid, physical and mental. How do agitated molecules of carbon and oxygen become the experience of redness and warmth of colour? The answer to this (hard) question lies in probably the most influential scientific metaphor of all times, namely, that the relationships between the two grades follow from the mere arrangement of the machine's organs every bit as naturally as the movements of a clock follow from the arrangements of its counterweights and wheels.[40] The third, mental grade of sense concerns the notions of formal systems and goes beyond the mechanistic conception just described. It took a few centuries for this quasi-rational symbol-manipulating process to catch on.

Before listing the influential assumptions originating in the seventeenth century, let us note that the current discourse around speculative realism is divided on the very issue of primacy of the first two grades of sense, derivative of the bifurcation of nature that Alfred North Whitehead denounced as the most serious error of modern Western thought.[41] The editors of the *Speculations* issue on twenty-first-century aesthetics offer a helpful broad-brush picture of a new struggle between rationalism and empiricism within contemporary speculative philosophy in general and its take on aesthetics in particular:

> For the contemporary rationalists, mathematics (Meillassoux) and science (Brassier) dictate the discourse on and the place of aesthetics within the larger framework of epistemology with the concomitant intent to hunt down any

manifestation of the, in their view, illusory 'immediacy thesis'. The empiricists (Harman and Grant, but also Shaviro and Morton) in turn insist upon 'immediacy' and a theory of taste in disguise holding that we immediately taste something before we conceptually know it.[42]

The authors concede that the dichotomy is too neat. Yet, it is symptomatic enough of the contrast between, on the one hand, the resilient seventeenth-century assumptions of inertness, context-independent parts and local (contiguous) cause and, on the other, the twenty-first-century hypotheses of self-organising matter, systems with irremovable impredicative loops and non-locality. Drawing upon Turvey, we will demonstrate that it is high time we dismantled the ghost-in-the-machine model so that neither the ghost nor the machine survives.[43] For this we need to update our inadequate all-too-representational toolbox. There is no better testing (groundless) ground for the task than the city. As Guattari put it, 'the aesthetic rupture of discursivity is never passively experienced. It leads to heterogeneous levels which must be related to a heterogenesis'.[44]

The Clock as the Image of Thought

Let us list the essential seventeenth-century mechanistic assumptions. First, locality dictates that all causes are local by contact. From the angle of aesthetics, the question is: what might be taken as the proximal, contiguous cause of some particular experience? Aesthetics is defined here in the most general sense of sensory or, *per negativum*, the opposite of anaesthetic.

Second, matter is passive and inert, lacking any morphogenetic capacity. If a thing itself moves, then one part of it must be the mover and another part that which is moved. It is in this way that the absence of self-cause or self-motion gets resolved. Here the ghost in the machine becomes the unmoved mover.

Third, the entailment assumption, the legacy of Newton, who proposed the single entailment mode, whereby the present entails the immediate future. In contrast to Aristotelian categories of causation, Newton holds that only an efficient cause is properly causal. Causal chains flow from parts to whole and never the other way around. This is the predicative direction, the way one writes computer programs. The lack of reflexivity effectively eliminates the possibility of autocatalysis with interdependent parts. It eliminates a quasi-formal cause related to Deleuze and Guattari's 'exteriority of relations', or the relation that is exterior to its terms and as such presents 'a vital protest against principles'.[45] There are two more (reductionist) assumptions that follow from the entailment assumption: the component and superposition assumptions. The former posits that parts are context-independent, while the latter states that the whole is the sum of its parts. In spite of the inadequacy that the interiority of relations suffers in the realm of biology and psychology, had it not been for these mechanistic hypotheses the whole enterprise of modern science would have been unimaginable. In the Deleuzian parlance the image of thought expressive of this paradigm is the clock. In the context of this chapter, we would have to imagine the city as the clock. If we take the clockwork city and break it into its constitutive parts, they retain their particular functions. In other words, synthesis becomes analysis in reverse. According to Turvey, the pure reversibility of putting together and taking apart prescribes both the ghost and the machine:

> The two assumptions of local contiguous cause and inert matter give us a prescribed ghost. Entailment is recursion in which the present, and only present, entails the immediate future. And, with context-independent components, analysis and synthesis are reciprocal and components entail function. These give us the machine, they prescribe the machine.[46]

What would be the 'thought without image', which rejects identity as the governing principle and instead embraces multiplicity, singularity and pure (non-dialectical) difference?[47] Perhaps the hypotheses of non-locality and active matter taken together will suffice to proscribe the ghost, while multiple entailment modes and reflexivity with context-dependency will proscribe the machine.[48] Of the two, the machine might turn out to be the tougher nut to crack. In the case of the city, the material, formal, efficient and final causes are not only indiscernible but also constantly mutating. The interacting parts produce the emergent distributed whole, which in turn constrains the parts. 'The parts compose the whole, which comprises the parts. The definition of what the parts are is dictated by the emergent distributed whole.'[49] Following the distinction which Deleuze appropriates from Henri Bergson, one ought to distinguish between the actual traits of a physical system and the virtual – real but abstract – thresholds at which it either adopts or changes those traits.

Cracks in the Street

It should be obvious by now that not all causes are by contact. Already in the mid-1950s Gibson challenged psychological orthodoxies by claiming that perception did not require a simultaneous composite in the brain, a representation.[50] Moreover, amodal and ambulant perception (of the indiscernible) is not an exception but the rule.[51] In other words, we do perceive the imperceptible (prehension). Life forms perceive potentials (for action) directly and never re-emerge as self-identical in becoming. They respond to perceptual signs, not to causal impulses.[52] As far as Gibson is concerned, the real problem is not the presupposed poverty of stimulation but the poverty of entailment, given that not all potentiality is (already) an accrued value. Georges Canguilhem cautions against facile analogies:

> Clearly, an organism has a greater range of activity than a machine. It is less bound by purposiveness and more open to potentialities. Every aspect and every movement of the machine is calculated; and the working of the machine confirms how each calculation holds up to certain norms, measures or estimates; whereas the living body functions according to experience. Life is experience, meaning improvisation, acting as circumstances permit; life is tentative in every respect.[53]

It is worth pointing out that non-local causation extends beyond the psychological register or existential grasp. It is coextensive with the lived experience but not reducible to it. It is a feature of all open hetero-poietic matter/energy systems as opposed to closed deterministic ones that exist only under laboratory conditions and in digital simulations. It is the feature of the impersonal non-organic life.

Vibrant matter as the second 'ghostbuster' is equally pertinent for its ability to wake architects from their correlationist slumber.[54] By endowing matter with agency of its own, the unbearable narcissism of the anthropos and the bad habit of hylomorphism start to evaporate. Self-organising matter does not need the imposition of a transcendent form to organise its putative chaos. The way Rem Koolhaas contrasted two paradigmatic cities is telling in this respect:

> Paris can only become more Parisian – it is already on its way to becoming hyper-Paris, a polished caricature. There are exceptions: London – its only identity a lack of clear identity – is perpetually becoming even less London, more open, less static.[55]

Finally we turn to the machinism of impredicativities, which is not to be confused with either organicism or mechanicism, agency or structure. We ought not to separate the doer from the deed, as the Nietzschean maxim goes. Complex systems, such as cities, contain impredicativities that cannot be removed. The term was introduced by the founder of non-linear dynamics, Henri Poincaré. Put simply, you cannot offer an understanding of actual parts in the absence of a virtual whole. Simpler still, what is defined participates in its own definition.[56] Yet, the abduction problem seems to have gone unnoticed in parametricist quarters, judging by their synoptic ambition to be achieved through simulation. In the words of the architect Ingeborg Rocker,

> the formal exuberance characteristic of parametricism's architecture and urban planning scenarios pretends to cope with societies' and life's complexities, while in fact they are at best expressions thereof, empty gestures of a form-obsessed and strangely under-complex approach to architecture and urbanity.[57]

Newtonian syntactic formalism is simply not abstract enough when it comes to complex systems. As we have argued, simple systems can be captured predicatively, complex systems cannot.[58] The most important logician of our times, Kurt Gödel, proved conclusively that one can never convert impredicative into predicative. It is not the result of the alleged limit of our minds, Turvey cautions. It is the limit of predicative perspectives on entailment: 'Predication without impredication is not powerful enough; syntax without semantics is too feeble for understanding explanation and entailment.'[59] To put it laconically, the digital can be generalised (logically formalised), while the analogue is always singular, that is eco-logical. In the words of the semiologist Paul Bains:

> Univocal, semiotic reality – the reality of experience – is not reducible to the mind's own workings (e.g., as in the Kantian synthesis) nor is it to that of a prejacent external physical world in which the mind has no part. It is a limitless interface where the line between what is and what is not, independent of interpretative activity, is a constantly shifting [asignifying] semiotic process.[60]

No wonder Deleuze insisted that the smallest unit of reality is the assemblage, *agencement*.[61] 'Thinking *with* AND . . . instead of thinking *for* IS: empiricism has never had another secret'.[62] The assemblage preserves certain symmetries and breaks others. Metastability rests on both difference and repetition in the relation of mutual determination. This is not an epistemological principle, but an ontological one. If the seventeenth-century concepts have given us remarkable discoveries, the next revolution based upon impredicativity will be nothing like what we have seen before.[63] It is key to most phenomena of the universe, not the few we have tackled thus far. The extension and comprehension of a concept are inversely proportional. The more specified the concept, the fewer the objects subsumed by it. By contrast to the vertical (transcendentally organised) state, we will never know conclusively what the horizontal city can do.[64] It is not about bringing all sorts of things under a single concept of the city, but about relating each city to the variables that determine its mutation, its becoming.[65] After the proscription of the a priori, the prescription of cartography becomes unavoidable. The non-mimetic mapping of affective capacities and virtual tendencies renders visible a condition 'that is no wider than what it conditions, that changes itself with the conditioned and determines itself in each case along with what it determines'.[66] Deleuze has never had another formula except for the N-1. It is an ecological formula that spells out: 'subtract the meta-signifier'. Bring into existence. Do not judge.[67] That is the injunction of immanence.

Notes

This essay, co-authored with Marc Boumeester, first appeared in *Deleuze and the City*, edited by Hélène Frichot, Catharina Gabrielsson and Jonathan Metzger (Edinburgh: Edinburgh University Press, 2016), 46–63.

1. Canguilhem, 'Machine and Organism', 56.
2. Koolhaas, *S, M, L, XL*, 1255.
3. Rosen, *Essays on Life Itself*, 292.
4. Guattari, *Schizoanalytic Cartographies*.
5. Deleuze and Guattari, *Anti-Oedipus*, 194.
6. Turvey, 'Theory of Brain and Behaviour'.
7. Deleuze, *Cinema 1*, 6.
8. Evans, *Translations from Drawing to Building*, 16–17.
9. Massumi, 'Perception Attack'.
10. Gibson, *The Ecological Approach to Visual Perception*.
11. Odling-Smee, 'Niche Inheritance'.
12. Wexler, 'Neuroplasticity, Culture and Society'.
13. Stiegler, *Technics and Time, 1*. 'The problem arising here is that the evolution of this essentially technical being that the human is exceeds the biological, although this dimension is an essential part of the technical phenomenon itself, something like its enigma. The evolution of the "prosthesis", not itself living, by which the human is nonetheless defined as a living being, constitutes the reality of the human's evolution, as if, with it, the history of life were to continue by means other than life: this is the paradox of a living being characterized in its forms of life by the nonliving – or by the traces that its life leaves in the nonliving.' Ibid., 50.
14. Bains, *The Primacy of Semiosis*.
15. Deleuze and Parnet, *Dialogues*, 55.
16. Guattari, *The Three Ecologies*.

17. Deleuze, *Difference and Repetition*, 222.

18. Braidotti, 'Elemental Complexity and Relational Vitality', 215.

19. Colebrook, *Sex after Life*, 63.

20. Gibson, *The Ecological Approach to Visual Perception*, 129.

21. Deleuze, *Difference and Repetition*, 89, 183.

22. A dynamic genesis moves from an encounter with intensity in sensation to the thinking of virtual ideas, while a static genesis moves from the virtual idea through an intensive individuation process to an actual entity.

23. McLuhan, *Understanding Media*.

24. Deleuze, *Cinema 1*, 4

25. By contrast to a scientific paradigm, Guattari characterised his meta-modelling activity as an 'ethico-aesthetic paradigm'. See Watson, *Guattari's Diagrammatic Thought*.

26. DeLanda, *A New Philosophy of Society*, 31.

27. Massumi, *What Animals Teach Us about Politics*, 36, 77.

28. Deleuze, *Kant's Critical Philosophy*, 148.

29. Cat's-eye effect.

30. Tomkins, *Exploring Affect*.

31. This neologism of Conrad Waddington's denotes the necessary path of any becoming. It is a 'figure of time'. As Sanford Kwinter explains, a Chreod refers to an invisible but not imaginary feature in an invisible but not imaginary landscape on which a developing form gathers the information and influence necessary for it to make itself what it is.

32. Kwinter, 'A Discourse on Method', 40–5.

33. Barad, *Meeting the Universe Halfway*, 33.

34. Massumi, *The Power at the End of the Economy*, 14.

35. Deleuze's reference to Bousquet's poem whereby the wound becomes not an effect but precisely a quasi-cause. Deleuze, *The Logic of Sense*, 148.

36. Deleuze referred to his book on Kant as 'a book on an enemy'. Deleuze, *Difference and Repetition*, 135.

37. Deleuze, *Pure Immanence*.

38. Deleuze and Guattari, *What Is Philosophy?*, 87.

39. Turvey, 'Theory of Brain and Behaviour', 57.

40. Whitehead, *The Concept of Nature*, 32. Cf. Descartes, 'Treatise on Man'.

41. Whitehead, *The Concept of Nature*, 26–48.

42. Askin, Hägler and Schweighauser, 'Introduction', 29–30.

43. Turvey, 'Theory of Brain and Behaviour'.

44. Guattari, 'Cracks in the Street'. On the issue of asignifying rupture, see Hauptmann and Radman, *Asignifying Semiotics*.

45. An autocatalytic process produces more of what is there. Autocatalysis drives pattern formation by making components interdependent. It is thus causal in the formal, not efficient, sense. See Deleuze and Parnet, *Dialogues*, 55.

46. Turvey, 'Theory of Brain and Behaviour', 59.

47. Deleuze, *Difference and Repetition*, 132, 147.

48. Turvey, 'Theory of Brain and Behaviour'.

49. Ibid., 64.

50. Gibson, *The Ecological Approach to Visual Perception*.

51. Amodal perception is a term that describes the full perception of a physical structure when it is only partially perceived; for example, a table will be perceived as a complete volumetric structure even if only part of it is visible. See: Noë, *Is the Visual World a Grand Illusion?*

52. Bains, *The Primacy of Semiosis*, 63.

53. Canguilhem, 'Machine and Organism', 58.

54. Bennett, *Vibrant Matter*.

55. Koolhaas, *S, M, L, XL*, 1248.

56. Wolfendale, *Object-Oriented Philosophy*, 246.

57. Rocker, 'Apropos Parametricism', 97.

58. In abductive reasoning, unlike in deductive reasoning, the premises do not guarantee the conclusion.

59. Turvey, 'Theory of Brain and Behaviour', 61.

60. Bains, *The Primacy of Semiosis*, 68.

61. Deleuze and Parnet, *Dialogues*, 51.

62. Ibid., 57.

63. Rosen, *Essays on Life Itself*.

64. Deleuze and Guattari, *What Is Philosophy?*, 89.

65. Deleuze, *Negotiations*, 31.

66. Deleuze, *Nietzsche and Philosophy*, 50.

67. Deleuze, *Essays Critical and Clinical*, 135.

7   Space Always Comes After: It Is Good When It Comes After; It Is Good Only When It Comes After

IF WE START paying attention to paying attention we will inevitably come to the same conclusion Walter Benjamin did in 'The Work of Art in the Age of Mechanical Reproduction': 'Architecture has always represented the prototype of a work . . . the reception of which is consummated by a collectivity in a state of distraction.'[1] Today, when artificial environments have become ubiquitous, with more than 50 per cent of the population living in cities, a state of absent-mindedness has turned into oblivion despite (or precisely because of) an ever more exuberant architectural production. The (in)famous modernist maxim 'Less is more' (*Weniger ist mehr*), a nineteenth-century proverbial phrase that underwent a number of mutations – from the postmodern reactionary 'Less is a bore' to the most recent excessive 'Yes is more' – also works in reverse.[2] More can indeed be less. This is, more or less, the lesson of contemporary ecological thought.[3]

We spend most of our lives in autopilot mode – walking, driving – and only a fraction in teleological mode. However, as the philosopher Hubert L. Dreyfus maintains, it is the intentional mode that we tend to notice, and its 'aboutness' has therefore been studied in detail.[4] Having acquired the capacity of understanding, we tend to see purposes and causes everywhere and thus remain oblivious to the profound non-linearity of the world.[5] This is to say that the invariants we rely on do not necessarily have specific causes that can be neatly identified. More often than not, they may only be mapped as a dynamic cascade of many processes operating over time.[6] However disadvantageous this lack of clarity and distinctness may seem to the architect, it will prove the opposite once we fully grasp the speculative turn and its implications for the discipline. It will become apparent that the royal road to the understanding of space is through the non-intentional, non-reflexive and non-conscious. It is through population thinking that we will undergo a biopolitical apprenticeship in spatialisation. As Michel Foucault phrases it, 'after a first seizure of power over the body in an individualizing mode, we have a second seizure of power that is not individualizing but, if you like, massifying, that is directed not at man-as-body but at man-as-species'.[7] Little wonder then that the architecture theorist Jeffrey Kipnis refers to the architect not as an engineer but as a trickster: 'So are we going to be better off trying to understand the neurophysiology of how we perceive things, or are we better off seeing that we're the magicians?'[8] Similarly, the self-proclaimed alchemist architect François Roche makes a case for deception and the forbidden, which have largely been absent from the architectural discourse in recent decades: 'We want to consider a premedical system, before Hippocrates, where temperament describes the body as a negotiation between the temperament of the black bile, the blood, the phlegm, etc.'[9] The unique capability of 'imagineers', film directors and magicians, to subordinate scientific aetiology to artistic symptomatology is largely unappreciated by the discipline of architecture save for these exceptions.[10] As long as architects remain reluctant to shake off the habit of privileging awareness over habit, they will continue to misplace concreteness in Whiteheadian terms.[11] As Félix Guattari already pointedly diagnosed in his plea for a new aesthetic paradigm, 'the paradigms of techno-science place the emphasis on an objectal world of relations and functions, systematically bracketing out subjective affects, such that the finite, the delimited and coordinatable, always takes precedence over the infinite and its virtual references'.[12]

This essay suggests that the dominant architectural history is not speculative enough. Its only merit is to translate a coexistence of becomings into a succession of neat, logically necessary types. A case will be made for the role of topology as an antidote to typological essentialism. This intensive geometry will help dispense with the merely representational in favour of the contingently obligatory becoming. The appeal that speculative philosophy holds for progressive architecture is not surprising, given that it resists subsuming the intensive under the extensive. Everything starts from an aesthetic encounter. Yet the task of speculative thinking is to go beyond the sensible to the potentials that make sensibility possible.[13] Hence, the basic medium of the discipline of architecture is the space of experience. This *spatium*, which is not to be confused with the experience of space, does not pre-exist. It subsists as a virtuality. According to Deleuze, the plane of composition – as a work of sensation – is aesthetic: 'It is the material that passes into the sensation.'[14] Once aesthetics is drawn into the context of production, its realm expands to become a dimension of being itself. While the relationship between technical and aesthetic planes of composition has varied historically, Deleuze and Guattari remain adamant that neither art nor sensation has ever been representational.[15] Consequently, the mereological relationship – which is perfectly suitable for the realm of the extensive – needs to be radically revamped in order to become capable of capturing (onto) topological transformations. However, I am not arguing for a formalisable or programmable model. Quite the contrary: mereotopology guarantees that technological determinism will be kept at bay. What we need instead is heuristics as a practice of material inference. Reza Negarestani has underscored Peircean abduction as one such form of material inference. In contrast to the classical, that is, formal logic, abduction is fallible, given that information is gathered by way of manipulation. His case is straightforward: one cannot understand a system unless one acts on it. The behaviour of a system is in turn dependent on the concept of tendencies that cannot be intuited unless one is to intervene in the causal fabric.[16] So, although logically one advances from space to affordance, developmentally the sequence runs in precisely the opposite direction. Affordance is J. J. Gibson's neologism for 'would-be action', which is always relational, that is, non-deterministic:

> An important fact about affordances of the environment is that they are in a sense objective, real, and physical, unlike values and meanings, which are often supposed to be subjective, phenomenal, and mental. But, actually, an affordance is neither an objective nor a subjective property; or it is both if you like. An affordance cuts across the dichotomy of subjective–objective and helps us to understand its inadequacy. It is both physical and psychical, yet neither. An affordance points both ways, to the environment and to the observer.[17]

Or, in a more philosophical vein:

> The theory of affordances rescues us from the philosophical muddle of assuming fixed classes of objects, each defined by its common features and then given a name. As Ludwig Wittgenstein knew, you cannot specify the necessary and sufficient features of the class of things to which a name is given. They have only a 'family resemblance'. But this does not mean you cannot learn how to use things and perceive their uses. You do not have to classify and label things in order to perceive what they afford.[18]

The founder of the ecological school of perception thus effectively sides with Deleuze, who insists that we go beyond the given (space), to that by which a given is given (*spatium*): 'Difference is not diversity. Diversity is given, but difference is that by which the given is given as diverse. Difference is not phenomenon but the noumenon closest to the phenomenon.'[19] However, by no means does temporal deployment merely actualise some pre-existing atemporal structure. The virtual itself is the product of immanence (contingent, temporal).[20] In his book on speculative realism, Steven Shaviro also makes a case for the detranscendentalisation of phenomenological aboutness whereby 'intentionality becomes an implicit striving toward, or a potential for becoming, *within* the world, rather than being an underlying principle or structure of correlation.'[21] Neither subject nor object is in control under the affordance theory either. They mutually constrain and even define one another.[22] Perhaps the best way to dispense with the substantialist prejudice is to see them both as derivative, as super-jects and object-iles. These neologisms evoke the sense of subjects and objects as events. The emphasis is on a field of immediate experience as being something and not an experience of something for someone. Conversely, the degree zero of spatial experience occurs at the level of the non-conscious. As such, it is proto-subjective and sub-representational: that is, a non-intentionalistic and non-correlational power of being. In the words of Katherine Hayles:

> In the posthuman view . . . conscious agency has never been 'in control'. In fact the very illusion of control bespeaks a fundamental ignorance about the nature of the emergent processes through which consciousness, the organism, and the environment are constituted. Mastery through the exercise of autonomous will is merely the story consciousness tells itself to explain results that actually come about through chaotic dynamics and emergent structures . . . emergence replaces teleology; reflexivity replaces objectivism; distributed cognition replaces autonomous will; embodiment replaces a body seen as a support system for the mind; and a dynamic partnership between humans and intelligent machines replaces the liberal humanist subject's manifest destiny to dominate and control nature.[23]

In anticipation of our speculative thesis, let us consider the following example as proof of how lethal our attachment to old conceptual baggage can be. It involves emergence, complex systems and topologies that have become a matter of interest for architectural discourse, philosophy and mathematical science alike. The neo-materialist Manuel DeLanda explains that emergent behaviour is to be expected of any dynamic system having the following three properties: multiple parts, extensive communication between them and substantial mobility.[24] In the early days of World War II, the German air force was arguably more successful than the British. As Jesse Reiser and Jason Payne show, British airborne manoeuvres were more concerned with symmetry-based representation than with efficiency, as if objects of experience resided in the head and were insulated from the environment. The common fighter pilot's slogan, 'If you have to think, you're dead', rings true. The RAF's insistence upon simple fixed formations had been more conditioned with the colonial aesthetics of pure two-dimensional geometries than the *nomos* of air combat. The Luftwaffe, on the other hand, were busy exploring the (phase) space to its full potential by keeping in direct touch with the milieu. The unmediated (direct) perception, according to ecological psychology, circumvents retinal, neural or mental pictures altogether.[25] Perhaps this is why German fighter formations were far more adaptive to contingencies and thus more capable of engaging the enemy by absorbing, deflecting or evading their tactics. The actions by pilots generated information for perception. What is at stake here is an emergent property of a dynamic system where the whole is not of the parts, but alongside and in addition to them.[26] In the words of Sanford Kwinter, 'extreme activities involve the mobilisation of every interacting part in a field, so that every moment of every part instantaneously changes the conditions of the unfolding whole'.[27] This, in a way, is a purely geometrical problem:

> When the British formation changed direction, for example, every plane would retain its fixed position within the assemblage throughout the turn, somewhat like rail-cars on a curving train track. The German formation, however, would rotate and fold over upon itself, the planes in the rear of the formation coming around to take up the front. Not only did this allow for a faster, tighter turn, but it also provided continual and ever-changing protection for each plane by some other in the formation. The shifting positions made it very difficult for an enemy to draw a bead on a single plane, especially one being defended by several others in rotation.[28]

The mapped manoeuvres of the two formations provide a perfect allegory for the difference between sedentary and nomadic distributions in an organisation of space. Namely, the difference between applying a preset, overarching principle in the case of the RAF, and tapping into the latent potentiality of an ad hoc assemblage on the part of the Luftwaffe: geometry of theorems vs geometry of problems.[29] It is a quintessentially architectural problem, not to be confused with the simple opposition between order and disorder. Rather, they are two different, perhaps even complementary, orders of what Deleuze and Guattari have famously called striated and smooth space. In contrast to sedentary space, which remains what it is and is then divided, nomadic space is produced through its very distribution. The dual nature of space is explained by Kwinter as follows:

> On the one hand, a fixed and extended milieu with metrical or dimensional properties and, on the other, a fluid and consistent field of intensities (e.g. forces, speeds, temperatures, colour). The resemblance to Bergson's two types of multiplicity, the numerical (discrete) and the qualitative (continuous), or, more generally, that of space and that of *durée*.[30]

The concept of nomadology is spelt out most explicitly in *A Thousand Plateaus*. Deleuze and Guattari take it to be 'the opposite of a history'.[31] To repeat, with nomadic distribution there is not a single law that stands outside and determines space ($N + 1$). Instead, the law is produced in the very traversal of space. This will be the basis of my critique of the all-too-transcendental and thus conservative concept of architectural typologies. Deleuze and Guattari offer a clear prescription: 'Subtract the unique from the multiplicity to be constituted; write at $N - 1$ dimensions.'[32] It is high time we lifted the military monopoly on the soft power of smooth space, where space is subordinate to time and object to relation. The notorious champions of *Noopolitik*, Arquilla and Ronfeldt, contrast the mighty soft power to the hard power of *Realpolitik*.[33] We ought to tap into the process of epigenesis for our own life-affirming purposes. Now that it is becoming increasingly difficult to rely on the classical political categories, Deleuze provides a crucial distinction between left and right. The political left wards off the hegemonic master signifier (nation, land). Simply put, it ponders the problem rather than let itself be driven by the solution.[34] Warren Neidich has issued a similar plea for the emancipatory process of environmentally directed neuromodulation.[35] Under the concept of epigenesis, space is no longer regarded as an enclosure but in terms of thresholds: 'Enclosures are *molds*, distinct castings, but controls are a *modulation*, like a self-deforming cast that will continuously change from one moment to the other, or like a sieve whose mesh will transmute from point to point.'[36]

Brian Massumi urges us to approach the problem of control in terms of an 'ecology of powers'.[37] In his work, this power of local-global becoming is defined as an ontopower, a creative power of becoming: 'The subject's situatedness becomes one of the deciding factors of what transpires. The double involuntary of the feedback and feedforward between the [molecular] dividual and the [supermolar] transindividual funnels through the situation, and is conditioned by the presuppositions and tendential orientations it highlights.'[38] This is to say that the modulation of control can itself be modulated. It will not be easy to live up to this speculative injunction, as metaphysics has always been concerned with the striated. The de-ontologist Peter Wolfendale has identified the three distinct post-Heideggerian rejections of metaphysics according to the concept of substance they hold responsible for its onto-theological legacy: presence (Derrida), unity (Badiou) and ground (Meillassoux).[39] According to Mark Wigley, the history of the ground 'is that of a succession of different names (*logos, ratio, archē,* etc.) . . . Each of them designates "being", which is understood as presence . . . "supporting presence" for an edifice.'[40] In other words, even before we begin the process of determination, certain things seem always already determined as enduring beyond their transitory predicates and are therefore precluded from affirming the original movement through which they themselves are affected. The cure is to bracket natural perception, in which everything appears as an already constituted body, quality or action.[41] Following Deleuze's (N − 1) advice: 'To make the body a power which is not reducible to the organism, to make thought a power which is not reducible to consciousness.'[42]

Clearly, a whole new vocabulary needs to be invented, as well as a new set of conceptual tools. Geometry becomes indispensable. Apart from being a branch of mathematics, geometry has always been a mode of rationality. Bernard Cache argues that it should be taken as a cultural reference.[43] This is no trivial matter, as we may depend upon a different rationality (not irrationality) where the law of the excluded middle or the principle of non-contradiction does not hold.[44] The distinction between linear and non-linear systems thus becomes fundamental. It constitutes what is arguably the single most important conceptual development in contemporary sciences. Whereas linear systems adhere to the superposition principle, non-linear systems do not lend themselves to such a simple addition of quantities. This is important if we want to avoid the fallacy of (mere) linear causation. For example, Henri Poincaré discovered, to his dismay, that the mechanics of no more than three moving bodies, bound by a single relation of gravity and interacting in a single isolated system, produced such complex behaviour that no differential equation, either known or possible, could ever describe it. In other words, causal theories need not be deterministic, not even in ideal cases, let alone when the situation is complicated by introducing a degree of chaos as chance into the picture.[45] Any theory of morphogenesis would thus need to confront novelty as an irreducible quality.[46] The three-body problem, as it came to be known, triggered a whole new approach to problem-solving that no longer focused on the solution, but on framing the (space of the) problem, which would then yield solutions. As is well known to readers of Deleuze, problems get the solutions that they deserve. This means that Poincaré bypassed exact solvability as a way of getting global information and used instead a novel method to investigate the space defining the problem itself.[47] The geometry fit for the purpose of dramatisation has been with us for over a century, and it is called topology.

Geometry and topology, while both concerned with space, are distinguished by their different mathematical provenances, explains Arkady Plotnitsky. While geometry has to do with measurement, topology disregards it altogether and deals only with the structure of space qua space. As long as one deforms a given figure continuously – that is, without separating the points previously connected and, conversely, without connecting the points previously separated – the resulting figure is considered the same.[48] The most common example is the topological isomorphism between a donut and a mug. From a topological point of view they are exactly the same. Although this particular example has been repeated ad nauseam, any object with a single hole would do. Topology may be considered as the most general (an exact yet rigorous) geometry whose suitability for thinking the (intensive) relation independent of its (metric) terms cannot be overstated. While perhaps inevitable, its current appeal for architects solely at the formal(ist) level is regrettable, as it rarely goes beyond (bio)mimicry.[49]

Consider Kees Doevendans's upgrading of Anthony Vidler's 1977 architectural history classic 'The Third Typology'.[50] Vidler discovered the first typology in the famous primitive hut of Laugier (1755). Nature thus became the model for architecture. The second typology coincided with industrial development. The machine was chosen as the model for architecture and figured as its legitimising agent. Form was to emerge from functional requirements. The third typology, introduced in the 1960s by Italian neo-rationalists, marked a break with the idea that architecture and urban design had to seek external legitimacy.[51] Instead of a metaphorical approach of representing the city as either natural (organicist fallacy), or mechanical (mechanicist fallacy), the emphasis was put on the city as form. Thus, the third typology ostensibly led to an ontology of the city (essentialist fallacy), which was to be found in its morphology as passed down through history. Its champion, Aldo Rossi, defined the type as the very idea of architecture, closest to its essence. The contemporary Dutch urbanist Doevendans, for his part, contributed the 'fourth typology'.[52] Notwithstanding his qualification to consider it in terms of a Kuhnian paradigm, the proposed 'typology of topology' must be challenged as a symptomatic case of category error. By its very nature, topology does not lend itself to typologising, and it is this elusiveness that endows it with the greatest conceptual power. Cache's valuable caution to fellow architects from 1998 continues to fall on deaf ears:

One single topological structure has an infinity of Euclidean *incarnations*, the variations of which are not relevant for topology, about which topology has nothing to say. New topological structures can be incarnated in Euclidean space as squared figures as well as curved figures. Topology cannot be said to be curved because it precedes any assignment of metrical curvature. Because topological structures are often represented with in some ways indefinite curved surfaces, one might think that topology brings free curvature to architecture, but this is a misunderstanding. When mathematicians draw those kinds of free surfaces, they mean to indicate that they do not care about the actual shape in which topology can be incarnated. In so doing, *they should open the mind of architects and allow them to think of spatial structures before styling them as either curved or squared.*[53]

Despite a number of references to Deleuze, Doevendans fails to recognise that it was precisely topological (continuous) modulation that helped Deleuze dispense once and for all with typological moulding.[54] *Pace* Cache's non-representationalist cry, there have been numerous pleas to 'typify topology' in the recent past. In spite of the proclaimed worthy ambition to collapse the figure/ground distinction by defining interstitial local connections, the field approach has only produced a myriad of field-like objects: 'A field condition would be any formal or spatial matrix capable of unifying diverse elements while respecting the identity of each. Field configurations are loosely bounded aggregates characterised by porosity and local interconnectivity. The internal regulations of the parts are decisive; *overall shape and extent are highly fluid.*'[55] One cannot but be struck by the irony of an effective reversal of Stan Allen's vector 'From Object to Field'. Field conditions as bottom-up phenomena were meant to introduce a degree of chaos as chance into the morphogenetic process precisely in order to yield novelty without precluding the overall shape.[56] Only in this way may we hope to avoid the fallacy of tracing (reified field syndrome), that is, conflating the actual product with the intensive process of individuation.

There simply is no common measure between topological content and typological form. There is an asymmetry between two odd, unequal, irreducible halves of the virtual and the actual, as beautifully illustrated by Henri Bergson's cone, in contrast to phenomenology, which maintains an isomorphic symmetry between the two branches of the empirico-transcendental double. Bergson's 'pure memory' is opposed to the most relaxed level of duration, that is, matter (space), in the most condensed contraction of the whole (time) into the present. By leaping into a virtual and not a chronological past, Bergson dispenses with the total actuality of teleological reflective judgement.[57] The question arises of the temporal interval between stimulus and response. What appears as a conscious de-cision (cut) or circumscribed perception (snapshot) constitutes an abundance of complex duration, an autonomy of affect replete with (subversive) potentials. The lack of symmetry is the clue to the radical nature of Deleuze's philosophy (of time), as James Williams argues:

> It is inherently anti-conservative and anti-reactionary due to its inbuilt and unavoidable asymmetries of time. There is no represented and original past to go to [Laugier's Nature]. There is no eternal realm to escape to in the future [either], where time stands still [Rossi's Type].'[58]

Vidler's three typologies all operate under the auspices of representation through analogies with nature, culture or history. In stark opposition, there is no re-presentation or any analogy in topological thinking. There is no homology between the engendered (type) and the engendering topology.[59] Topologically, a thing can no longer be considered as one, a unity, but as a multiplicity, always increasing its lines of connection with other things. It is no longer defined by a form or by functions, but by affordance. The consistency of the thing is not dependent on any logical or psychophysical compounding, 'rather, the very elements to which such compounding is applied are themselves the results of cognitive abstractions from the wholes in question'.[60]

Lars Spuybroek provides an apt diagnosis of the problem. According to him, architects have difficulties understanding order and contingency in an onto-logical relationship, as one producing the other. Rather, they see them both as (quasi-stable) structures. The notion of structure can entail many things and is thus difficult to define. Structure itself is often comprised of components that in turn have their own structure. So, in terms of an ordered composition or artic-ulation, structure applies both to the whole and to its constituent parts. Each part may have a recognisable identity, and together the parts form a whole, a unity, with a molar identity. An architectural structure is usually taken to be the totality of form, measure, scale, function, space and materials. Be that as it may, the key aspect of structure is the relationship. If mereology is interested in the relationship between the parts, and the relationship of the parts to the whole, the key aspect of structure is 'structuration', or in our terms, mereotopology, where, somewhat counter-intuitively, relations remain external to their terms. It should not come as a surprise that Gibson too considered the notion of struc-ture inadequate.[61] The better part of our technological and aesthetic tradition has been oriented towards structure as stable and homeostatic. But a system is more accurately defined by the events as incorporeal effects than by a mere description of the physical substrate in which these events act as quasi-causes (dark precursors). This has become inconveniently evident with the arrival of the Anthropocene and its de-ontologisation of the binary opposition between culture and nature: 'If the will to knowledge characteristic of modernity provided the assurance that the fault line between human culture and nature was indeed factual, the production of the Anthropocene counter-factuality relieves our contemporaneity of the burden of perpetuating this epistemic illusion.'[62] From a Gibsonian point of view, what is required is a concept of structure that is not detached from what it structures. It has to be neither a priori as in organicism, nor a posteriori as in mechanicism.[63] In other words, rather than asking to typologise topology in the vein of Doevendans, it will always be necessary to topologise type as in (abstract) machinism.[64] For Deleuze following Spinoza, all individuation is based upon movement and rest.[65] The distinction between the seemingly opposed strata on the one hand, and the fluid plane of nature or body without organs on the other, is simply a question of varying speeds and slownesses within a single system (monism). All this is evidence that we have yet to distinguish between the three Ts: the essentialist typology, the extensive topography and the intensive topology.[66] Spuybroek provides a helpful image of the solid–structure–configuration–pattern–rhythm cascade that may be taken as a diagram of the concrescence of Cartesian space out of topological *spatium*, albeit in reverse:

> Let's put all the forms between solid and liquid on a line. *Solid* is on one side. That's how architects generally understand form: idealised, crystallised, *a priori*, archetypal. No dynamics, no contingency, only memory. . . . The first one after solid form going in the direction of liquid is *structure*: it's more open, not necessarily Platonic. It's not the dead clay of Platonism; there are forces, points and lines involved, but it is as static. Then we have *configuration*; it's the word some of the Gestaltists used for form. There is a going back and forth between actual perceptions and virtual memories; it's much more dynamic than structure. Next to configuration, we have the modern notion of *pattern*, which is sort of between information and form; it is generally considered as fully emergent. . . . Then, I guess, closest to completely liquid, we have Deleuze's *rhythm*, his continuous variation and modulation. Waves, turbulences, swerves.[67]

A parallel may be drawn with language. Deleuze explains, 'language has no significance of its own. It is composed of signs, but signs are inseparable from a whole other element, a non-linguistic element, which could be called "the state of things" or, better yet, "images."'[68] Language always comes after. Process philosophy, or the ontology of becoming, identifies metaphysical reality with change and dynamism. Ever since Plato and Aristotle, processes have either been denied or subordinated to timeless substances. Change has been seen as purely accidental. Consequently, classical ontology denies any full reality to change as such and continues to impinge upon our epistemologies to this day. By contrast, Deleuzian anti-correlationism *avant la lettre* grants full reality to becoming.[69] It grants full reality to an ontopower which is environmental yet proto-territorial and both logically and onto-logically prior to the categories of (passive) nature and (active) culture.[70]

Despite the all-too-hastily declared dislike of the non-non-Euclidean geometries, contemporary architecture has not yet broken its allegiance with the arborescent schema in favour of its rhizomatic counterpart. The cart of semantic signification thus precedes the horse of pragmatic significance and will continue to do so until the discipline has fully absorbed the conceptual power of the smooth space (*spatium*) that is both emergent and constructed by way of inclusive disjunction. For a genuine change to occur, the relation between space (perception) and movement (action) ought to be inverted. My plea for topologising has no other purpose than to adequately conceptualise the event: it is not about what happens, but what is going on in what happens. Similarly, Kwinter advocates 'radical anamnesis' to recall not the (contingent) past that has happened but the past that has not happened but could have. This position resists the allure of allowing common sense (*doxa*) to govern all our encounters: 'Through (selective) memory the future becomes possible, a future that the past could not think and that the present – alone – dares not.'[71] Having propositional knowledge about reality does not render the nature of reality propositional.[72] Thinking does not go from proposition to proposition. When we communicate by reference to and with socially coded stimuli, we are not (yet) thinking. Rather, thinking becomes creative by tracing back propositions to the non-propositional field of problems that engender them. Only through the non-apodictic, that is, aesthetic experimentation, can we determine whether an encounter is ethical or not, whether it augments or diminishes our power of action. Hence the necessity of topologising as the only plausible ethico-aesthetic strategy to (provisionally) 'rid ourselves of ourselves' or break the vicious circle of correlationism in which no-thing can be independent of thought and where space is a priori.[73]

An architect's desire to be nameless is no false modesty.[74] Under the commitment to flat ontology it becomes an expression of the highest ambition.

Notes

This essay first appeared in *Speculative Art Histories: Analysis at the Limits*, edited by Sjoerd van Tuinen (Edinburgh: Edinburgh University Press, 2017), 185–201.

1. Benjamin, 'The Work of Art in the Age of Mechanical Reproduction', 239.
2. The maxim 'Less is a bore', a postmodern antidote to Mies van der Rohe's famous modernist dictum 'Less is more', was coined by Robert Venturi. 'Yes is more' is a title from Copenhagen-based architectural practice Bjarke Ingels Group, or BIG. See: Ingels, *Yes Is More*.
3. Morton, *The Ecological Thought*. See also: Morton, *Ecology without Nature*.
4. Dreyfus, 'Heidegger's Critique of Husserl's (and Searle's) Account of Intentionality'.
5. Bashour and Muller, 'Exploring the Post-Darwinian Naturalist Landscape', 2.
6. Kwinter, 'Hydraulic Vision'.
7. Foucault, *Society Must Be Defended*, 243.
8. Kipnis and Martin, 'What Good Can Architecture Do?'.
9. Roche, 'Matters of Fabulation', 199. Cf. Roche, 'Alchimis(t/r/ick)-machines'.
10. Deleuze, 'Coldness and Cruelty', 133.
11. Whitehead, *Process and Reality*, 7–8.
12. Félix Guattari, *Chaosmosis*, 100.
13. Radman, 'Sensibility Is Ground Zero' (Chapter 4 in this volume).
14. Deleuze and Guattari, *What Is Philosophy?*, 192.
15. Ibid., 193.
16. Negarestani, 'Frontiers of Manipulation'.
17. Gibson, *The Ecological Approach to Visual Perception*, 129.
18. Ibid., 134.
19. Deleuze, *Difference and Repetition*, 202.
20. Žižek, *Event*, 144.
21. Shaviro, *Universe of Things*, 81.
22. Chemero and Withagen, 'Naturalising Perception'.
23. Hayles, *How We Became Posthuman*, 288.
24. DeLanda, *Philosophy and Simulation*, 1–6.
25. Gibson, *The Ecological Approach to Visual Perception*, 147.
26. Massumi, 'The Thinking-Feeling of What Happens'.
27. Kwinter, 'Flying the Bullet', 71.
28. Payne and Reiser, 'Chum', 23.
29. Deleuze and Guattari, *A Thousand Plateaus*, 387–467.
30. Kwinter, 'La Cittá Nuova', 593.
31. Deleuze and Guattari, *A Thousand Plateaus*, 23.
32. Ibid., 6.

33. Arquilla and Ronfeldt, *The Emergence of Noopolitik*, x.
34. Deleuze, *Negotiations*, 126–7.
35. Neidich, 'Neuropower'.
36. Deleuze, 'Postscript on the Societies of Control', 4.
37. Massumi, 'National Enterprise Emergency'.
38. Massumi, *The Power at the End of the Economy*, 15, 42.
39. Wolfendale, *Object-Oriented Philosophy*, 222.
40. Wigley, 'The Translation of Architecture', 662.
41. Boumeester and Radman, 'The Impredicative City' (Chapter 6 in this volume).
42. Deleuze and Parnet, *Dialogues*, 124. See also: Deleuze, *Two Regimes of Madness*, 92.
43. See: Peter Macapia, 'Interview with Bernard Cache in *Saint Ouen l'Aumône*'. Cache and Macapia discuss several conceptual changes in the contemporary use of geometry in the field of architecture.
44. A term borrowed from Scott Lash's book *Another Modernity*. For the relation between the principle of sufficient reason and the principle of non-contradiction, see: Van Tuinen, 'Deleuze'.
45. Plotnitsky, 'Chaosmologies', 45.
46. Kwinter, 'Landscapes of Change', 52.
47. DeLanda, *Intensive Science and Virtual Philosophy*, 154.
48. Plotnitsky, 'Algebras, Geometries and Topologies of the Fold', 99.
49. The same concern is expressed by Kwinter in 'A Discourse on Method', 46.
50. Vidler, 'The Third Typology'.
51. Rossi, *The Architecture of the City*. Rossi's book sketches out the concept of rational architecture further developed in the book *Architettura razionale*, published in 1973 on the occasion of the fifteenth Milan Triennale.
52. Doevendans, 'Sustainable Urban Development and the Fourth Typology'.
53. Cache, 'Plea for Euclid', 40; emphasis added.
54. Kwinter, *Architectures of Time*, 26–8.
55. Allen, 'From Object to Field', 24; emphasis added.
56. For examples of non-formalist architecture, see: Hauptmann and Radman, 'Northern Line' (Chapter 3 in this volume).
57. Bergson, *Matter and Memory*.
58. Williams, *Gilles Deleuze's Philosophy of Time*, 4.
59. Churchland, *Plato's Camera*, 110.
60. Smith, 'Values in Contexts', 17.
61. Gibson, *The Ecological Approach to Visual Perception*.
62. Turpin, 'Who Does the Earth Think It Is, Now?', 4.
63. Braund, *From Inference to Affordance*, 67.
64. Spuybroek, 'Machining Architecture', 9.

65. DeLanda, 'Nonorganic Life'. See also: Deleuze, *Spinoza, Practical Philosophy*, 123; Deleuze and Guattari, *A Thousand Plateaus*, 254, 261.

66. Lury, 'Topology for Culture'.

67. Spuybroek in an interview by Arjen Mulder, 'The Aesthetics of Variation', 141–2.

68. Deleuze, *Two Regimes of Madness*, 201.

69. Rosi Braidotti in an interview by Timotheus Vermeulen, 'Borrowed Energy'.

70. Massumi, 'National Enterprise Emergency', 27, 29.

71. Kwinter, *Far from Equilibrium*, 142.

72. Brassier, 'Nominalism, Naturalism, and Materialism'.

73. Meillassoux, *After Finitude*, 5.

74. Van Berkel and Bos, *Move: (3)*, 26.

8   Zigzagging: Bound by the Absence of a Tie

Empathy and Abstraction

THIS CHAPTER UNPACKS Deleuze and Guattari's machinic conception of consistency, which is determined neither by the naïve, organic autonomy of the vitalist whole, nor by the crude, reductionist expression of the whole in the sum of its mechanical parts. Machinism entails the dark precursor's zigzagging between the immanent limits of both empathy and abstraction, nature and culture, the extensive and the intensive, signification and significance, as well as the political and the libidinal. To talk of multiplicities is to avoid subsuming a number of particulars under the universal concept. Instead, each multiplicity is to be related to the variables that determine its mutations.[1] We start from the hypothesis that the current digital turn in architecture effectively reproduces the Cartesian duality of mind and body. It removes the mind from the concerns of coping with the environment and treats the body as no more than a kind of recording mechanism. The role of the body is relegated to converting the stimuli that impinge upon it into data to be processed.

It is for this reason that I want to revamp the legacy of Deleuzian transcendental empiricism in general and Gibsonian ecological perception in particular.[2] The American psychologist J. J. Gibson vehemently rejected the reductionist information-processing view because of its implied separation of the activity of the mind in the body from the re-activity of the body in the world. Instead, he argued that perception is part and parcel of the total system of relations constituted by the ecology of the life form, or its mode of existence.[3] Let us make it, after Guattari, ecologies in the plural: environmental, social and psychic.[4] Life forms perceive the world directly, by moving about and discovering what the 'annexed milieu' affords, rather than by representing it in the mind.[5] Hence, meaning is not the form that the mind contributes to the flux of raw sensory data by way of its acquired schemata. Rather, it is continually becoming within relational contexts of pragmatic engagement or speculative extrapolation. To put it succinctly, empathy and abstraction are mutually constitutive.

Although everything starts from the sensible, one must quickly reach towards that which makes sensibility possible.[6] In other words, sensations mobilise the differential forces that, in turn, make thinking possible. This is what Deleuze meant by referring to the 'pedagogy of the senses'.[7] One is at the mercy of the more or less contingent encounters. The profound consequence of the epigenetic turn did not pass unnoticed by the media guru Friedrich Kittler: 'it's funny, this thing turning back on itself. It's called feedback (and not, as should be noted, reflection).'[8] (Dis)cognition is extended and not interiorised or centralised, embedded and not generalised or decontextualised, enacted and not passive or merely receptive, embodied and not logocentric, affective and not unprovoked.[9] If architects ever stopped to consider how much of life is constrained by the ego-logical intentionality and how much enabled by the eco-logical gratuitous encounters, they would certainly pay more attention to the relational properties. If they paid attention to paying attention, they would concede that there could be a bind in spite of the absence of an a priori tie.

Nature and Culture

We commence with a problem statement. Is there a way to overcome techno-determinism without regressing to relativism, and conversely, how is one to escape relativism without regressing to determinism? In contemporary architectural discourse, the crypto-modernist logic of dominating abstraction goes by the name of parametricism.[10] A parametricist's wet dream is total formalisation/simulation: Intelligent City, Big Data, Infrastructure, to name but a few. The crypto-PoMo relativism is associated with neo-phenomenologists such as Steven Holl and Peter Zumthor, who privilege the poetics of space, the subjective, the haptic and similar emphatic submissions.[11]

The answer lies in the transversal approach of eco-logic as advanced by the Ecologies of Architecture (æ), a neo-materialist architecture research group at TU Delft.[12] New materialism is the umbrella term for a series of movements that distance themselves from anthropocentrism, rethink subjectivity and ethics in terms of inhuman forces within the human, emphasise heteropoiesis as the organising power of transversal processes and explore the political ramifications of these processes for cultural practices such as architecture. According to this view, architecture does not represent culture but is a mechanism of culture. Better still, it is machinism, or what Guattari named the 'collective equipment'.[13]

Let us return to the opposition between the all-too-abstract parametricism and the not-abstract-enough neo-phenomenology.[14] Once again, we are offered a false choice between the territory-as-map and the map-as-territory; objective reality or subjective illusion; the red or the blue pill from *The Matrix*.[15] I opt for a third pill, as does Slavoj Žižek in *The Pervert's Guide to Cinema*.[16] Yet, this is as far as I am prepared to follow his Hegelian/Lacanian trajectory that insists on human exceptionalism. Instead, I turn to Spinozian ethics as a mode of existence, for it is in ethology – as a theory of capacity – that the distinction between abstraction and empathy finally collapses.[17] As I have already underscored, binaries such as subject and object are never to be taken as general abstractions, but as divergent processual destinations.

The æ also follows the lead of the process philosopher Whitehead, who rejected the solipsistic self – the liberal humanist subject – in favour of its developmentally constructed counterpart.[18] Whitehead launched his (in)famous plea for substituting super-ject for sub-ject, or the ontogenetic effect for the substantialist cause.[19] Sanford Kwinter has reiterated Whitehead's critique of the reversed ontology. Moreover, according to Kwinter, the essential human engagement in the environment is geared towards extraction of sensory stimulation, not food.[20] The thesis reverses the orthodoxy of urban metabolism, with its presumed primacy of incorporation over sensation as the vehicle of our experience of the world.[21] Guattari's prodigious statement on architectural enunciation in his *Schizoanalytic Cartographies* is worth quoting at length:

> Reinventing architecture can no longer signify the relaunching of a style, a school, a theory with a hegemonic vocation [*pace* parametricism], but the recomposition of *architectural enunciation*, and, in a sense, the trade of the architect, under today's conditions.

He continues:

> Once it is no longer the goal of the architect to be the artist of built forms [*pace* neo-phenomenology] but to offer his services in revealing the virtual desire of spaces, places, trajectories and territories, he will have to undertake the analysis of the relations of individual and collective corporeality by constantly singularizing his approach. . . . In other words, he will have to become an artist and an artisan of sensible and relational lived experience.[22]

Not only do humans realise 'natural' ends, they do so by creating the means of their realisation. They creatively transform these ends into those of culture. The transformation allows a deterritorialisation from the organic strata and its subsequent non-organic reterritorialisation, fraught with the dangers of ex-futurism and neo-archaism, respectively. Once again, it is eco-logic that will help us navigate between the evident schizophrenia of the revolutionary parametricism and the equally evident paranoia of the reactionary neo-phenomenology. Deleuze and Guattari anticipated the impasse in their first volume of *Capitalism and Schizophrenia*:

> The social axiomatic of modern societies is caught between two poles and is constantly oscillating from one pole to the other. Born of decoding and deter-ritorialization, on the ruins of the despotic machine, these societies are caught between the Urstaat that they would like to resuscitate as an overcoding and reterritorializing unity [as in neo-phenomenology], and the unfettered flows [as in parametricism] that carry them toward an absolute threshold. . . . They are torn in two directions: archaism and futurism, neoarchaism and ex-futur-ism, paranoia and schizophrenia. . . . They are continually behind or ahead of themselves.[23]

The Extensive and the Intensive

The term ecology is as political as it is scientific. Departing from the logic of discreteness and its principle of non-contradiction, ecological thinking endorses the logic of continuity. There is discreteness, to be sure, but the finite always consists of an infinity under a certain relation.[24] The discrete and the continuous – digital and analogue – are not to be taken as mutually exclusive, but rather as effectively codetermining, albeit asymmetrically.[25] The content is always too big for the form, given that the reality is in excess to the phenomenal.

The general lesson of the logic of the included middle is that the quasi-stable regularities we see in actuality – objects – do not have a specific cause that can be demarcated and isolated, but may only be understood as a heteropathic cas-cade of many processes operating over time.[26] Gregory Bateson:

> we used to ask: Can a computer simulate all the processes of logic? The answer was yes, but the question was surely wrong. We should have asked: Can logic simulate all sequences of cause and effect? The answer would have been no.[27]

After all, if effects were reducible to their causes, novelty would be impossible. The ethico-political lesson of the logic of intensity is that all things are contingently obligatory and not logically necessary. Therein lies the possibility of pursuing a project of defatalisation or anti-teleology.[28]

Resetting ourselves in a metaphysical perspective, as the speculative realist Quentin Meillassoux suggests, permits us to reconstruct our existence beyond faith alone or the sole opportunism of interest.[29] Artistic researchers beware: it is not just that all things could have been different, but what might have happened virtually subsists in what actually exists. The time has come to unyoke the architect from Newtonian physics and Cartesian metaphysics in favour of the intensive and relational – ecological – approach. In the words of Guattari, 'there is no longer a tripartite division between the realm of reality, realm of representation or representativity, and the realm of subjectivity. You have a collective set-up which is, at once, subject, object, and expression.'[30] Yet, this is not to be taken as a call for the homeostatic conception of ecology. In the words of Žižek, 'after the death of the God-Father, the masculine Reason, we should also endorse the death of the Goddess-Nature'.[31]

The æ starts from the middle, *par le milieu*: 'the assemblage extracts a territory from the milieu; it is the assemblage that allows us to think the coevolution of the human and nature in terms of milieu, the back-and-forth of modulation'.[32] *Pace* cognitivism, we must avoid reducing the world to our own conceptual schemes and instead be 'primed for non-recognition'.[33] If we hold a hammer, we should not treat everything as if it were a nail. Both Deleuzian transcendental empiricism and Gibsonian ecological perception ward off the reductionist information-processing view, with its implied mutual exclusivity of active abstraction and reactive empathy. Instead, they advocate the metastable plasticity whereby the condition is never greater than the conditioned.[34]

The lesson of the assemblage theory is that capacities do depend on the properties of their components but cannot be reduced to them.[35] This is how Gibson conceptualises the externality of relations:

> The affordances of the environment are what it offers the [human], what it provides or furnishes, either for good or ill. . . . I mean by [affordance] something that refers to both the environment and the [human] in a way that no existing term does.[36]

It would be difficult to imagine a more elegant shift of focus from the extensive space of properties to the intensive non-local *spatium* of capacities, or in Deleuzian parlance, from the actual manifest reality to the real-yet-incorporeal virtual. This is crucial, because the actual experience-of-space bears no resemblance to the (phase) space-of-experience. A mode of existence never pre-exists an event.[37]

Signification and Significance

In his review of Deleuze's early works – *Difference and Repetition* and *The Logic of Sense* – Foucault praises Deleuze for challenging the three conditions that make it impossible to think through the event, namely the world, the self and god (a sphere, a circle and a centre).[38] First, Deleuze introduces a metaphysics of the virtual, which is irreducible to the physics of the world (the actual). Second, the logic of neutral meaning (affect/affordance) replaces the phenomenology of signification based on the subject and her sense-bestowing. Finally, the tethering of the conceptual future to a past essence is rejected in favour of a thought of the present infinitive.

Consequently, the prerogative of the æ is to renounce any order of preference, any goal-oriented organisation, any signification, any a priori tie.[39] In *What is Philosophy?* Deleuze and Guattari would characterise the auto-unifying form (*survol*) in the following terms:

> It is a primary, 'true form' as Ruyer has defined it: neither a Gestalt nor a perceived form, but a form in itself [N – 1] that does not refer to any external point of view, ... it is an absolute consistent form that surveys itself independently of any supplementary dimension [N + 1], which does not appeal therefore to any transcendence.[40]

Semiology is only one of the many regimes of signs and certainly not the most important for architecture. After all, 'natural stimuli cannot be understood by analogy and with reference to socially coded stimuli, for that would be like putting the cart before the horse'.[41] A sign, according to Spinoza, can have several meanings, but it is always an effect. An effect is first of all the trace of one body upon another, the state of a body insofar as it suffers the action of another body.[42] For the æ, singularities come before identities and participation precedes cognition. A body ought to be defined not by its form, nor by its organs or functions, but by its capacity for affecting or being affected, because 'the limit of something is the limit of its action and not the outline of its figure'.[43] This is what it means to be bound in the absence of tie and, perhaps, by the very absence of tie.

Things are powers, not forms, and there may be consistency in spite of incongruence or isomorphism without correspondence.[44] Deleuze gives an example which seems counter-intuitive at first and proves just how much we are accustomed to Aristotelian categorisation (of genera and species): 'There is a greater difference between a racehorse and a work horse than between a work horse and an ox.'[45] This is because the racehorse and the work horse do not have the same affects. Things are no longer defined by qualitative essence, as in 'man as a reasonable animal', but by quantifiable power.

The Political and the Libidinal

For radical empiricism, thought cannot be richer than reality and non-conscious experience is not an oxymoron, because much more is felt than is known. The æ is interested in an encounter between thought and that which forces it into action. While accepting multiple scales of reality, it opposes the alleged primacy of the physical world. We cope with the environment more or less skilfully.[46] The emphasis is on the encounter, where experience is seen as an emergence which returns the body to a process field of exteriority.

Sensibility introduces an aleatory moment into thought's development. It effectively turns contingency into the *conditio sine qua non* for thinking. Contingency upsets logical identity and opposition, and places the limit of thinking beyond any dialectical system. Thought cannot activate itself by thinking. It has to be provoked. It must suffer violence. Architecture as 'the first art' may inflict such violence because it bears the potential for breaking up the faculties' common function by placing them before their own limits: 'thought before the unthinkable, memory before the immemorial, sensibility before the imperceptible, etc.'[47]

As already argued, the eco-logical perspectivist assault on the ego-logical representational thinking inevitably impinges upon the identity of the subject. While Kant founded the representational unity of space and time upon the formal unity of consciousness, difference fractures consciousness into multiple states not predicable of a single subject. According to Deleuze, Leibniz's great lesson is that, counter-intuitively, it is points of view that engender a subject, rather than the other way around.[48] In the words of Anne Sauvagnargues, 'subjectivity proceeds through framing'.[49] Always already social desiring machines connect, disconnect and reconnect with one another without (private or personal) meaning or intention.[50] There may be 'entention', or intention without intentionality, desire without volition and a smile without a cat.[51] Individuality is not characteristic of a self or an ego, but a perpetually individualising differential, a dark precursor. As Claire Colebrook put it, 'I love you not because of the predicates that personalize you, but rather for that absolutely singular event of your existence that is irreducible to determination.'[52] As we have seen at the outset, this constitutes Deleuze's famous 'pedagogy of the senses': 'Each faculty, including thought, has only involuntary adventures', and 'involuntary operation remains embedded in the empirical'.[53]

To turn the theatre of re-presentation into the machine for desiring-production is to recognise a (r)evolutionary potential in creating the new, that which is not-as-yet captured or (over)codified as in clichés and opinions.[54] The emancipatory political potential lies, quite literally, in the pure agency of transcendental causality, or the difference in itself – ontopower – that relates heterogeneities. The concept of quasi-causality – the dark precursor – prevents regression into simple reductionism of the sensible (empathy) to the intelligible (abstraction). To think differently one has to feel differently. The first step towards the reversal of the reversed ontology is to 'ask not what's inside your head, rather what your head's inside of'.[55]

Notes

This essay first appeared in *The Dark Precursor: Deleuze and Artistic Research*, edited by Paulo de Assis and Paolo Giudici (Leuven: Leuven University Press (Orpheus Institute Series), 2017), 182–91.

1. Deleuze, *Negotiations*, 31.
2. *Pace* Spencer, contemporary architecture is not 'Deleuzist' enough. See: Spencer, *The Architecture of Neoliberalism*.
3. Gibson, *The Ecological Approach to Visual Perception*.
4. Guattari, *The Three Ecologies*.
5. Deleuze and Guattari, *A Thousand Plateaus*, 51. Cf. Radman, 'Involuntary Architecture' (Chapter 11 in this volume).
6. Colebrook, 'Derrida, Deleuze and Haptic Aesthetics'. 'Once we try to think the origin of all that is, the very ground of being, then we arrive properly not at the origin of sensibility, but sensibility as origin.' Ibid., 29.
7. Deleuze, *Difference and Repetition*, 237.
8. Kittler, *Literature, Media, Information Systems*, 144.
9. For more information on 4EA cognition, see John Protevi's '4EA' blog. Cf. Shaviro, *Discognition*. 'I use this neologism [discognition] to designate something that disrupts cognition, exceeds the limits of cognition, but also subtends cognition.' Ibid., 10–11.
10. For an account of parametricism, see: Schumacher, 'Patrik Schumacher, Promoter of Parametricism', interview by Flavien Onfroy. See also: Schumacher, 'The Parametricist Epoch'.

11. For an account of neo-phenomenology, see: Holl, Pallasmaa and Perez-Gomez, *Questions of Perception*. See also: Otero-Pailos, *Architecture's Historical Turn*.

12. See: 'Research and Publications', <www.tudelft.nl/en/architecture-and-the-built-environment/about-the-faculty/departments/architecture/organisation/groups/architecture-theory/research-publications> (accessed 13 March 2021).

13. Guattari, *Lines of Flight*.

14. McKim, 'Radical Infrastructure?'.

15. Wachowski siblings (dir.), *The Matrix* (1999).

16. Finnes, *The Pervert's Guide to Cinema*.

17. Deleuze, *Spinoza, Practical Philosophy*.

18. Whitehead, *Process and Reality*, 29.

19. Brassier, 'Prometheanism and Its Critics'.

20. Kwinter, 'Neuroecology', 329.

21. Maas and Pasquinelli, 'Accelerate Metrophagy'.

22. Guattari, *Schizoanalytic Cartographies*, 232.

23. Deleuze and Guattari, *Anti-Oedipus*, 260. See also: Deleuze, *Two Regimes of Madness*. 'Unlike the paranoid whose delirium consists of restoring codes and reinventing territories, the schizophrenic never ceases to go one more step in a movement of self-decoding and self-deterritorialization.' Ibid., 28.

24. Deleuze, *Cours Vincennes*, 'Sur Spinoza: The Actual Infinite-Eternal' (10 March 1981).

25. The concept of the double bind was coined by Gregory Bateson. See: Bateson, *Steps to an Ecology of Mind*, 199–204.

26. Unlike homopathic laws that have an additive character – producing highly predictable patterns of causal interactions – heteropathic laws are somewhat idiosyncratic – linking quite different classes of homopathic properties across levels. See: Deacon, *Incomplete Nature*, 155. Cf. Kwinter, 'Hydraulic Vision'.

27. Bateson, *Mind and Nature*, 58.

28. Radman, 'Sensibility Is Ground Zero' (Chapter 4 in this volume).

29. Meillassoux, 'Interview with Meillassoux'.

30. Guattari, *Chaosophy*, 160.

31. Žižek, *Disparities*, 31. Cf. Wark, *Molecular Red*, 209.

32. Sauvagnargues, *Artmachines*, 83.

33. Massumi, 'Of Microperception and Micropolitics', 10.

34. The concept of plasticity has been revamped by Catherine Malabou. See: Malabou, *What Should We Do with Our Brain?*

35. DeLanda, *Assemblage Theory*.

36. Gibson, *The Ecological Approach to Visual Perception*, 127.

37. Manning and Massumi, 'Coming Alive in a World of Texture for Neurodiversity'.

38. Foucault, 'Theatrum Philosophicum'. Cf. Deleuze, *Difference and Repetition*; Deleuze, *The Logic of Sense*.

39. Deleuze, *Essays Critical and Clinical*, 153.

40. Deleuze and Guattari, *What Is Philosophy?*, 210. Cf. Ruyer, *Neofinalism*. Cf. Hauptmann and Radman, 'Northern Line' (Chapter 3 in this volume).

41. Gibson, 'The Concept of the Stimulus in Psychology', 702.

42. Deleuze, *Spinoza, Practical Philosophy*, 124.

43. Deleuze, *Cours Vincennes*, 'Sur Spinoza' (17 February 1981).

44. Deleuze and Guattari, *A Thousand Plateaus*, 51–2.

45. Deleuze and Parnet, *Dialogues*, 60.

46. Dreyfus, *Skillful Coping*. 'In our most basic way of being – i.e., as skillful copers – we are not minds at all but one with the world . . . The inner–outer distinction becomes problematic. There's no easily askable question about where the absorbed coping is – in me or in the world.' Ibid., 259.

47. Deleuze and Guattari, *What Is Philosophy?*, 186.; Cf. Deleuze, *Difference and Repetition*, 227.

48. 'It's the point of view that explains the subject and not the opposite.' Deleuze, *Cours Vincennes*, 'Sur Leibniz' (4 April 1980).

49. Sauvagnargues, *Artmachines*, 103.

50. Guattari, 'A Liberation of Desire'. 'For Gilles Deleuze and me desire is everything that exists before the opposition between subject and object, before representation and production. It's everything whereby the world and affects constitute us outside of ourselves, in spite of ourselves. It's everything that overflows from us. That's why we define it as flow.' Ibid., 142.

51. Deacon, *Incomplete Nature*. 'I propose that we use the term ententional as a generic adjective to describe all phenomena that are intrinsically incomplete in the sense of being in relationship to, constituted by, or organized to achieve something non-intrinsic. By combining the prefix en- (for "in" or "within") with the adjectival form meaning something like "inclined toward", I hope to signal this deep and typically ignored commonality that exists in all the various phenomena that include within them a fundamental relationship to something absent.' Ibid., 27.

52. Colebrook, 'Who Comes after the Post-Human?', 229.

53. Deleuze, *Difference and Repetition*, 145.

54. Ibid., 271.; cf. Deleuze and Guattari, *Anti-Oedipus*, 379.

55. Mace, 'James J. Gibson's Strategy for Perceiving'.

9 3D Perception ≠ 2D Image + 1D Inference: or Why a Single Precise Shot Would Often Miss the Target, Whereas a Series of Imprecise Shots Will Eventually Lead to a Hit

> The world does not speak to the observer. Animals and humans communicate with cries, gestures, speech, pictures, writing, and television [and the Internet], but we cannot hope to understand perception in terms of these channels; it is quite the other way around. Words and pictures convey information, carry it, or transmit it, but the information in the sea of energy around each of us, luminous or mechanical or chemical energy, is not conveyed. It is simply there. The assumption that information can be transmitted and the assumption that it can be stored are appropriate for the theory of communication, not for the theory of perception. (James Jerome Gibson, 1986)[1]

AT THE WHAT Images Do network's inaugural meeting, in Copenhagen in December 2012, I addressed the overarching question literally. My answer was: 'images move'. The subtitle of my presentation contained a caveat that this was 'More Than a Facile Rejoinder to the Question (of What Images Do)'. Not only do images cause things to move, I argued, they are constantly in movement themselves. Simpler still, image equals movement. The crypto-essentialist question of 'what images are' will unavoidably continue to be pondered elsewhere. However, it is high time to consider the problem in pragmatist terms, despite the fact that we will never be able to answer the question of 'what it is that images do' conclusively. After all, it is not about bringing all sorts of other things into the concept of the image, but about relating the concept to the variables that determine its mutation.

My argument draws on what Gilles Deleuze diagnosed as the historical crisis of psychology caused by the 'ontological iron curtain' between the mind and the body, which keeps the images in consciousness separated from the movements in space.[2] Such a dualist position is not sustainable, for there has never been such a thing as a bounded body coupled to the world. The 'movement-image' as a pure event is antecedent to the formation of the border between the inside and the outside. To escape the pernicious reversed ontology whereby the cart of representation is placed before the horse of morphogenesis, we need to draw on the 'reversal (of the reversal)'. The realist account of metastable structures as being produced out of material flows requires that we put the event before and beyond meaning and organism altogether. Images cannot be reduced to their all-too-human semiotic function in a cultural system. It is not about the world of design, but about the design of a world.[3]

Kinaesthesia

In his essay 'Birth', Michel Serres recounts the dramatic story of a sailor whose vessel is on fire. In an attempt to escape through a porthole, he becomes trapped between the inferno of the burning cabin and the freezing cold of the rough seas. Struggling to squeeze himself out, the sailor begins to contemplate the sense of 'I'. At which point, he wonders, do I consider myself to be effectively outside; is it when the head alone is sticking out, or when the whole chest emerges, or . . .? This is a problem of coenaesthesia.[4]

Echoing Maurice Merleau-Ponty, Gregory Bateson goes even further (and I mean this literally) in his *Steps to an Ecology of Mind*: 'Consider a blind man with a stick. Where does the blind man's self begin? At the tip of the stick? At the handle of the stick? Or at some point half-way up the stick?'[5] Kinaesthesia – which is even antecedent to coenaesthesia – is not *like* something, explains the champion of the corporeal turn, Maxine Sheets-Johnstone: it is what it is.[6] At around the same time (early 1980s), Serres's compatriot Deleuze diagnosed the historical crisis of psychology: it was no longer attainable to place images in consciousness and movements in space.[7] How is one to pass from one order to another once the 'ontological iron curtain' is up?[8]

The Affective Turn

The Frenchmen did not seem to be aware of the parallel efforts by the American psychologist J. J. Gibson, who published his masterpiece *The Ecological Approach to Visual Perception* in 1979. In what turned out to be his last book, Gibson set the course for a radical anti-representationalist approach to perception.[9] If we agree with Deleuze that film-makers, painters, architects and musicians are all essentially thinkers, then the difference is that, unlike philosophers, they do not create concepts. They create percepts (would-be perceptions) and affects (capacities to affect and be affected). Hence the pertinent question of what images are capable of – what is it that they do? Gibson famously cautioned that the course in 'basic design' with which architects normally begin their training is a setback. It teaches graphics on the assumption that an understanding of form is as necessary for architects as it is presumably for painters. But in his opinion the use of the term form only adds to the confusion. Instead, what architects ought to be concerned with are affordances – Gibson's neologism for 'would-be action'.[10] According to him, it is safe to suggest that

> men had not paid attention to the perspectives of things until they learned to draw and perceive by means of drawings. Before that time they needed only to detect the specifying invariants of things that differentiated them – their distinctive features, not their momentary aspects or frozen projections. Young children are also . . . not aware of aspects of forms as such until they begin to notice pictures as surfaces.[11]

There is a strong resonance between Gibson's ecological approach and Deleuze's theses from the first *Cinema* book. It is, however, unfortunate that in Deleuzian scholarship the movement-image seems to be overshadowed by the subsequent volume dedicated to the time-image.[12] Notwithstanding the theoretical capacity of the latter, the time is right – at least from the point of view of architectural discipline – to reopen the former. The Bergsonian trope 'Image = Movement' from *Cinema 1*, which might as well be attributed to Gibson, is yet to be unpacked.[13]

Speculative Pragmatism

Movement is a phenomenon *sui generis* which may detach itself from the objects of sight. Nothing 'comes through' the sense organs, according to Gibson, neither signals nor pictures, since these organs are components of perceptual systems that extract invariants from the flux of stimulus energy surrounding the observer. Invariants are specific to the world but not to the receptors stimulated. Perception is therefore a skill, not a constructing of the mental world out of psychic components. It needs no mediation through memory, inferences or any other cognitive process. Put succinctly, the information does not have to be processed, it need only be detected.[14]

In his *Cinema* books Deleuze relies heavily on Charles Sanders Peirce's 'three principles of Logic': Firstness, Secondness and Thirdness.[15] This is how Peirce himself explains the triad:

First is the conception of being or existing independent of anything else. Second is the conception of being relative to, the conception of reaction with, something else. Third is the conception of mediation, whereby a first and second are brought into relation ... The origin of things, considered not as leading to anything, but in itself, contains the idea of First, the end of things that of Second, the process mediating between them that of Third.[16]

For Henri Bergson, famously, there is also a 'degree zero' – *the plane of immanence* – from which signs take shape. Deleuze follows the lead of Bergson, for whom the image is more than what the idealist calls a representation and less than what the realist calls a thing. He thus identifies a dead end in the macro- and micro-reductionist approach of idealism and materialism respectively.[17] In the case of Gibson, the imperative was to navigate between exo-reductionist (quasi-materialist) behaviourism and endo-reductionist (crypto-idealist) gestalt.[18] The key is to go beyond the given (product), to that by which a given is given (process).[19] Let us for the sake of simplicity limit our enquiry to visual perception:

Icon: Ambient Optic Array

Under the conventional theory, the starting point for perception is the retinal image. According to Gibson, however, the starting point is the 'ambient optic array' that provides direct information about the media, surfaces, substances and events for an observer. This 'compiled knowledge' is rich and reliable and not in need of mediating processes. The optical structure is generated by the layout of surfaces. It is potentially and not necessarily effectively available for perception. Each edge and each surface in the environment projects a unique and specific pattern of optical discontinuities in a visual solid angle to each potential point of view. The concept of ambient optic array could be said to fall under Peirce's firstness.

Index: Optical Flow Field

Gibson's concept of 'optical flow field' corresponds with Peirce's secondness. The optical flow field results from the locomotion of an organism in a cluttered environment. When an organism moves forward there is a global transformation of the solid angle that produces a vectorial movement of each optical texture. The law of optical expansion (looming) gives a basis for goal-directed movement: 'To start moving, make the optic array flow. To stop, cancel the flow. To go back, make the flow reverse.'[20]

Symbol: Affordance

Finally, thirdness is the mode of being which brings interaction into relationship with a third thing, a context of constraint (quasi-cause) akin to Gibson's concept of affordances (for example, walk-through-ability). Traditionally, a shape has been seen to be perceived through two instantaneous values: static retinal form (image) and the momentary distance value of depth cues (inference). But the affordance perceived is not based on a static property such as form, but rather upon an invariant embedded in change (hence the title of this chapter).

The concept of the invariant, as a figure of time (and not space), might prove indispensable for answering difficult questions such as: what is the ontological status of looming and locomoting as the *relata* of the ecological law, that is, the relation that is exterior to its terms? It is this sort of ontological question that the ecological approach addresses. Before we deal with them, let us dwell a little longer on some contemporary realist speculations.[21]

Abduction

In his contribution to the Speculations on Anonymous Materials symposium, Reza Negarestani underscored Peircean abduction as a form of material inference. In contrast to classical, that is, formal logic, abduction is fallible, given that information is gathered by way of manipulation. His case is straightforward: one cannot understand a system unless one acts on it. The behaviour of a system is in turn dependent on the concept of tendencies which cannot be intuited unless one is to intervene in the causal fabric (by locomotion in the case of perception).

Another term for such a device of manipulation is heuristics, neither deductive nor inductive, but material inference. It is material in the sense that it is non-formal, as it does not abide by logical norms. It preserves neither foundation nor truth. The problem of non-entailment is overcome by turning the system into a living hypothesis. As with our threefold example, to render anything intelligible one just needs to deepen the scope of one's manipulation. The constructability then becomes isomorphic with the understanding of what this or that is, or better, what it affords (what its affects are). In the words of Negarestani:

> Heuristics are not analytical devices. They are synthetic operators. They treat material as a problem. But they don't break this problem into pieces. They transform this problem into a new problem. And this is what the preservation of invariance is. . . . the problem now can be approached and solved on

a simpler, more optimal level. Hence, the understanding that the system is nothing but its behavior and behavior is a register of constructability.[22]

Radical Empiricism

A healthy dose of scepticism led Gibson to conclude that the perplexing lack of correlation between proximal stimulation and perception is due to the mere arbitrariness of physical dimensions that have been chosen for the description of the stimulus.[23] This, in turn, led him to a further conclusion that the appropriate level of describing perception is ecology, and not physics or geometry, as adopted in the conventional theory of perception. 'Perception has no object' is an assertion by Deleuze which might as well be attributed to Gibson.[24] It is hallucinatory, because it has no object and presupposes no object, because it has not yet been constituted (constructed). There is, of course, no (fully constituted) subject either.

The ecological ontology, which Gibson developed to displace Cartesian dualism, is therefore circumscribed by invariant relations or patterns of becoming that need to be defined relative to an appropriate domain of validity. This direct perception is based on the ecological realist position which takes things to appear as they do because that is the way they are, as taken in reference to the acting perceiver at the ecological (meso) scale. The stance is not to be confused with naïve realism that is absolute, where things appear exactly as they are and unconditionally so. As William James defined it, there are five guidelines of radical empiricism. In the words of Brian Massumi:

1. Everything that is, is in perception.
   (Please note that the first guideline also applies to classical empiricism; radical empiricism begins to part company with classical empiricism in the second guideline).
2. Take everything as it comes. You cannot pick and choose according to a priori principles or pre-given evaluative criteria.
3. Relations must be accounted as being as real as the terms related. In other words, relations have a mode of reality distinct from that of the discrete objects we find in relation.
4. Relations are not only real, they are really perceived, and directly so. Relations not only have their own mode of reality, but each has its own immediate mode of appearance [for instance, looming].
5. 'Ninety-nine times out of a hundred' the terms and relations that appear 'are not actually but only virtually there'.[25]

Our engaged understanding of the world is based not on simulation or matching what we see, but on enactive perceptual and interactive processes. Steven Shaviro explains a kindred contribution to the enactive approach to cognition by the process philosopher Alfred North Whitehead:

> Western philosophy since Descartes gives far too large a place to 'presentational immediacy', or the clear and distinct representation of sensations in the mind of a conscious, perceiving subject. In fact, such perception is far less common, and far less important than what Whitehead calls 'perception in the mode of causal efficacy', or the 'vague' (nonrepresentational) way that entities affect and are affected by one another through a process of vector transmission. Presentational immediacy does not merit the transcendental or constitutive role that Kant attributes to it. For this mode of perception is confined to 'high-grade organisms' that are 'relatively few' in the universe as a whole. On the other hand, causal efficacy is universal; it plays a larger role in our own experience than we tend to realize, and it can be attributed 'even to organisms of the lowest grade'.[26]

Inserting the Interval

Representational theories of perception postulate an isolated and autonomous subject which is set apart from its milieu and is thus utterly dependent on the process of mental representation. Furthermore, this process is often seen to be staged for another interiorised subject. Gibson repeatedly cautioned against the homunculus thesis: 'The movements of the hands do not consist of responses to stimuli . . . This is surely an error. The alternative is not a return to mentalism. We should think of the hands as neither triggered nor commanded but controlled.'[27] As Massumi puts it, a 'zone of indeterminacy' is glimpsed in the hyphen between the stimulus and response (S-R): 'Thought consists in widening that gap, filling it fuller and fuller with potential responses.'[28] The task of the architect, as I see it, is to widen the gap between perception and action, for what is affordance if not the hyphen between the two? In opposition to a deterministic schema of perception leading to a certain action, affordance is always relational, that is, non-deterministic. Here is the definition by Gibson himself:

> An important fact about affordances of the environment is that they are in a sense objective, real, and physical, unlike values and meanings, which are often supposed to be subjective, phenomenal, and mental. But, actually, an affordance is neither an objective nor a subjective property; or it is both if you like.

An affordance cuts across the dichotomy of subjective–objective and helps us to understand its inadequacy. It is both physical and psychical, yet neither. An affordance points both ways, to the environment and to the observer.[29]

Conclusion

Unfortunately, a great deal of artificial intelligence research with direct influence on contemporary architectural discourse continues to be based on template-matching strategies, making Karl Popper's famous metaphor of the 'bucket theory of mind' difficult to dispense with.[30] It unwittingly perpetuates the Platonic division between the visible appearances and the intelligible essences.

By way of conclusion, let us briefly remind ourselves of what constitutes the pernicious representational view. In order for a life form to perceive X, it relies on the concept of X. Furthermore, if inputs require concepts to be meaningful, then concepts must precede inputs, as in nativism. Conversely, if concepts require input for their content, then inputs must precede concepts, as in empiricism. A hopeful way out of this deadlock might be to consider a different form of universality, one that is no longer grounded on commonality.

Representation as the very term is considered to be utterly misleading. What if drawing is not copying, if it is impossible to copy (re-present) a piece of environment, if information is unlimited and the concept of projection useless – all from the point of view of perception? Ignorance is no defence. We are in need of a critique of the conception of the world as an optical phenomenon.[31] Our all-too-ocularcentric theories require major updating.[32] According to Gregory Flaxman, the image is neither a representation of an object nor a visual impression, the first of which connotes mere re-cognition and the second a limited sensory bandwidth. Rather, the image is a collection of sensations – a 'sensible aggregate', or what Deleuze will ultimately call a sign. As Deleuze himself explains, 'the movement-image is the modulation of the object itself'.[33]

Curiously enough, the ambulatory dimension of vision seems to have eluded the greatest of authorities in the field.[34] Architects are known to be keen readers of the sci-fi writer William Gibson.[35] However, if we are to unlock the real virtuality, rather than the crypto-Cartesian virtual reality, another Gibson is in order. I will conclude with his caveat, which seems timelier than ever: 'Being intellectually lazy, we try to understand perception in the same way we understand communication, in terms of the familiar.'[36]

Notes

This essay first appeared in *What Images Do*, edited by Henrik Oxvig, Jan Bäcklund, Michael Renner and Martin Søberg (Aarhus: Aarhus University Press, 2018), 145–55.

1. Gibson, *The Ecological Approach to Visual Perception*, 242.
2. Deleuze, *Cinema 1*, 56.
3. The maxim is borrowed from the subtitle of the book by Bruce Mau and the Institute without Boundaries, *Massive Change*.
4. Serres, 'Birth'.
5. Bateson, *Steps to an Ecology of Mind*, 318. Cf. Merleau-Ponty, *Phenomenology of Perception*, 152.
6. Sheets-Johnstone, *The Primacy of Movement*, 139, 146–50. See also: Sheets-Johnstone, *The Corporeal Turn*.
7. Deleuze, *Cinema 1*, 56.
8. Pierre Lévy's expression from Guattari, *Chaosmosis*, 108.
9. Gibson was well aware of the philosophical implications of his work. As the Gibsonian Edward Reed explains, by the time Gibson obtained his BA in philosophy in 1925, such great thinkers as John Dewey, William James, Bertrand Russell and Alfred North Whitehead had all struggled with this problem of body/mind dualism: 'Once a dualism was erected it seemed impossible to eliminate it: If matter is purely physical, then how can aggregates of matter evolve into minds (and surely the brain – mere matter – is the basis of mind)? Yet, if awareness is purely mental, of what relevance to it are the physical trappings of the body?' Reed, *James J. Gibson and the Psychology of Perception*, 287.
10. Gibson, *Reasons for Realism*, 415.
11. Ibid., 286.
12. Which, in turn, is challenged by 'the third kind' of image. See for example: Pisters, *The Neuro-Image*.
13. Deleuze is referring to the first chapter of Bergson, *Matter and Memory*.
14. 'The act of picking up information . . . is a continuous act, an activity that is ceaseless and unbroken. The sea of energy in which we live flows and changes without sharp breaks. Even the tiny fraction of this energy that affects the receptors in the eyes, ears, nose, mouth, and skin is a flux, not a sequence. The exploring, orienting, and adjusting of these organs sink to a minimum during sleep but do not stop dead. Hence, perceiving is a stream, and William James's description of the stream of consciousness applies to it. Discrete perception, like discrete ideas, are as mythical as the Jack of Spades.' Gibson, *The Ecological Approach to Visual Perception*, 240. Cf. James, *The Principles of Psychology*, Vol. 1, 224–90 (chapter 9).

15. Peirce placed icons under firstness, indices under secondness and symbols under thirdness.

16. Peirce, *Philosophical Writings of Peirce*, 322.

17. Deleuze, *Cinema 1*, 56.

18. Behaviourist psychologists solved the problem of dualism by eliminating all concepts of mind and explaining them away as forms of behaviour. Conversely, the gestaltists made the fundamental mistake of treating observers as passive recipients of stimuli. Their approach was essentially nativistic, explaining perception by means of innate principles of organisation. An insightful comparison of the two parallel traditions was provided by Paul Stenner in his lecture on 'Deep Empiricism' at the Topological Approach to Cultural Dynamics conference.

19. 'Difference is not diversity. Diversity is given, but difference is that by which the given is given as diverse. Difference is not phenomenon but the noumenon closest to the phenomenon.' Deleuze, *Difference and Repetition*, 202.

20. Gibson, *The Ecological Approach to Visual Perception*, 233.

21. Realist in the sense that it is asymptotic to the contingent reality that drives the universe, and speculative in the sense of not driven by our reflection but by the exteriority and contingency of a universe that always antedates and postdates us.

22. Negarestani, 'Frontiers of Manipulation'.

23. The thesis was set out by Gibson in his earlier book, *The Senses Considered as Perceptual Systems*.

24. 'Conscious perception is always a hallucination which refers back to differential relations established between minute perceptions, and that these perceptions express only affections of our material bodies by other material things, never in the form of complete objects, but as "molecular movements".' Deleuze, *The Fold*, 107.

25. Massumi, *Parables for the Virtual*, 85–6.

26. Shaviro, 'The Actual Volcano', 291.

27. By mentalism Gibson means the approach which appeals to mental representations whereby each of us supposedly builds up his or her own cognitive map of the real world, based on his or her relation to it. It is allegedly this cognitive map or representation we are aware of, not the world itself. See: Gibson, *The Ecological Approach to Visual Perception*, 235.

28. Massumi, *A User's Guide to Capitalism and Schizophrenia*, 99.

29. Gibson, *The Ecological Approach to Visual Perception*, 129.

30. Popper, 'The Bucket and the Searchlight'.

31. Under the Western metaphysics of presence, or the privileging of the *logos*, everything that appears is determined or synthesised in advance from some prior ground. For Plato, this ground or source of appearing, or what allowed sensation to

make sense, was the *logos*, that which could be said of anything, that which would remain the same (Heidegger's onto-theology).

32. Western ocularcentricity has blinded us and prevented us from considering other senses. The tendency to privilege sight as the sense that gives us access to the truth has been elaborated by Martin Jay in *Downcast Eyes*.

33. Flaxman, 'Introduction', 12–15. Cf. Deleuze, *Cinema 2*, 27.

34. See contributions by Hal Foster, Martin Jay, Jonathan Crary, Rosalind Krauss, Norman Bryson and Jacqueline Rose in Foster, *Vision and Visuality*.

35. In *Neuromancer*, William Gibson defined cyberspace as 'consensual hallucination', where all the media converge. In this (cyber)space, computer 'cowboys' travel disembodied across the world of data. Boyer, *CyberCities*, 14.

36. Gibson, *The Ecological Approach to Visual Perception*, 63. It calls to mind a Žižekian story about a drunkard who lost his car keys in the dark but looked for them under the streetlight.

10   Double Bind: On Material Ethics

We are made of contracted water, earth, light and air – not only prior to the recognition or representation of these, but prior to their being sensed. Every organism, in its receptive and perceptual elements, but also in its viscera, is a sum of contractions, of retentions and expectations. (Deleuze, 1968)[1]

The task of abstraction . . . is to liberate the virtual subject – the designated force of thought – from the trap of the material. But this liberation is conducted precisely by utilizing the resources of the material, with the aid of its tendencies, properties and parameters, that determine and govern the behavior of the material system and, correspondingly, constrain the dynamic of thought, forcing it to revise its formation and to triangulate new affordances for conception and action. (Negarestani, 2014)[2]

Introduction

ETHICS IS DERIVED from the Greek word *ēthos* meaning dwelling or habitat. But rather than the question of where, the emphasis must be placed on the question of how, on habit.[3] Habit is not to be regarded as a mere passive knee-jerk response to a stimulus, but as a creative power. It is more than obvious that we cannot be said to *have* habits. Rather it is habits that have us.[4] Moreover, it is habits that we *are*. The urdoxa of the 'transcendental unity of perception' prevents an account of the genesis of sense. As Rosi Braidotti has argued, the enabling 'power to' as *potentia* needs to be distinguished from the hindering 'power over' as *potestas*. I see this as a plea to set environmentality apart from governmentality:

> I do not think it acceptable . . . to raise any issues related to ethics or to moral-
> ity independently of considerations of power and power relations. . . . At times
> contemporary moral philosophy comes across as comfortably installed in a
> consensus about the *context free* nature of its deliberations. As a materialist
> nomadic feminist philosopher, I want to stress the urgency of rewriting issues
> of power.[5]

Aesthetics has to be rescued from the province of reactive undisciplined sensu-
ality. In order to do so, as Jane Bennett argues, we ought to stop overlooking and
'underfeeling' a realm between a striking reality and a stricken body. This third
realm she calls sensibility. '*This* aesthetics – aesthetics as sensibility-formation
– has implications for ethics that are irreducible to fascism, hedonism, or
indiscriminateness. For as a form of *askeis*, a sensibility establishes the range
of possibility in perception, enactment, and responsiveness to others.'[6] The
approach draws on the Foucauldian practice of the self, 'in its Greek sense
of self-discipline rather than a Christian sense of self-denial.'[7] The founder of
ecosophy, Félix Guattari, coined the term ethico-aesthetic precisely in order
to underline the inseparability of action and perception.[8] The neologism was
his subtle way of arguing that it is practice and experimentation that actively
shape the subject. Until recently the sentient has been considered as a mere
supplement to the sapient. The ranking order in major philosophical systems
clearly reveals a historical bias towards the cognitive over the affective. But as
Terry Eagleton remarked, it is in the manner of such lowly supplements to end
up supplanting what they are meant to subserve.[9]

Ecological Thinking

We start from the hypothesis that the digital turn in architecture effectively reproduces the duality of mind and body, removing the former from contexts of engagement with the environment while treating the latter as no more than a kind of
recording mechanism, converting the stimuli that impinge upon it into data to
be processed. The Cartesian view of action as the bodily execution of innate (or
acquired) programmes is replaced with the kindred albeit more contemporary cognitivist view of perception as the operation of the mind upon the deliverance of the
senses. The architecture theorist Ingeborg Rocker protests against the reductionist
tendency in the parametricist disregard of sociopolitical issues:[10]

> Only if architecture and urbanism are viewed from more than one –
> currently the formal – vantage point, only if sociopolitical as well as

technological-material and organizational aspects are taken into the equation, will parametricism be able to achieve those changes to our modes of thinking, designing, and producing the architecture and urbanity that [we hope for].[11]

Parametricism in its current state, in other words, is too formal and hence not abstract enough. Let us recall that the opposite of the concrete is not the abstract but the discrete.[12] Even though the champion of parametricism, Patrik Schumacher, has in the meantime conceded the problem, the question of formalisation of the non-discursive remains open at best.[13] I cannot but reiterate Guattari's puzzlement from thirty years ago: 'But where does the idea that the socius is reducible to the facts of language, and that these facts are in turn reducible to linearizable and "digitalizable" signifying chains, come from?'[14] It is for this reason that I want to revamp the legacy of radical empiricism in general and that of J. J. Gibson's ecological perception in particular.[15] Gibson similarly cautions: 'we cannot hope to understand natural stimuli by analogy with socially coded stimuli, for that would be like putting the cart before the horse'.[16] The American psychologist vehemently rejected the reductionist information-processing view, with its implied separation of the activity of the mind in the body from the reactivity of the body in the world, arguing instead that perception is part and parcel of the total system of relations constituted by ecology. Let us follow Guattari and call it ecologies in the plural: environmental, social and psychical.[17] As the author of *Nihil Unbound*, Ray Brassier, underscores, the structure of reality includes but is not exhausted by the ego-logical structure of discretely individuated objects:

> The question is why those who are so keen to attribute absolute or unconditional reality to the activities of self-consciousness (or of minded creatures) seem so loath to confer equal existential rights upon the unconscious, mindless processes through which consciousness and mindedness first emerged and will eventually be destroyed.[18]

Perceivers get to know the world directly by moving about and discovering what the environment affords rather than by representing it in the mind.[19] Hence, meaning is not the form that the mind contributes to the flux of raw sensory data by way of its acquired schemata. Rather it is continually becoming within the relational contexts of engagement. 'The materiality of each organism, its historical thickness, and the density of its internal and external relations, rule out any dualism between "software" and "hardware" that is specific to the notion of computer programs.'[20] Because everything starts from the sensible, cognition is extended and not interiorised or centralised, embedded and not generalised or decontextualised, enacted and not passive or merely receptive, embodied and not logocentric, and affective and not unprovoked.[21] Architects should pay close attention to the panexperientialist implications of the 4EA approach (extended, embedded, enacted, embodied and affective) that dispenses not only with the biological/social dichotomy but also with that between evolution and history.[22] The key is to expand the explanatory framework 'out of our heads'.[23] According to the social anthropologist Tim Ingold, this approach explains human capacities as the properties not of genetic or cultural programming but of the self-organising dynamics of developmental systems:

> It follows from this approach that if people raised in different environments perceive different things, this is not because they are processing the same sensory data in terms of alternative representational schemata, but because they have been trained, through previous experience of carrying out various kinds of practical tasks, involving particular bodily movements and sensibilities, to orient themselves to the environment and to attend to its features in different ways. Modes of perception, in short, are a function of specific ways of moving around . . . these forms of motility are not added to, or inscribed in, a pre-formed human body, but are rather intrinsic properties of the human organism itself, developmentally incorporated into its modus operandi through practice and training in a particular environment. Hence capacities of perception, as of action, are neither innate nor acquired but undergo continuous formation within processes of ontogenetic development.[24]

The actual content of architecture is thus movement and not message.[25] It is movement that is space-making and thus literally ontogenetic. This is why, according to Gibson, learning is but the education of attention, based on continuous variation and selection rather than enrichment through schematisation.[26]

Nomadic Ethics

The current affective turn renders some traditional issues obsolete but introduces new problems, most notably those concerning the 'source of normativity'. After all, as Deleuze and Guattari diagnose in the first volume of *Capitalism and Schizophrenia*, 'unlike previous social machines, the capitalist machine is incapable of providing a code that will apply to the whole of the social field'.[27] When pondering the issue of whether there can be a material ethics, Deleuze advanced an infamous tongue-in-cheek proposal that morality needed to be replaced with physics. What he meant, of course, is that the source of any critique must not come from the outside, as in a transcendental intrusion: 'the conditions of a true critique and a true creation are the same: the destruction of an image of thought [cliché] which presupposes itself and the genesis of the act of thinking in thought itself'.[28] It has to operate at the level of production of the very concept (or affect), on its own terms. 'Thus the question is not how architectural criticism can serve architecture, but of how architecture can be a medium for critical activity.'[29] To paraphrase the film-maker Jean-Luc Godard, not a just architecture, just an architecture.[30] Braidotti explains how to set desire for becomings at the centre of the political agenda:

> In keeping with their reading of advance capitalism as a supple and dynamic system, Deleuze and Guattari diversify their notion and practice of politics. Politics for them consists not so much in 'LA politique' (politics as usual, i.e. institutional or Majoritarian politics) as in 'LE politique' (the political movement in its diffuse, nomadic and rhizomic forms of becoming). This distinction between politics and the political is of crucial importance.[31]

Truth and falsity are not values that exist outside the constitutive problematic fields that give them sense.[32] Ethics, framed in this way, is a problem of power and not of duty. An ontological event is to supersede epistemological law. Rather than relying upon *logos*, the emphasis shifts to the 'natural law' of *nomos*.[33] In the undivided shared space of the cosmos everything becomes a matter of dosage. The neo-materialist philosopher Manuel DeLanda explains the main tenets of Spinozian ethics, where the moral dichotomy of good and evil is replaced by the concept that goes by the name of *pharmacon*:

> In an ethics of nourishing [joy] versus degrading [sadness] assemblages, real-life experimentation (not a priori theorization) is the key. To use an obvious example from environmental ethics: a little phosphorous feeds the soil; too much poisons it. Where exactly the threshold is varies with type of soil so it cannot be known a priori. But the normative statement 'do not poison the soil' is there nevertheless. Similarly for society: too much centralization poisons (by concentrating power and privilege; by allowing corruption; by taking away skills from routinized command-followers etc.) but exactly how much is to be decided by social experiments, how else?[34]

A double bind is a concept proposed by Gregory Bateson to account for a particular condition of *aporia*, which results from a kind of split loyalty or mutual determination.[35] We raise it to address a particular concern about the alleged tendency of some proponents of the affective turn to undermine intelligence in favour of instinct, the difference being that instinct presupposes instantaneous payoff, while intelligence is about a deferred higher efficiency. A possible consequence of pursuing a narrow instinct-driven interest may have an unintended effect in the long run. With its impulsive will to survive (*élan vital*), humanism might indeed turn out to be suicidal, as Claire Colebrook cautions. To prevent this scenario she proposes to counter the old (Luddite) active vitalism with the so-called passive vitalism, where the emphasis needs to be on the non-organic life as a dynamic creativity rather than on the homeostatic environment:

> Vitalism in its contemporary mode therefore works in two opposite directions. The tradition that Deleuze and Guattari invoke is opposed to the organism as subject or substance that would govern differential relations; their concept of 'life' refers not to an ultimate principle of survival, self-maintenance and continuity but to a disrupting and destructive range of forces. The other tradition of vitalism posits 'life' as a mystical and unifying principle. It is this second vitalism of meaning and the organism that, despite first appearances, dominates today.[36]

The existential territory is not a given.[37] Rather, life forms actively construct and are constructed by existential niches (sets of affordances) that hold together as assemblages.[38] The evolutionary biologist Richard Lewontin explains:

> This view of environment as causally prior to, and ontologically independent of, organisms is the surfacing in evolutionary theory of the underlying Cartesian structure of our world view. The world is divided into causes and effects, the external and internal, environments and the organisms they 'contain'. While this structure is fine for clocks, since main-springs move the hands and not vice versa, it creates indissoluble contradictions when taken as the meta-model of the living world.[39]

Passive Vitalism

It should be easy enough for architects to empathise with the above deferred payoff reasoning, since their job is not merely allographic and tactical. It is also strategic, if not logistical, as in the case of urbanism and physical planning.[40] There is hardly anything immediate or instantaneous in architectural design. Architects don't (even) make buildings, they make drawings and models of buildings.[41] But the analogy with artistic practices is simply far-fetched. Richard Sennett rightly dismisses the cult of the artefact as implausible:

> Architecture forms a special case in relation to the ideal of integrity, for it comes into being in ways paintings, sculptures, and poems do not. The making of a piece of urban architecture is a messy process, involving an army of specialist designers and technicians at war with opposing armies of government officials, bankers and clients.[42]

Put succinctly, architectural design is action at a distance in a profound sense.[43] If 'assemblage' has been the core concept of Deleuze and Guattari ever since *A Thousand Plateaus* (1980), then what they call a territory is simply its limit condition, as in stratification:

> Just as milieus swing between a stratum state and a movement of destratification, assemblages swing between a territorial closure that tends to restratify them and a deterritorializing movement that connects them to the Cosmos. Thus it is not surprising that the distinction we were seeking is not between assemblage and something else, but between two limits of any possible assemblage, in other words, between the system of strata and the plane of consistency.[44]

Any deterritorialisations and reterritorialisations are to be considered as mere dimensions of the very assemblage, which is beyond the full control of the designer. Given the asymmetry between the actual territory and the virtual assemblage, it should not come as a surprise that 'what holds an assemblage together is not the play of framing forms or linear causalities but, actually or potentially, its most deterritorialised [abstract] component'.[45] What gives integrity to an assemblage, in other words, is Nietzschean eternal return, which does not allow for the return of identity, since this would ultimately come down to a final stasis, but must instead stand for the eternal return of differentiation. 'All our potential futures are fully real (if virtual) as are all the non-actualized pasts, and yet the actualization of any event transforms the whole, always and eternally.'[46] In the words of Guattari: 'Repetition is not the law, the finality of something; on the contrary, it marks the threshold to "deterritorialization", the indication of a desiring mutation.'[47] He continues:

> Schizoanalysis . . . meets with the revolutionary struggle to the extent that it strives to free the flows, to remove the bolts – the axiomatics of capitalism,

the overcoding of the superego, the primitive territorialities artificially reconstructed, etc. The work of the analyst, the revolutionary, and the artist meet
to the extent that they must constantly tear down systems which reify desire,
which submit the subject to the familial and social hierarchy (I am a man, I am
a woman, I am a son, I am a brother, etc.). No sooner does someone say, 'I am
this or that' than desire is strangled.[48]

Deleuze and Guattari's favourite example of the 'cutting edge of deterritorialisation' is the refrain (*ritornello*). 'In a general sense, we call a refrain any aggregate
of matters of expression that draws a territory and develops into territorial
motifs and landscapes.'[49] They insist that it is the difference that is rhythmic, not
the repetition.[50] 'Rhythm is the milieus' answer to chaos.'[51]

To meet the challenge of the double bind, there needs to occur a fundamental change in the architect's role from a synoptic visionary – a psychological
subject whose private meanings and public expressions are crucial to understanding his work and its effects – to a more humble (synaptic) explorer of the
machinic phylum where resingularisation may occur.[52] A paradigmatic example
of a synoptic visionary is Ayn Rand's architect Howard Roark.[53] By contrast, the
'intensification of events' also known as dramatisation can best be illustrated
with an example of the periodic table.[54] DeLanda explains: 'What constitutes
Mendelev's great achievement is that he was the first one to have the courage
to leave *open gaps* in the classification instead of trying to impose an artificial
completeness on it.'[55] The sedentary pigeonholing has given way to the nomadic
distribution. According to the topology connoisseur Bernard Cache, 'one of the
great failings of architectural theory has been its inability to go beyond a theory
of proportions, a striking case being Le Corbusier with his Modulor',[56] which
is a mereological issue. Conversely, the architecture theorist Manfredo Tafuri
identifies the great mereotopological merit of American urban planning since
the mid-eighteenth century: 'in the United States, absolute freedom is granted
to the single architectural fragment, which is situated in a context that is not
formally conditioned by it. . . . Here urban planning [whole] and architecture
[part] are finally separated from each other.'[57] The whole is not *of* the parts, but
alongside them and in addition to them, ever open and divergent.

A determinant interconnection between obeying and commanding (empathy
and abstraction) requires not surrendering to the matter but 'meeting it halfway'.[58] 'It is the concurrent organization of matter by the force of thought, and
the reorientation of thought by material forces. It is the mutual penetration and
destabilization of thought and matter.'[59] Many a Deleuzian epigone will frown at
such a proposal of a semi-automatic mode of operation, as if immanence were

only guaranteed by taking the architect out of the loop, together with the right angles and the rest of the superseded toolkit. Very often one hears arguments in favour of processual automatism that Robert Somol sums up as 'look, ma', no hands'. In his view, this is just not convincing enough. The process is just a device. It ought to become a technique to generate other effects that are not reducible to or explainable by the context of function arguments.[60] Furthermore, while formalism certainly knows what probability means, it does not know what realisation means, and to presume otherwise is to commit a category error.[61] An event that is unforeseen in fact is unforeseeable in principle:

> The future doesn't consist of future possibilities. The future is real, when possibility . . . is only a fabrication made up after the real. The real future (as opposed to our toy-idea of a future) is made up of events, which emerge out of nothing that may anticipate them. Such events are real and create the possibilities that 'will have led' to them.[62]

Those opposed to the partnership with matter also forget that the architect is but an effect quasi-caused by the conceptual persona or aesthetic figure. The former is the power of concepts and the latter is the powers of affects and percepts. 'Philosophy's sole aim is to become worthy of the event, and it is precisely the conceptual person who counter-effectuates the event.'[63] Counter-actualisation is the highest power of the principle of sufficient reason (as an intrinsic genesis, not an extrinsic conditioning) in its turning against the principle of non-contradiction. It marks the passage from the exclusive to the inclusive disjunction.[64]

The architectural audience does not come ready-made either. We are in need of a people, Deleuze and Guattari say, a people yet to come. Not to address the one who is missing, but the one who will arrive.[65] Colebrook's distinction between active and passive vitalisms becomes crucial. In order to take a step forward we need not take a step back, as in the former, but start from the middle (*par le milieu*), as in the latter:

Active
In the beginning we created the world, we subjected ourselves to systems and now we have to *reclaim* the world we created.

Passive
In the beginning there is a 'system'. It is through the system that we think. One has to understand the *emergence* of the system.[66]

It is certainly not enough to replace the quasi-objective Cartesian space with the quasi-subjective *Umwelt*.[67] In everyday German *Umwelt* means surroundings or environment, but through the work of Jakob von Uexküll the term has acquired the meaning of the phenomenal world. Instead, we need to tap into the mutual becoming, of two transcendental illusions formerly known as self and world. The champion of the concept of radical auto-affection, Raymond Ruyer, takes this to be the most delicate point:

> We should vehemently deny the existence of a geometric dimension that pro-
> vides a point of observation external to the sensory field. But we should affirm
> no less vehemently the existence of a sort of 'metaphysical' transversal to the
> entire field, whose two 'extremities' are the 'I' (or the x of organic individual-
> ity), on one hand, and the guiding Idea of organization, on the other.[68]

By contrast to the two paralogisms that bestow extensive properties of actual products on the intensive production process, we need to tap into the dynamic creativity or Ruyer's 'absolute survey' instead. It is always the difference – sub-representational will to power – that is the condition of identity and not the other way around.[69] The mechanicist part-to-whole relationship has to be supplanted by the one-all machinic concept of multiplicity:

> Multiplicities are made up of becoming without history, of individuation with-
> out subject (the way in which a river, a climate, an event, a day, an hour of the
> day, is individualized). That is, the concept exists just as much in empiricism as
> in rationalism, but it has a completely different use and a completely different
> nature: it is a being-multiple, instead of a being-one, a being-whole or being
> as subject.[70]

If metaphysics is concerned with the beginning/totality, and epistemology with foundation/ground, our task is to address consistency/consolidation. At the meso level (formerly known as environment) the commitment to passive vitalism turns our attention to ecology, not as a tree-hugging pathos (the Gaia hypothesis), but as an ethos of irreducible complexity.[71] By irreducible we mean non-transcendental, non-universal, non-eternal and non-discursive. This is how Lewontin underscores the emergent (yet constructed) wholes that could not be understood by being broken down into parts:

> Over the last three hundred years the analytic model has been immensely
> successful in explaining nature in such a way as to allow us to manipulate

and predict it. It seems abundantly clear to us now that the holistic view of the world obstructs any possibility of a practical understanding of natural phenomena. But the success of the clock model, in contrast to the failure of obscurantist holism, has led to an overly simplified view of the relations of parts to wholes and causes to effects ... Taken together, the relations of genes, organisms, and environments are reciprocal relations in which all three elements are both causes and effects. Genes and environment are both causes of organisms, which are, in turn, causes of environments, so that genes become causes of environments as mediated by organisms.[72]

In other words, synthesis is not analysis in reverse. As the dystopian novelist J. G. Ballard noted, 'the obsession with the specific activity of quantified functions is what science shares with pornography'.[73] By contrast, each concept ought to be related to the variables that determine its mutations, rather than construed a priori or a posteriori. Rationalism and empiricism are not opposed but co-constitutive.[74] It is high time to put the horse of intensity and its affective catalytic operators before the cart of intentionality or 'aboutness' of reason.[75] Society is not an ensemble of rational individuals who are each aiming at the maximisation of profit. The unconscious investment of desire always counts for more than the conscious investment of interest.[76] Consequently, what architects create first and foremost are ethico-aesthetical affordances, a certain existence which is more than the idealist's representation, but less than the realist's thing.[77]

The recomposition of what Guattari refers to as architectural enunciation transforms the trade of the architect who becomes its relay by assuming analytic and pragmatic responsibility for the production of subjectivity.[78] We are in need of a practice that will reunite the quasi-objective theory of perception with the quasi-subjective theory of art, where particular situations are not subsumed by universal forms. According to the Whiteheadian scholar Judith Jones, subjectivation is a creative act: 'the subject is not *having* emotional *reactions to* an object but is a subject in virtue of the provoked activity of a reactive incorporation of objects in the coming to be of an entity which would not come to be unless those provocative objects [affordances] were working in it'.[79] What we are in need of is the architecture of immanence where the condition is no greater than the conditioned. In the words of the author of *Cyclonopedia*, Reza Negarestani, 'proceeding becomes a matter of following a new choice of disequilibrium that opens up a new path or transit, and with that new constraints which bring into view new affordances of action'.[80] To rethink Hume's challenge is to be concerned not with the epistemological stability of logically necessary theories but with the metastabilities of contingently obligatory ontological processes of singularisation themselves.[81] Not only will this keep us from cheating by overcoding, but it will also release us from the bad habit of tracing the transcendental from the empirical. Most importantly, it will allow for the long overdue unyoking of coherence from congruence.

Notes

An abridged version of this essay first appeared in *Schizoanalysis and Ecosophy: Reading Deleuze and Guattari*, edited by Constantin V. Boundas (London: Bloomsbury, 2018), 241–56.

1. Deleuze, *Difference and Repetition*, 73.
2. Negarestani, *Torture Concrete*, 11.
3. Magnani, *Abductive Cognition*, 320.
4. Massumi, *Ontopower*, 64.
5. Braidotti, *Transpositions*, 30; emphasis added.
6. Bennett, '"How Is It, Then, That We Still Remain Barbarians?"', 654.
7. Simons, *Foucault and the Political*, 77.
8. Ecosophy is defined as science of ecosystems. See: Guattari, *Chaosmosis*, 91.
9. Eagleton, *The Ideology of the Aesthetic*, 45.
10. 'Parametricism: A term used in a variety of disciplines from mathematics to design. Literally, it means working within parameters of a defined range. Within the field of digital design, it refers broadly to the utilization of parametric modeling software. In contrast to standard software packages based on datum geometric objects, parametric software links dimensions and parameters to geometry. It therefore describes the incremental adjustment of a part that is able to impact on the whole assembly.' Parisi, *Contagious Architecture*, 265.
11. Rocker, 'Apropos Parmetricism', 100–1.
12. Deleuze, *Cours Vincennes*, 'Sur Kant: Synthesis and Time' (14 March 1978).
13. 'That parametricism "goes social" is not a concession to the prevailing winds of political correctness (that divert and dissolve the innovative thrust of architectural discourse). Rather, it is a sign of parametricism's maturity, confidence and readiness to take on the full societal tasks of architecture, i.e. it implies the inauguration of Parametricism 2.0.' Schumacher, 'Parametricism with Social Parameters'.
14. Guattari, 'The Postmodern Impasse', 11.
15. Gibson, *The Ecological Approach to Visual Perception*.
16. Gibson, 'The Concept of the Stimulus in Psychology', 702.
17. Guattari, *The Three Ecologies*.
18. Brassier, 'Concepts, Objects, Gems', 290.
19. 'The affordances of the environment are what it offers the animal, what it provides

or furnishes, either for good or ill. The verb to afford is found in the dictionary, but the noun affordance is not. I have made it up. I mean by it something that refers to both the environment and the animal in a way that no existing term does. It implies the complementarity of the animal and the environment.' Gibson, *The Ecological Approach to Visual Perception*, 127.

20. Longo, 'The Consequences of Philosophy', 11–12.

21. Radman, 'Sensibility is Ground Zero' (Chapter 4 in this volume).

22. For more information on ways of thinking about cognition that depart from standard cognitivist models, see Protevi's blog, '4EA Cognition'.

23. Noë, *Out of Our Heads*.

24. Ingold, 'From Complementarity to Obviation', 267–8.

25. Massumi, 'Building Experience', 322.

26. Gibson, *The Senses Considered as Perceptual Systems*, 270.

27. Deleuze and Guattari, *Anti-Oedipus*, 36.

28. Deleuze, *Difference and Repetition*, 139.

29. Bouman and Van Toorn, *The Invisible in Architecture*, 15.

30. A paraphrased line from Deleuze's text covering a series of TV programmes made in 1976 by Godard and Anne-Marie Miéville. Deleuze adjusted Godard's formula, 'not a just image, just an image', in order to advocate experimentation as a way of escaping normalisation according to dominant orders. Deleuze, *Negotiations*, 38.

31. Braidotti and Dolphijn, *This Deleuzian Century*, 25.

32. Contra Henri Lefebvre, spatialisation has a dynamism that escapes the theoretical abstraction that he joins Marx in imposing: 'By using a nineteenth-century historiography, Lefebvre's system of thought ... ties "*l'espace*" and spatialisation to a model of extrinsic periods derived from economic rather than spatial analysis.' Shields, *Spatial Questions*, 34.

33. 'Deleuze and Guattari use the term in its earliest form; *nomos* as pasture or steppe. ... The distinction that Deleuze and Guattari want to use is that between the carefully controlled city and the unregulated expanse of the steppe. For them, *nomos* "stands in opposition to the law or the *polis*, as the backcountry, a mountainside, or the vague expanse around a city".' Sellars, 'Nomadic Wisdom', 71.

34. DeLanda, '1000 Years of War'.

35. Gregory Bateson, *Steps to an Ecology of Mind*, 199–204.

36. Colebrook, *Deleuze and the Meaning of Life*, 137.

37. Turner, 'Extended Phenotypes and Extended Organisms', 345. According to Turner, ecological niches are an outward extension of the physiology of an organism.

38. Boumeester and Radman, 'The Impredicative City' (Chapter 6 in this volume).

39. Lewontin, 'Organism and Environment', 159.

40. In contrast to autographic arts such as sculpting, allographic arts are those capable of being reproduced at a distance from the author.

41. Allen, *Practice*, 1.

42. Sennett, 'The Technology of Unity', 563.

43. Evans, *The Projective Cast*, 363.

44. Deleuze and Guattari, *A Thousand Plateaus*, 337.

45. Ibid., 374. See also: Williams, 'Deleuze's Ontology and Creativity', 211–12.

46. Colebrook, 'Futures', 205.

47. Guattari, *Chaosophy*, 150.

48. Ibid., 152.

49. Deleuze and Guattari, *A Thousand Plateaus*, 356.

50. Ibid., 346.

51. Ibid., 313. 'Chaos is not the opposite of rhythm, but the milieu of all milieus.' Ibid.

52. Radman and Sohn, 'Preface: The Four Domains of the Plane of Consistency'.

53. Rand, *The Fountainhead*.

54. Debaise, 'The Dramatic Power of Events', 7.

55. DeLanda, 'Deleuzian Ontology'.

56. Cache, 'Geometries of Phàntasma', 90.

57. Tafuri, 'Toward a Critique of Architectural Ideology', 13.

58. Stengers, 'The Symbiosis between Experiment and Techniques', 17. Cf. Barad, *Meeting the Universe Halfway*.

59. Negarestani, *Torture Concrete*, 5.

60. Schmid and Vrhunc, 'Interview: Robert E. Somol', 126.

61. Poincaré's resolution of the three-body problem destroyed Laplace's myth of complete determination. See: Longo, 'The Consequences of Philosophy', 6–12.

62. Ayache, *The Medium of Contingency*, 21.

63. Deleuze and Guattari, *What Is Philosophy?*, 160.

64. 'The groundless ground is neither a known unknown nor an unknown unknown, but a felt unknown'. Van Tuinen, 'Deleuze', 105.

65. Deleuze and Guattari, *A Thousand Plateaus*, 345.

66. Based on: Colebrook, *Deleuze and the Meaning of Life*, 126.

67. Von Uexküll, 'A Stroll through the Worlds of Animals and Men'. See also: Buchanan, *Onto-Ethologies*.

68. Ruyer, *Neofinalism*, 99.

69. The expression 'will to power' is Nietzschean anthropomorphism for forces.

70. Deleuze and Parnet, *Dialogues*, viii.

71. Herzogenrath, *An [Un]Likely Alliance*. According to James Lovelock's Gaia hypothesis, the biosphere, atmosphere and geosphere form 'a totality constituting a

feedback or cybernetic system which seeks an optimal physical and chemical for life on this planet.' See: Lovelock, *Gaia*, 11.

72. Lewontin, *The Triple Helix*, 72, 100–1.

73. Quoted in: Crary, 'Eclipse of the Spectacle', 292.

74. Deleuze, *Negotiations*, 25–34.

75. Sloterdijk, *In the World Interior of Capital*, 70.

76. Deleuze and Guattari, *Anti-Oedipus*, xviii.

77. A paraphrase of Bergson: 'An existence placed half-way between the "thing" and the "representation".' Bergson, *Matter and Memory*, vii–viii.

78. 'Architectural enunciation doesn't only involve diachronic discursive components. It equally implies a taking consistency of synchronic existential dimensions or levels of ordinates.' Guattari, *Schizoanalytic Cartographies*, 237.

79. Jones, 'Provocative Expression', 264, emphases in the original.

80. Negarestani, *Torture Concrete*, 10. Cf. Negarestani, *Cyclonopedia*.

81. Hume's problem – also known as the problem of induction – is the problem of causal necessity or the potential changeability of natural processes themselves. See: Meillassoux, *Science Fiction and Extro-Science Fiction*, 15.

Involutionary Architecture:
        Unyoking Coherence from Congruence

Men are conscious of their own desire, but are ignorant of the causes whereby
that desire has been determined. (Spinoza, 1764)[1]

In solipsism, you are ultimately isolated and alone, isolated by the premise 'I
make it all up.' But at the other extreme, the opposite of solipsism, you would
cease to exist, becoming nothing but a metaphoric feather blown by the winds
of external 'reality'. (But in that region there are no metaphors!) Somewhere
between these two is a region where you are partly blown by the winds of reality and partly an artist creating a composite out of the inner and outer events.
(Bateson, 1977)[2]

It would no longer involve raising to infinity or finitude but an unlimited
finity, thereby evoking every situation of force in which a finite number of
components yields a practically unlimited diversity of combinations. It would
be neither the fold nor the unfold that would constitute the active mechanism,
but something like the Superfold . . . And is this unlimited finity or superfold
not what Nietzsche had already designated with the name of eternal return?
The forces within man enter into a relation with forces from the outside.
(Deleuze, 1988)[3]

Annexed Milieu as a Site of Resistance to the Present

This chapter is devoted to the involutionary relation of the forces from within
with the forces from without.[4] It starts from the premise that the interior as a
given needs to be set aside until the issue of how the given is given has been

addressed. Only then will it be possible to make sense of the superfold's (eternal) giving. When the explanatory ladder is turned upside down, what has figured as an explanation – namely interiority as a datum – becomes that which begs the question. To give due prominence to interiorisation it is necessary to stop treating structure and agency independently. To discount the facile rejoinder that evolution is imposed design, focus must be given to the mutation of boundary conditions.[5] In the words of Didier Debaise: 'It is as if the universe, in its creative advance, never ceases to create new constraints, which are the existents themselves, canalizing how they inherit what is possible, in a new way.'[6]

To think the moving by way of the unmovable is to privilege homeostasis over and above homeodynamics. This is a misconception, since the latter bears the capacity to learn. The idea of a progressive constraint, as captured in Félix Guattari's concept of ethico-aesthetics, will require a step further in order to substitute the gregarious morphodynamics for the parochial metabolic concerns of homeodynamics.[7] As Guattari's radical empiricist predecessor William James surmised, only if sentience is involved do ethical considerations come into play.[8] Sentience inevitably implies a valence (response-ability),[9] and that raises the question of immanent normativity. Physics may be value-free, but ecology is certainly not.[10] By positing that there are good and bad encounters, Spinoza paved the road for such a nomadic version of normativity. The encounters can be distinguished as the empowering powers of life and the hindering powers over life.[11] His ethics equals ethology. Consequently, niche construction could have taken another course, because no thing is logically necessary but only ever contingently obligatory.

The truth of the relative, which is not to be confused with the (postmodern) relativity of truth, has profound consequences for design in general and architecture in particular. In his preface to Bernard Cache's *Earth Moves*, Michael Speaks draws a diagram of architecture's enabling constraints. Building a wall is to disconnect first and then reconnect differently by punching holes in it.[12] Crucially and somewhat paradoxically, architectural relation is always antecedent to its *relata*, the interior and exterior. While the interior and exterior are interior to the actualised systems of strata, the process of dividing remains exterior to both regardless of whether they are inorganic (geological), organic (biological) or alloplastic (cultural).[13]

The thesis of Gerald Raunig's book aptly named *Dividuum* rests on a kindred premise.[14] By introducing a third term, namely the singular-one, Raunig overcomes the impasse of the binary opposition between the individual-one and the all-one. In his *Cartography of Exhaustion: Nihilism Inside Out*, Peter Pál Pelbart joins Raunig in refusing to take sides between (what effectively is the conceptual double of) individualism and communalism: 'neither fusion, nor intersubjective dialectic, nor metaphysics of alterity, but rather an enveloping composition, a disjunctive synthesis, a polyphonic game'.[15] For my own purposes it is worth emphasising that interiority does not entail detachment from the world. Rather, the interior is inconceivable as non-reciprocally presupposed with, or non-mutually constitutive of, the exterior.

Notoriously, Deleuze and Guattari never settled for diacritical solutions either. That is why they proposed a further con-division of every stratum into metastable epistrata and parastrata.[16] The former relate to territorialities and movements of de-re-territorialisation, while the latter relate to codes and processes of de-re-coding. Material and discursive activity is all there is.[17] The epistrata are just as inseparable from the movements that constitute them as are the parastrata from their processes of semiosis. The entanglement of epistrata and parastrata is known as the ecumenon. This unity of composition is opposed to the plane of consistency, or the planomenon.

To bring the concept of the ecumenon down from a high register of abstraction, the authors of *Deleuze and Geophilosophy* provide a helpful diagram.[18] In the case of religion, the unity of composition is not established solely by the faithful who make up the interior and the unfaithful from the exterior. It also includes the membrane that both protects the ecumenon's integrity and projects its messages. In this particular diagram (the ecumenon need not be religious), the epistrata are different internal stable states or organisational nuances and the parastrata are different affects, or capacities for becomings when encountering other assemblages.

Drawing on Gilbert Simondon's work, Deleuze and Guattari do not merely distinguish between the interior and exterior milieus mediated by the milieu of the membrane. They introduce the fourth – annexed – milieu, whereby sources of energy, different from the material that will make up the interior, are annexed to the organism. Crucially for my thesis, apart from being defined by the capture of energy sources, the fourth milieu is related to action-perceptions.[19]

According to Deleuze and Guattari, the development of associated milieus with all their active-perceptive and energetic characteristics culminates in Jacob von Uexküll's *Umwelt*.[20] They provide a graphic example which was also a favourite of Gregory Bateson's.[21] The annexed milieu of the tick is threefold and consists of (1) the gravitational pull (climbing the tree), (2) the olfactory field (perception: scenting the prey) and (3) the haptic sense (action: locating a hairless spot to latch on to). Although much more is to be found there, it is blatantly disregarded, because it does not matter for the life of ticks. Here one recognises a Bergsonian trope where perception is a function of *ascēsis*, and not of enrichment.[22] Existential niches are subtracted from the intensive space (*spatium*).[23] In contrast to phenomenology, which maintains the isomorphic symmetry between the two prongs of the empirico-transcendental double, we ought to insist on the 'vital' asymmetry between the actual territory and the virtual milieu-of-milieus. The disparation is literally ontogenetic (in this region there are no metaphors!).

Deleuze never tires of expressing his preference for lines over points. This is his subtle way of distinguishing between the milieu's dimensions that are directional (topological) and those of territories that are dimensional (metric). While accepting multiple scales of reality, this view opposes the alleged primacy of the physical world. What we cope with is the *Umwelt*. The *Umwelt* is an ethological concept insofar as it is defined by capacities or affects. Affect is shorthand for to-affect-and-be-affected. The animal is prone to fight as much as it is to flight. By this curious assertion Deleuze and Guattari target the vulgar view of the supposed evolutionary drive known as the survival of the fittest. Flights of those supposedly less fit are also conquests and creations in their own right:

> A . . . kind of line of flight arises when the associated milieu is rocked by blows from the exterior, forcing the animal to abandon it and strike up an association with new portions of exteriority, this time leaning on its interior milieus like fragile crutches. When the seas dried, the primitive Fish left its associated milieu to explore land, forced to 'stand on its own legs', now carrying water only on the inside, in the amniotic membranes protecting the embryo.[24]

Although the process of natural selection decreases variety and increases constraints on form and function, the resultant consistency provides a certain resilience that in turn allows new forms of cultural variety to emerge in parallel to the natural. The new means by which new information – defined as difference that makes a difference – can emerge open up new higher-order combinatorial possibilities. These new possibilities, however, come under the constraining influence of the natural selection process. In the words of the biological anthropologist Terry Deacon: 'such back-and-forth interplay between [evolutionary] selection and [involutionary] morphodynamics thus opens the door to indefinite complexification and ever higher-order forms of teleodynamic organization'.[25] Deacon's concept of 'teleonomy' from *Incomplete Nature* is valuable for describing the kind of action that is intentional without being intended (by someone, least of all the fully constituted self-identical subject):

Teleonomy implies law-like behavior that is oriented toward a particular target state in systems where there is no explicit representation of that state (much less an intention to achieve it), but only a regular predictable orientation toward an end state.[26]

In conformity with Deleuzian static genesis, teleonomy is propelled by teleodynamics. Static genesis is pitted against its counterpart, which qualifies as dynamic by virtue of its movement from a sensation-intensive encounter to the thinking of abstract-yet-real ideas. Conversely, static geneses move from the virtual idea to an intensive individuation process to an actual entity.[27] The concept genesis, which is static, is meant to challenge the bad habit of privileging the mechanistic (push–pull) efficient causality over the quasi-final braided causality.[28] This prematurely disqualified non-linear causal efficacy is teleonomic or tendential (that is, neofinalist),[29] rather than teleological or axiomatic. It is important to stress that in terms of coping with (the constraints and opportunities of) the environment, interactions are triggered as much kinematically – without reference to force or mass – as they are kinetically or techno-deterministically. Put simply, response-able life forms respond as much to signs as they do to causal impulses, if not more.[30] Better still, what Karen Barad refers to as intra-action[31] – the mutual constitution of entangled agencies – depends on the flow of epistemic engines as much as it does on the force of thermodynamic engines, where engine stands for any system that supplies dynamics for another system.[32]

Due to its dependence on abstract tools (for production) and concrete social purpose (of consumption), the discipline of architecture has a unique insight into the entanglement of the pathic and ontic, the kinematic and kinetic. We argue that it is the incommensurability of the non-discursive and discursive that makes involution possible and superfolding thinkable. As Bateson emphatically argued, 'confusing information processes [pathic epistemic engines] with energetic processes [ontic thermodynamic engines] was one of the most problematic tendencies of twentieth-century science. . . . they are in fact warp and weft of a single causal fabric'.[33]

An example is in order. Let us once again refer to the animal *Umwelt*. Not a tick or fish this time, but a cat. According to Bateson, to exist is to be engaged in a certain form of play which, as he effectively argues, has a teleonomic structure: a cat's nip means a 'non-bite'.[34] This, however, is not to be confused with language. The concept of involution becomes instrumental in putting the non-discursive intensity and its affective catalytic operators before intentionality or the aboutness of reason. In the words of David Roden, 'if the encounter gives non-inferential knowledge of the structure of reality, then it must do so without situating this categorical insight within the "space of reasons" secured by the inferential proprieties of language'.[35] After all, the development from bacteria to Bach was achieved through 'competence without comprehension', that is, relying on significance without signification.[36]

While meaning is traditionally defined in terms of an organism's perceptions governed by intentionality, J. J. Gibson proposes an alternative approach by way of affordance that is apersonal, pre-subjective, extra-propositional and sub-representative, that is, immanent. This is how he introduces the neologism in his major work *The Ecological Approach to Visual Perception*:

> The affordances of the environment are what it offers the animal, what it provides or furnishes, either for good or ill. The verb to afford is found in the dictionary, but the noun affordance is not. I have made it up. I mean by it something that refers to both the environment and the animal in a way that no existing term does. It implies the complementarity of the animal and the environment.[37]

The frequent reference to animals in both Gibson's and Deleuze's work is not accidental. It is meant to emphasise the shared continuum of humans and animals rather than the break so dear to the rationalist tradition that insists on human exceptionalism. Social implications ensue. Society is not an aggregate of Hobbesian rational individuals as agents who are each aiming to maximise profit by way of communication. In the words of Debaise, 'what communicates are not subjects between themselves, but regimes of [subjectivation] which meet'.[38] The always-already-collective unconscious investment of desire – where desire implies rupture with linear causality – counts for more than the individual conscious investment of interest. The annexed milieu thus becomes a potential site of resistance to the hegemony of representational and instrumental thinking. The *Umwelt* is a locus of creation, rather than communication. As certified niche constructionists, what architects modulate first and foremost are ethico-aesthetical affordances.

The primacy of temporal boundedness (affect/affordances) over spatial boundedness (shelter) becomes more evident as we ascend to the level of biological and mental selfhood.[39] Beth Lord identifies the moment in which Kant approaches the theory of immanent differential genesis: 'it is a matter of *producing* my being by internally differentiating it from my thinking'.[40] This kind of determination does not presuppose re-cognition, as in subsuming a given being under an external concept that would determine it as my being. Ernst Cassirer would qualify it as a move from the generic to the genetic principle of determination.[41] This bootstrapping moment occurs when the 'I think' generates itself from its own differential relation to itself. Dan Smith espouses Deleuze's self-declared indebtedness to Kant.[42] When desire is no longer defined in terms of lack, but in terms of production, the already miraculous bootstrapping transforms itself into an even more miraculous substantiation of sorts whereby one produces the object because one desires it.[43]

By contrast to evolution, involution is not only irreducible to mechanistic causality but also free from any parochial fatalism, including that of self-preservation. After all, if effects were reducible to their causes, novelty would be ruled out in advance. As Sanford Kwinter underscored, the essential human engagement in the environment is geared towards extraction of sensory stimulation, not nourishment.[44] In this he sides with Nietzsche, who took issue with the Darwinist emphasis on the all-too-reactive adaptation. He argued for the will to power that provides life with new self-overcoming directions and interpretations.[45] A contemporary version of the 'power of the false' is best exemplified by the slogan concluding the *Xenofeminist Manifesto*: 'If nature is unjust, change nature!'[46]

It ought to be clear by now that the exterior milieu is equally inconceivable as non-correlative of the interior milieu. As we have argued, both interior and exterior are exterior to the relation of exchange (porosity) between them. This is the crux of radical empiricism. The terms of the relation are determined only *ex post facto*. First comes the *ritornello*, minimally defined as the relation which is free of conceptual prejudices. In the words of Anne Sauvagnargues from her superb *Artmachines*:

> Neither objective, cosmological time, nor a time of consciousness 'in general', ritornellos express time less as it is lived (*vécu*) than as it is inhabited (*habité*), as bundles of sensory signs by which we extract a territory from surrounding milieus through consolidation and habit. For habit very much concerns the temporal milieu in the form of repetition, but valorises the attainment of consistency as well as the crisis by which we attain consistency when we interiorise time as a power of transformation, by stabilising it as a milieu and as a habitation.[47]

In the next two sections I will position the discipline of architecture in relation to affect theory and demonstrate that the so-called perceptual illusions are not illusions at all. It is not a surprise then that Deleuze and Guattari underscored the (molecular) revolutionary capacity of op art.[48]

Reclaiming the Affect Theory for Architectural Enunciation

Incorporeal materialism knows no ultimate foundation but the immanence of powers, relations and bodily compositions. There is no need to postulate the existence of a more fundamental realm. To embrace radical empiricism is to see cognition as belonging to the same world as that of its objects.[49] In Spinozian parlance, *natura naturans* and *natura naturata* – the engendering and engendered – are inseparable.

To embrace the affective turn is to acknowledge that, unlike affections (feelings), affect is impersonal, pre-individual and unmediated. Paradoxically, feelings are states produced by thoughts, while thoughts are actually produced by affects. 'Not a thought that is assembled individually,' Guattari stresses, 'but an n-dimensional thought in which everything thinks at the same time, individuals as well as groups, the "chemical" as well as the "chromosome", and the biosphere.'[50]

Instead of focusing on the all-too-human meaning (signification), the posthuman architect ought to focus on affect (affordance). In contrast to representation, expression is singularly determined (univocal). Architecture is effective not because of its predicates, but rather for the absolutely singular event of its relationality that remains irreducible to any conclusive determination. Consequently, the built environment affects without a priori determining any meaning. It neither solicits nor precludes consensus.

In this approach I side with Jeffrey Kipnis, who insists on the cleavage between engineering and architecture, that is, between the subjugating effect of the former and the liberating affect of the latter.[51] While engineering – as science – delivers the greatest good for most people by reducing difference (geodesic principle), architecture – conceived as art – offers emancipatory potential by constructing new existential niches, that is, a new set of affects/affordances. Arguably, architects produce nothing but affordances, or a way of affecting which recasts them as psychotropic practitioners. Psychotropy is Daniel Smail's version of what Daniel Stern called the modulation of affective tonality.[52] It includes the mood-shaping of others (teletropy), things we do to ourselves (autotropy) and things we ingest.

> The mood-altering practices, behaviors, and institutions generated by human culture are what I refer to, collectively, as psychotropic mechanisms. Psychotropic is a strong word but not wholly inapt, for these mechanisms have neurochemical effects that are not all that dissimilar from those produced by the drugs normally called psychotropic or psychoactive.[53]

To exemplify the difference between tele- and autotropic practices, Smail refers to Christianity. This particular faith, with its teletropic practices, such as liturgy and confession, is famously hostile to a range of 'sinful' autotropic practices, such as masturbation and alcohol consumption.[54] It could be argued that psychotropy is one of the fundamental posthuman conditions. Smail makes a connection with the advent of civilisation, which 'brought with it an economy and a political system organized increasingly around the delivery of sets of practices, institutions, and goods that alter or subvert human body chemistry. This is what gives civilizations their color and texture.'[55]

The reference to colour and texture is not coincidental. As far as I am concerned, any attempt to undermine the so-called qualia would result in the fallacy of what Whitehead called the bifurcation of nature, or the untenable split of primary from secondary qualities. Gibson was adamant: 'It is . . . a mistake to separate the cultural environment from the natural environment, as if there were a world of mental products distinct from the world of material products. There is only one world.'[56] Likewise, the privilege of presentational immediacy (discretion) over causal efficacy (becoming) would lead to the Whiteheadian fallacy of misplaced concreteness. As Deleuze's caveat goes, the true opposite of the concrete is not the abstract, but the discrete.[57]

In contrast to the metaphysical viewpoint of nominalism, affect theory embraces realism according to which virtualities or state spaces – not just actual instances – are important in determining what happens in the world. In the concluding section we will give a concrete example of such abstract space with real efficacy, akin to Karen Barad's 'agential realism'.[58] Recasting the realism/ nominalism debate in terms of dynamics and constraints eliminates the need to pit generalities against particulars and communalism against individualism. Deacon: 'What exist are processes of change, constraints exhibited by those processes, and the statistical smoothing and the attractors (dynamical regularities that form due to self-organizing processes) that embody the options left by these constraints.'[59]

Once again, I want to carve out a third line, which diverges from both the totalising wholes and constitutive parts.[60] The all-too-structuralist mereology ought to give way to the conception of the open whole that is not *of* the parts, but alongside them.[61] We thus turn our attention to mereotopology defined in terms of progressive constraint (teleodynamics). Given the growing prestige of contemporary neurosciences it has become impossible to continue to rely on armchair theorising. As Catherine Malabou argues, the reinvigorated interest in the cerebral is not to be dismissed as neuro-reductionism.[62] Quite the opposite: it is the locus of the most promising research trajectory that places biology and history – nature and culture – on the same footing.[63] Only humans are biologically compelled to modify and redesign their environment in an innovative and historical manner.[64] The (neo-)Lamarckian accelerationist nature of cultural involution exposes the vulnerability of purely Darwinian explanations. The mode of relating itself, rather than any adaptationist end, is arguably the dominant ontopower. We are not just evolutionary products, but also evolving causes of involution. Deacon's espousal is worth quoting at length:

> The shift from simple autogen replication to information-based reproduction, though it might be a rare evolutionary transition in a cosmic sense, is one that would make a fundamental difference wherever and whenever it occurred. The capacity to offload, store, conserve, transmit, and manipulate information about the relationship between components in a teleodynamic system and its potential environmental contexts is the ultimate ententional revolution.

By combining the prefix en- (for 'within') with the adjectival form meaning something like 'inclined toward', Deacon coins the word ententional to define intention minus intentionality. He continues:

> It marks the beginning of [asignifying] semiosis as we normally conceive of it, and with it a vast virtual representational universe of possibilities, because it marks a fundamental decoupling of what is dynamically possible from immediately present dynamical probabilities – the point at which the merely probable becomes subordinate to representational possibility. This is the source of the explosive profligacy of biological evolution.[65]

To put it succinctly, passive ('evo') adaptation to the environment is complemented by active modulation of (and by) the annexed milieu, hence 'evo-devo'. In this light we might want to recast involution as becoming active out of constitutive passivity:

> The evolution of this 'anticipatory sentience' – nested within, constituted by, and acting on behalf of the 'reactive (or vegetative) sentience' of the organism – has given rise to emergent features that have no precedent. Animal sentience is one of these. As brains have evolved to become more complex, the teleodynamic processes they support have become more convoluted as well, and with this the additional distinctively higher-order mode of human symbolically mediated sentience has emerged. These symbolic abilities provide what might be described as sentience of the abstract.[66]

Geno-reductionists were wrong to privilege filiation over alliance.[67] It has now become undeniable that the phenotypical expression of genes is shaped by the *Umwelt*.[68] Unsurprisingly, the rates of phenotypical change are greater in urbanising systems than in natural and non-urban anthropogenic systems.[69] The Gibsonian aproach was ahead of the epigenetic curve by focusing on affordances: 'ask not what's inside your head, but what your head's inside of'.[70] A contemporary version of this motto spells 'ask not what's inside the genes you inherited, but what your genes are inside of'.[71] Epigenesis, let us remind ourselves briefly, is the theory of development in which forms are influenced and modified by the milieu. It provides for the often overlooked link between the genotype and phenotype. The fatally missing link is the process of development itself, that is, progressive differentiation.

Conrad Waddington is credited with coining the term epigenetics in 1942 for the branch of biology that studies causal interactions between genes and their products, giving rise to the phenotype. While the question of the extent to which we are pre-programmed – by filiation – versus developmentally shaped – in alliance – awaits universal consensus, it is safe to suggest that the field of epigenetics has helped bridge the gap between nature and nurture.[72] No wonder that it should appeal to architects, as niche constructionists who could be said to sculpt brains by way of sculpting neither the genetic, nor the epigenetic, but the epi-phylo-genetic nature-cultures. The distinction between the three mnemo-technics comes from Bernard Stiegler, who urges us to rethink the relationship between ontogeny and phylogeny, that is, between development at organismic scales and branching at evolutionary scales.[73] If epigenetics is the concept of non-genetic heritability, such as language acquisition, then epi-phylo-genetic means that the rhetoric of 'we build our cities and in return they build us' is to be taken literally.[74]

> Epiphylogenetics ... designates the appearance of a new relation between the organism and its environment, which is also a new state of matter. If the individual is organic organized matter, then its relation to its environment (to matter in general, organic or inorganic) ... is mediated by the organized but inorganic matter of the *organon*, the tool with its instructive role ... It is in this sense that the *what* invents the *who* just as much as it is invented by it.[75]

It is time for the discipline of architecture to awaken from the slumber of anthropocentrism and fully embrace the posthumanist involution. By opposing the ecumenon to the planomenon, Deleuze and Guattari propose that we drop anthropomorphism for geomorphism. The problem with our inherited abstractions is not that they are too abstract. On the contrary, they are not abstract enough. The ecological approach to cognition must not rely on representation, which typically comes in the form of a model. The problem is not to understand how to construct a simulacrum of the world, but how to cope with it. Or better, make with it, sympoietically. According to Donna Haraway, we ought to learn to be truly present by staying with the trouble. There is no awful or Edenic past to go to. There are no apocalyptic or salvific futures either. There are only 'myriad unfinished configurations of places, times, matters, meanings'.[76]

James's fellow pragmatist Charles Sanders Peirce recognised the limit of formal if-then logic (induction and deduction) and argued for the hands-on what-if logic of abduction.[77] This form of material inference or speculative extrapolation presupposes an intervention into the causal fabric of reality. Paraphrasing the famous Marxist dictum, Maria Puig de la Bellacasa writes: 'theory has only observed the world; the point is to touch it'. She elaborates:

> Awareness that knowledge-making processes are inseparably world making and materially consequential evokes the power to touch of knowledge practices, and therefore a feminist concern to keep in touch with the politics and ethics at the heart of scientific and academic conversations.[78]

As I have argued, radical empiricism takes relations to be as real as objects. Furthermore, relations as higher-order facts or invariants are not only real but also directly perceivable. Under speculative pragmatism, reality is subject to scrutiny, that is, indefinite differentiation. It unfolds in experience, rather than sitting behind experience.

Let us consider a simple but illustrative what-if example. Take three snapshots of a frame within a frame (A, B, C) defined not merely by outlines, but by two superimposed textured surfaces (patterned, as they usually are in the environment)[79] (Figure 11.1). Let us now imagine that the surfaces start looming (as a result of the beholder's forward locomotion), which comes across as continuous transformation of the pattern (self-induced optical flow) both within and without the inner frame (A', B', C'). If the rate of change of the inner and outer patterns is the same, the frames are flush (A-A'). If the rate of change of the inner pattern is faster, it is a protruding obstacle (B-B'). If the rate of change of the inner pattern is slower, it is a recess which affords 'walk-through-ability' (C-C'). Curiously, even here at the level of *Umwelt* (action-perceptions) we are relying on none other than the two greatest Darwinian contributions to mereotopology, namely the substitution of populations for (eternal) types and the substitution of rates-of-change (intensity) for degrees.

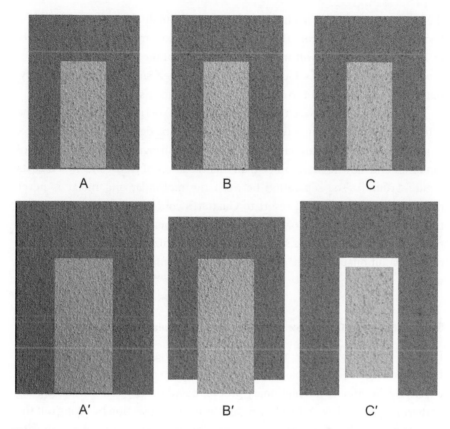

Figure 11.1 Occlusion as a higher-order invariant. Based on Turvey, 'Perception: The Ecological Approach'.

Source: author.

In line with our previous argument, we could go as far as to suggest a reversal of the logic that rests on the substantive conception of the subject. As Leibniz knew, it is not the subject that has a point of view. Rather, the subject is second in relation to the point of view.[80] In our concrete example it would entail the following reversal: to make the optic array flow is to start moving; to cancel the flow is to stop; to make the flow reverse is to go back (and not the other way around!). By consuming these states (make/cancel/reverse flow) – the third passive synthesis of consumption – one gradually becomes aware of one's selfhood (larval subject): the experience is 'mine', hence there is also 'me'.[81]

Senses fold upon each other, intensively cross-referencing disparate planes of experience. They are neither separate nor discrete. Nor are ethics and aesthetics, action and perception, movement and image. In *Gesture and Speech*, André Leroi-Gourhan shows that encephalisation begins from the feet more than from the head, since the brain profits from locomotion but does not provoke it.[82] The teleodynamism of the brain that evolved to guide locomotion and the capacity to modify the *Umwelt* will inevitably sculpt the brain itself. Not only does a special emergent form of self continually create its self-similarity and continuity, but it does so with respect to its alternative virtual forms.[83]

The isomorphism between the virtual space of experience (*Umwelt*) and the actual experience of space (environment) does not depend on resemblance. It requires continuum-thinking attuned to transformations of states (field of rapidities and slownesses), rather than identification of transcendental objects (figure–ground). The separation between the molecular and molar is never clear-cut, and that is why I resort to Guattari's concept of transversality, akin to Haraway's making-with (sympoiesis) rather self-making (autopoiesis). Let us now turn to the concluding section in order to (schizo)analyse a concrete case of the involutionary immanent relation of forces from within with forces from without.

Speculations on Complex Interiors and (Speculative) Ententionality

In their article 'Symmetry and Symmetry-Breaking in Thermodynamic and Epistemic Engines', the ecological psychologists Peter Kugler and Robert Shaw effectively describe an involutionary process based on the non-linear coupling of thermodynamic laws.[84] I will start this third and last section by laying out the key terms, with the exception of symmetry-(breaking), which will be dealt with subsequently.

First comes the difference between the first and the second law. The first law of thermodynamics is that of conservation of matter and energy, which stipulates that matter and energy cannot be created or destroyed. They can be transformed, and energy can be converted from one form into another, but the total of the equivalent amounts of both must always remain constant. The second law of thermodynamics, aka entropy, states that energy of all sorts tends to change itself spontaneously into more dispersed, random or less organised forms. No wonder then that entropy is seized upon by artists, such as Robert Smithson, who used it to create a new kind of geophilosophical continuity between the interior and exterior, one that involved the immediate present and the most remote geological past alike.[85] The second law is nearly ubiquitous, yet not universal. Precisely because it is not absolutely necessary, there can be special circumstances where it does not obtain, at least locally. It is this loophole that allows the possibility of life and mind.[86]

To talk of tendency rather than law is to describe a process of falling towards regularity (contingent *nomos*), rather than being forced into it (necessary *logos*). When this 'memory of the future' is conflated with more generic notions of causality, it yields a troubling implication, especially for those with eliminativist leanings. Deacon does not shy away from the (inconvenient) truth of the involutionary effect: 'Such phenomena as life and cognition might be changing or adding to the fundamental physical laws and constants, or at least be capable of modifying them.'[87]

Traditionally, physics is taken to be the study of thermodynamic engines (movement/action), while psychology is the study of its epistemic counterparts (image/perception). By contrast to psychology and physics, biology is meant to suture the gap between the systems with and without complex interiors. By complex interiors we mean systems with ententional dynamics, vital and (non-consciously) cognitive. In the wake of the transdisciplinary turn, it is no longer possible to place images in consciousness and movements in space, for how is one to pass from one order to another once the 'ontological iron curtain' between them is up?[88] The downfall of the disciplinary apartheid has given birth to ecology, the cross-scale science par excellence.

By contrast to the egological categories of time and space, ecologic is concerned solely with symmetry as the measure of consistency, that is, 'what on a given stratum varies and what does not'.[89] The transversal coupling (sympoiesis) remains reversible across the same scale (symmetry-preserving), but crucially, it is irreversible across different scales (symmetry-breaking). The former can be summed up in the famous mereological maxim: 'the whole is the sum of its parts'. The latter is ecological by virtue of not offering such reassurance. Simply put, the superfold stands for irreducible complexity of the singular-one. Deacon: 'What we interpret as parts are in most cases the consequence of differentiation processes in which structural discontinuities and functional modularization emerged from a prior, less-differentiated state, whether in evolution or development.'[90] In contrast to agglomerations – that can be dissected into their synchronic parts and reconstructed without loss – superfolds suffer the Humpty-Dumpty problem when taken apart. In diachronic superfolding, synthesis is not analysis in reverse.

Whereas the second law has traditionally been seen as a destructive agency, a new view has emerged that considers it an active participant in constructive processes. Systems open to the replenishing and dissipative processes can develop new symmetries that lead to new ententions manifested as fitness landscapes. As Waddington discovered, 'we will find that the system resists some types of changes more than others, or restores itself more quickly after changes in some directions than in others'.[91] The new attractors (*ritornellos*) that emerge out of the competition between import of high-grade energy and export of low-grade energy are invariant solutions (symmetries) that relate the molecular and molar states of a system. Kwinter elucidates:

> The relentless cleaving and changing of the universe's 'matter-flow' establishes *the rule of the differential* in nature, and following from it the irrepressible, some might even say divine reality of the gradient without which nothing would ever happen, and thanks to which so many wonderful things not yet imagined, easily could.[92]

Therein lies the most profound (negentropic) lesson for posthuman architects. There is no such thing as simple part-to-whole relationship. This is what Spinoza expressed in his oft-quoted maxim 'we don't know what a body can do'.[93] However, if we substituted mereotopology for mereology, it would become possible to find a subset of solutions for multiple interacting systems in spite of their dynamic relationship. The Gibsonian affordance, which is akin to the Deleuzian affect, is such a critical set, which specifies the symmetries shared by the systems of acting-perceiving organisms and their associated milieus. Affect always cuts both ways. The affordance of 'sit-on-ability' depends as much on the quasi-objective layout (structure formerly known as a chair) as it does on the quasi-subjective entention (agency wrongly attributed to intention).

Affordance is best described as a higher-order invariant (invariant of invariants). Deacon describes invariants with reference to constraints, as something less than varying without limit. If there is a bias in the probability of the occurrence of states, not all of them are realised.[94] Any long-term tendency of a system (attractor) is but a Peircean habit. In this sense, gravity is the habit of the earth. Even things could be said to have propensities, or sympathies.[95] So do situations. The presence of constraints entails the absence of certain potential states. The nature of the constraint determines 'which differences can and cannot make a difference in any interaction'.[96] Consequently, an increase in entropy is a decrease in constraint, and vice versa, or, as Stuart Kauffman put it, 'constraints are information and information is constraint'.[97] Most importantly for our thesis, constraint propagation – which can be translated as habits-begetting-habits – is the ultimate locus of vicarious causality, or what Deleuze calls becoming (*devenir*).

Where does it all leave us in terms of niche construction? To adopt a mereotopological approach to posthuman architecture and urbanism is to think in terms of intensive capacities rather than mere extensive properties. This understanding of response-able life is tied to Deleuze's analysis of sensation that exceeds the bounds of the organic body because it is registered at an antecedent level. Sensation is not representational. It is not *like* something, explains the champion of the corporeal turn, Maxine Sheets-Johnstone.[98] However, to claim that it-is-what-it-is is not a tautology, since things are powers, not forms. As we have argued, agency cannot be segregated from structure nor can it be possessed; it can only be produced ad hoc, as implied in the concept of assemblage (*agencement*). By the same token, the so-called perceptual illusions are not illusions, but locally generated geometro-dynamic real effects. Crucially, these curvature-based effects are forceless. They are kinematic.

I will conclude by considering a well-known but wrongly qualified optical illusion. I shall argue that it is not a self-induced effect on the part of the observer, but an effect yielded by the observer's state space, which literally gets warped by what it detects (Figure 11.2). Kugler and Shaw explain:

> By tracking the equidistant, parallel lines depicted by the trivial gradient sets of a flat space (B) to the left (A) and to the right (C), we see what failure of our nervous systems to solve the cohomology problem means perceptually.

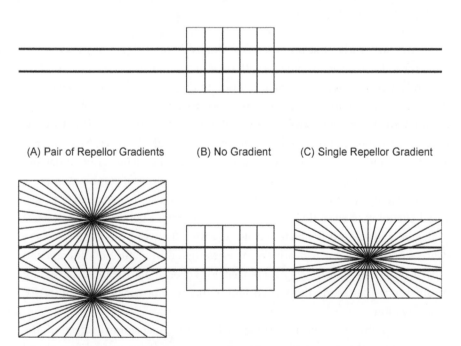

(A) Pair of Repellor Gradients   (B) No Gradient   (C) Single Repellor Gradient

Figure 11.2 Kinematic effect manifested as warping of manifolds. Based on Kugler and Shaw, 'Symmetry and Symmetry-Breaking in Thermodynamic and Epistemic Engines'.
Source: author.

What cohomology actually measures, at its most elementary, is a failure of local solutions to glue together to form a global (cross-scale) solution. As in the process of tessellation (planification), the problem is how modular quantities (tiles), when distributed under local constraints only, fit together globally over the manifold that they attempt to cover (floor). Cohomology reveals the impossibility of patching locally consistent data into a consistent whole. Simpler still, it demonstrates the impossibility of totalisation. Transversal onto-heterogenesis, or what I referred to as the superfold, provides a frame-free means for explaining discrepancies between local and non-local constraints. Kugler and Shaw continue:

> The information for change in curvature of the lines is due to the failure of gradient sets (A), (B), and (C) to share a common homological solution. Hence the pair of lines conforms locally to the direction and distance metrics of the manifold to which they are most proximal. Our state space as observers is being warped by what it detects rather than causing the effect itself. The critical set properties [affordances/affects] have as much reality status as any other physical property, and more than most. Hence the lines are indeed curved, and they are not illusions![99]

It was the Stoics who first proposed that things themselves are bearers of ideal events that do not exactly coincide with their properties. Any actual incarnation may in fact be seen as a provisional solution to the virtual problem posed by the state space, in the same way that lightning is the solution to the problem of electrical potential differences between the cloud and the ground.[100] It is why the virtual is qualified as problematic, real yet incorporeal. However, by no means am I proposing the Manichean opposition between the quantitative actual and qualitative virtual. Likewise, a paralogism of psycho-physical commensurability of extensive magnitudes and intensive differences must be debunked, a generalised economy of equivalences refused. The difference between the difference in degree and in kind is not reducible to either: 'between the two are all the degrees of difference – beneath the two lies the entire nature of difference in other words, the intensive'.[101] And indeed, for Deleuze it is the intensive nature of difference that binds the virtual and actual and provides the catalyst for subjectivation.

The geometro-dynamical warping is the Stoic incorporeal effect of the kinetic corporeal cause, which in turn operates as an ontopowerful formal and kinematic quasi-cause.[102] Our conjecture is that there could be no teleonomy without mereotopology (against mereology), which in turn is a problem of sympoiesis (against autopoiesis), the hallmark of ethico-aesthetics. The concept of quasi-cause (dark precursor) prevents regression into simple reductionism. It designates the pure agency of vicarious causality, the difference in itself that relates heterogeneities. Deacon too is unambiguous about the fact that 'all efficient causes ultimately depend on the juxtaposition of formal [quasi-]causes!'[103] The warped-state space of the observer from the earlier example is of the same ilk as the process by which mass singularities curve space-time. 'It is, crucially, not a matter of curves in a flat space but of the curvature of the space itself.'[104] The major difference is that such effects may be induced through neuro-perceptual fields into the abstract machines of thought and experience. In Andy Clark's terms, these are 'optimal illusions' quasi-caused by predictions.[105] These pockets of inconsistency, Kugler and Shaw insist, are like local inertial frames. They show up as non-linearities (not perceptual errors) at the more exacting level of systems integration.[106] They are wrongly assumed to be self-induced alterations in the mind that distort the perception of the world. Quite the contrary: the imperceptible is virtually perceived, albeit as actually inconsistent over local frames. The failure of homologies to mesh across scales is unsurprising, since the molar has fewer degrees of freedom (that is, less symmetry) than the molecular.

In contrast to rationalists who believe that nature has solved the cohomology problem, speculative pragmatists see reality more like a harlequin's coat, 'an infinite patchwork with multiple joinings'.[107] The joinings stand for entanglements of epi- and parastrata. The ontological question of what-there-is cannot be separated from its ethical counterpart of how-to-live, nor from the aesthetic imperative of constructing a new sensorium. The question of interior, interiority and interiorisation is ultimately a matter of sensibility, not of judgement.[108] It is a matter of radical auto-affectivity sustained by an ongoing artistic, conceptual and historical involution: not of pleasure, but of self-enjoyment defined as immediacy without objectification. If we can accept as really real only that which is cohomologically systematic across our experience (*partes extra partes*), perhaps the fault lies more with our all-too-phenomenological conception of possible experience than with the real unlimited finity.

Notes

This essay first appeared in *Posthuman Ecologies: Complexity and Process after Deleuze*, edited by Rosi Braidotti and Simone Bignall (London: Rowman & Littlefield, 2019), 61–86.

1. Spinoza, 'Letter 62 (P03)'.

2. Bateson, 'Afterword', 245.

3. Deleuze, *Foucault*, 131.

4. Deleuze and Guattari, *A Thousand Plateaus*, 238–9.

5. Deacon, *Incomplete Nature*, 426.

6. Debaise, *Nature as Event*, 66.

7. Guattari, *Chaosmosis*.

8. James, *The Will to Believe*, 198.

9. Haraway, *Staying with the Trouble*, 29.

10. Gibson, *The Ecological Approach to Visual Perception*, 137–40.

11. Deleuze, *Spinoza, Practical Philosophy*, 17–29.

12. Speaks, 'Folding toward a New Architecture', xviii.

13. Deleuze and Guattari, *A Thousand Plateaus*, 57–60.

14. Raunig, *Dividuum*.

15. Pelbart, *Cartography of Exhaustion*, 18.

16. Deleuze and Guattari, *A Thousand Plateaus*, 53.

17. Foucault and Deleuze, 'Intellectuals and Power', 205–7.

18. Bonta and Protevi, *Deleuze and Geophilosophy*, 81.

19. Deleuze and Guattari, *A Thousand Plateaus*, 51.

20. Von Uexküll, 'A Stroll through the Worlds of Animals and Men'.

21. Bateson, 'Afterword', 241.

22. Meillassoux, 'Subtraction and Contraction'.

23. Radman, 'Space Always Comes After' (Chapter 7 in this Volume).

24. Deleuze and Guattari, *A Thousand Plateaus*, 54–5.

25. Deacon, *Incomplete Nature*, 462.

26. Ibid., 116.

27. Deleuze, *Difference and Repetition*, 183.

28. Massumi, 'Virtual Ecology and the Question of Value', 353–4.

29. Ruyer, *Neofinalism*.

30. Bains, *The Primacy of Semiosis*, 61.

31. Barad, *Meeting the Universe Halfway*, 33.

32. Kugler and Shaw, 'Symmetry and Symmetry-Breaking', 312.

33. Bateson, 'Afterword', 241.

34. Bateson, *Steps to an Ecology of Mind*, 141–6.

35. Roden, 'A Post-Sellarsian Encounter'.

36. Dennett, *From Bacteria to Bach and Back*.

37. Gibson, *The Ecological Approach to Visual Perception*, 127.

38. Debaise, 'What Is Relational Thinking?', 7.

39. Deacon, *Incomplete Nature*, 470.

40. Lord, 'Deleuze and Kant', 92.

41. Cassirer, *Rousseau, Kant, Goethe*, 69, 93.

42. Smith, *Essays on Deleuze*, 117.

43. Ibid., 187.

44. Kwinter, 'Neuroecology', 331.

45. Ansell-Pearson, 'Nietzsche's Brave New World of Force', 26.

46. Laboria Cuboniks, 'Xenofeminism'.

47. Sauvagnargues, *Artmachines*, 126.

48. Deleuze and Guattari, *A Thousand Plateaus*, 478.

49. Heft, *Ecological Psychology in Context*, 73.

50. Guattari, *Lines of Flight*, 205.

51. Kipnis et al., '2015 Grad Thesis Prep Symposium'.

52. Smail, *On Deep History and the Brain*. Cf. Stern, *The Interpersonal World of the Infant*.

53. Smail, *On Deep History and the Brain*, 161.

54. Ibid., 177–8.

55. Ibid., 162.

56. Gibson, *The Ecological Approach to Visual Perception*, 130.

57. Deleuze, *Cours Vincennes*, 'Sur Kant: Synthesis and Time' (14 March 1978).

58. Barad, *Meeting the Universe Halfway*, 132–85.

59. Deacon, *Incomplete Nature*, 197.

60. Bateson, 'Afterword', 244.

61. Deleuze and Guattari, *A Thousand Plateaus*, 266.

62. Malabou, *What Should We Do with Our Brain?*, 72.

63. It has become unimaginable to circumvent the brain conceived as the intersection of the three *chaoids*, namely philosophy, science and art. See Deleuze and Guattari, *What Is Philosophy?*, 208.

64. Kwinter, 'Neuroecology', 329.

65. Deacon, *Incomplete Nature*, 458.

66. Ibid., 504–5.

67. Deleuze and Guattari, *A Thousand Plateaus*, 238.

68. Wexler, 'Neuroplasticity, Culture and Society'.

69. Alberti et al., 'Global Urban Signatures'.

70. Mace, 'James J. Gibson's Strategy for Perceiving'.

71. Stotz, 'Why Developmental Niche Construction Is Not Selective Niche Construction'.

72. Kwinter, 'A Discourse on Method', 40.

73. Stiegler, *Technics and Time, 1*.

74. Ibid., 134–79.

75. Ibid., 177.

76. Haraway, *Staying with the Trouble*, 1.

77. Peirce, *Philosophical Writings of Peirce*, 302–5.

78. Bellacasa, 'Touching Technologies, Touching Visions', 298–9.

79. Turvey, 'Perception', 340.

80. Deleuze, *Cours Vincennes*, 'Sur Leibniz' (4 April 1980).

81. Deleuze, *Difference and Repetition*, 78–9.

82. Leroi-Gourhan, *Gesture and Speech*, 229.

83. Deacon, *Incomplete Nature*, 484.

84. Kugler and Shaw, 'Symmetry and Symmetry-Breaking', 296–331.

85. Smithson, *Robert Smithson: The Collected Writings*, 23.

86. Deacon, *Incomplete Nature*, 237.

87. Ibid., 368.

88. Guattari, *Chaosmosis*, 108.

89. Deleuze and Guattari, *A Thousand Plateaus*, 45.

90. Deacon, *Incomplete Nature*, 135.

91. Waddington, *Tools for Thought*, 113.

92. Kwinter, 'Sensing the Aerocene'.

93. Deleuze and Guattari, *A Thousand Plateaus*, 283.

94. Deacon *Incomplete Nature*, 202.

95. Jullien, *The Propensity of Things*. Cf. Spuybroek, *The Sympathy of Things*.

96. Deacon, *Incomplete Nature*, 198.

97. Ibid., 228, 392.

98. Sheets-Johnstone, *The Primacy of Movement*, 139, 146–50.

99. Kugler and Shaw, 'Symmetry and Symmetry-Breaking', 328.

100. Deleuze, *Difference and Repetition*, 119.

101. Ibid., 239.

102. Deleuze and Guattari, *A Thousand Plateaus*, 86.

103. Deacon, *Incomplete Nature*, 232.

104. Plotnitsky, 'Algebras, Geometries and Topologies of the Fold', 101–2.

105. Clark, *Surfing Uncertainty*.

106. Kugler and Shaw, 'Symmetry and Symmetry-Breaking', 329–30.

107. Deleuze, *Essays Critical and Clinical*, 86.

108. Deleuze, *Nietzsche and Philosophy*, 94.

Bibliography

Abou-Rihan, Fadi, *Deleuze and Guattari: A Psychoanalytic Itinerary* (London: Continuum, 2011).

Adkins, Taylor, 'A Short List of Gilbert Simondon's Vocabulary', *Fractal Ontology* (2007), <http://fractalontology.wordpress.com/2007/11/28/a-short-list-of-gilbert-simondons-vocabulary/> (accessed 5 April 2020).

Alberti, Marina, et al., 'Global Urban Signatures of Phenotypic Change in Animal and Plant Populations', *Proceedings of the National Academy of Sciences* 114, no. 34 (2016), <www.pnas.org/content/early/2017/01/01/1606034114.full.pdf> (accessed 5 April 2020).

Alexander, Christopher, *Notes on the Synthesis of Form* (Cambridge, MA: Harvard University Press, 1964).

Allen, Stan, 'From Object to Field', *AD (Architectural Design)* 67 (May–June 1997): 24–31.

Allen, Stan, *Practice: Architecture, Technique and Representation* (Amsterdam: Gordon and Breach, 2000).

Allen, Stan, 'Pragmatism in Practice', manuscript from Pragmatist Imagination conference, Museum of Modern Art, New York, November 1999.

Allen, Stan, commentary in 'Stocktaking 2004: Nine Questions about the Present and Future of Design', *Harvard Design Magazine* 20 (Spring/Summer 2004): 5–52.

Alliez, Éric, Claire Colebrook, Peter Hallward, Nicholas Thoburn and Jeremy Gilbert, 'Deleuzian Politics? A Roundtable Discussion', *New Formations* 68 (2010): 143–87.

AMO and Rem Koolhaas, eds, *AMO/Rem Koolhaas: Countryside – A Report* (Cologne: Guggenheim and Taschen, 2020).

Ansell-Pearson, Keith, *Germinal Life: The Difference and Repetition of Deleuze* (London: Routledge, 1999).

Ansell-Pearson, Keith, 'Nietzsche's Brave New World of Force: Thoughts on Nietzsche's 1873 "Time Atom Theory" Fragment and on the Influence of Boscovich on Nietzsche', *Pli* 9 (2000): 6–35.

Arquilla, John and David Ronfeldt, *The Emergence of Noopolitik: Toward an American Information Strategy* (Santa Monica: RAND, 1999).

Ascott, Roy, 'Syncretic Strategies', paper presented at the Ideology of the Imaginary in the 21st Century symposium, March 2007, <https://web.archive.org/web/20091003144329/http://eaf.asn.au/2007/symposium_p_ascott.html> (accessed 26 June 2020).

Askin, Ridvan, Andreas Hägler and Philip Schweighauser, 'Introduction: Aesthetics after the Speculative Turn', in *Speculations V: Aesthetics in the 21st Century*, ed. Ridvan Askin et al. (New York: Punctum Books, 2014), 6–38.

Assis, Paulo de and Paolo Giudici, eds, *The Dark Precursor: Deleuze and Artistic Research* (Leuven: Leuven University Press (Orpheus Institute Series), 2017).

Ayache, Elie, *Blank Swan: The End of Probability* (Chichester: John Wiley and Sons, 2010).

Ayache, Elie, *The Medium of Contingency: An Inverse View of the Market* (Palgrave Macmillan, 2015).

Bains, Paul, *The Primacy of Semiosis: An Ontology of Relations* (Toronto: University of Toronto Press, 2006).

Banham, Reyner, *Los Angeles: The Architecture of Four Ecologies* (London: Allen Lane, 1971).

Barad, Karen, 'Intra-Actions', interview by Adam Kleinman, *Mousse* 34 (2013): 76–81.

Barad, Karen, *Meeting the Universe Halfway: Quantum Physics and the Entanglement of Matter and Meaning* (Durham, NC: Duke University Press, 2007).

Bashour, Bana and Hans D. Muller, 'Exploring the Post-Darwinian Naturalist Landscape', in *Contemporary Philosophical Naturalism and Its Implications*, ed. Bana Bashour and Hans D. Muller (New York and London: Routledge, 2014), 1–14.

Bateson, Gregory, 'Afterword', in *About Bateson* (New York: E. P. Dutton, 1977), 233–47.

Bateson, Gregory, 'The Cybernetics of "Self": A Theory of Alcoholism', *Psychiatry* 34, no. 1 (1971): 1–18.

Bateson, Gregory, 'Lecture on Epistemology' (1974), <www.archive.org/details/GregoryBatesonOnEpistemology> (accessed 5 April 2020).

Bateson, Gregory, *Mind and Nature: A Necessary Unity* (New York: E. P. Dutton, 1979).

Bateson, Gregory, *Steps to an Ecology of Mind: Collected Essays in Anthropology, Psychiatry, Evolution and Epistemology* (London: Jason Aronson, 1972).

Beaucé, Patrick and Bernard Cache, 'Objectile, towards a Non-Standard Mode of Production', in *Time-Based Architecture*, ed. Bernard Leupen, René Heijne and Jasper van Zwol (Rotterdam: 010, 2005), 116–25.

Beistegui, Miguel de, *Immanence: Deleuze and Philosophy* (Edinburgh: Edinburgh University Press, 2010).

Bellacasa, Maria Puig de la, 'Touching Technologies, Touching Visions: The Reclaiming of Sensorial Experience and the Politics of Speculative Thinking', *Subjectivity* 28, no. 1 (September 2009): 297–315.

Benjamin, Walter, 'The Work of Art in the Age of Mechanical Reproduction', in *Illuminations*, ed. Hannah Arendt (New York: Knopf Doubleday, 1968 [1936]), 245–55.

Bennett, Jane, '"How is It, Then, That We Still Remain Barbarians?": Foucault, Schiller, and the Aestheticization of Ethics', *Political Theory* 24, no. 4 (1996): 653–72.

Bennett, Jane, *Vibrant Matter: A Political Ecology of Things* (Durham, NC: Duke University Press, 2010).

Bergson, Henri, *Creative Evolution*, trans. Arthur Mitchell (New York: Dover Publications, 1998 [1907]).

Bergson, Henri, *Matter and Memory*, trans. N. Margaret Paul and W. Scott Palmer (London: George Allen and Unwin, 1911 [1896]).

Berkel, Ben van, 'The New Understanding', *Kenzo Tange Lecture at Harvard University Graduate School of Design* (3 March 2011), <http://harvard.vo.llnwd.net/o18/gsd/03032011_Berkel.mp4> (accessed 15 October 2018).

Berkel, Ben van and Caroline Bos, 'Corporal Compactness', in *Mobile Forces*, ed. Kristin Feireiss (Berlin: Ernst und Sohn, 1994), 176–81.

Berkel, Ben van and Caroline Bos, 'Deep Planning', in Ben van Berkel and Caroline Bos, *UN Studio – Unfold*, ed. Véronique Patteeuw (Rotterdam: NAi Publishers, 2002), 38–9.

Berkel, Ben van and Caroline Bos, eds, *Move: (1) Imagination: Liquid Politic* (Amsterdam: UN Studio and Goose Press, 1999).

Berkel, Ben van and Caroline Bos, eds, *Move: (2) Techniques: Network Spin* (Amsterdam: UN Studio and Goose Press, 1999).

Berkel, Ben van and Caroline Bos, eds, *Move: (3) Effects: Radiant Synthetic* (Amsterdam: UN Studio and Goose Press, 1999).

Besset, Maurice, *Le Corbusier: To Live with the Light* (Geneva: Skira, 1987).

Betsky, Aaron, 'Unfolding the Forms of UNStudio', in Ben van Berkel and Caroline Bos, *UN Studio – Unfold*, ed. Véronique Patteeuw (Rotterdam: NAi Publishers, 2002), 6–13.

Birnbaum, Daniel and Greg Lynn, 'In Conversation with Ben van Berkel and Caroline Bos: "Digital Conversation"', in Ben van Berkel and Caroline Bos, *UN Studio – Unfold*, ed. Véronique Patteeuw (Rotterdam: NAi Publishers, 2002), 14–21.

Bogue, Ronald, *Deleuze on Literature* (New York and London: Routledge, 2003).

Bonfanti, Ezio et al., *Architettura razionale* (Milan: Franco Angeli 1973)

Bonta, Mark and John Protevi, *Deleuze and Geophilosophy: A Guide and Glossary* (Edinburgh: Edinburgh University Press, 2004).

Boogst, Ian, *Alien Phenomenology, or What It's Like to Be a Thing* (Minneapolis: University of Minnesota Press, 2012).

Bouman, Ole and Roemer van Toorn, eds, *The Invisible in Architecture* (London: Academy Editions, 1994).

Boumeester, Marc and Andrej Radman, 'The Impredicative City: or What Can a Boston Square Do?', in *Deleuze and the City*, ed. Hélène Frichot, Catharina Gabrielsson and Jonathan Metzger (Edinburgh: Edinburgh University Press, 2016), 46–63. (Chapter 6 in this volume.)

Boundas, Constantin V., ed., *Schizoanalysis and Ecosophy: Reading Deleuze and Guattari* (London: Bloomsbury, 2018).

Boyer, Christine M., *CyberCities: Visual Perception in the Age of Electronic Communication* (New York: Princeton Architectural Press, 1996).

Braidotti, Rosi, 'Borrowed Energy', interview by Timotheus Vermeulen, *Frieze* 165 (2014), <www.frieze.com/issue/article/borrowed-energy/> (accessed 5 April 2020).

Braidotti, Rosi, 'Elemental Complexity and Relational Vitality: The Relevance of Nomadic Thought for Contemporary Science', in *The Force of the Virtual: Deleuze, Science, and Philosophy*, ed. Peter Gaffney (Minneapolis: University of Minnesota Press, 2010), 211–28.

Braidotti, Rosi, *The Posthuman* (Cambridge: Polity Press, 2013).

Braidotti, Rosi, *Transpositions: On Nomadic Ethics* (Cambridge: Polity Press, 2006).

Braidotti, Rosi and Simone Bignall, eds, *Posthuman Ecologies: Complexity and Process after Deleuze* (London: Rowman & Littlefield, 2019).

Braidotti, Rosi and Rick Dolphijn, eds, *This Deleuzian Century: Art, Activism, Society* (Leiden and Boston: Brill/Rodopi, 2014).

Brassier, Ray, 'Concepts, Objects, Gems', in *Theory after 'Theory'*, ed. Derek Attridge and Jane Elliot (New York: Routledge, 2011), 278–93.

Brassier, Ray, 'Nominalism, Naturalism, and Materialism: Sellars's Critical Ontology', in *Contemporary Philosophical Naturalism and Its Implications*, ed. Bana Bashour and Hans D. Muller (New York and London: Routledge, 2014), 101–14.

Brassier, Ray, 'Prometheanism and Its Critics', in *#Accelerate: The Accelerationist Reader*, ed. Robin MacKay and Armen Avanessian (Berlin and London: Urbanomic and Merve Verlag, 2014), 467–87.

Brassier, Ray, 'The Pure and Empty Form of Death: Deleuze and Heidegger', *A/V Journal* 2 (2006), <www.hssr.mmu.ac.uk/deleuze-studies/journal/av-2/> (accessed 22 June 2012).

Brassier, Ray, 'Stellar Void or Cosmic Animal? Badiou and Deleuze on the Dice-Throw', *Pli* 10 (2000): 200–16.

Bratton, Benjamin H., '18 Lessons of Quarantine Urbanism', *Strelka Mag* (2020), <https://strelkamag.com/en/article/18-lessons-from-quarantine-urbanism> (accessed 5 April 2020).

Bratton, Benjamin H., *The Terraforming* (Moscow: Strelka Press, 2019), <https://s3.eu-west-1.amazonaws.com/strelka.storage/2020/4/8100070b-5651-4409-bc4c-cac813e51124/the_terraforming_fin.epub> (accessed 5 April 2020).

Braund, Michael J., *From Inference to Affordance: The Problem of Visual Depth-Perception in the Optical Writings of Descartes, Berkeley and Gibson* (Ottawa: Library and Archives Canada, 2009), 67.

Brockman, John, 'The Third Culture' (1995), <www.edge.org/3rd_culture/> (accessed 5 April 2020).

Bryant, Levi, Nick Srnicek and Graham Harman, *The Speculative Turn: Continental Materialism and Realism* (Melbourne: re.press, 2011).

Buchanan, Brett, *Onto-Ethologies: The Animal Environments of Uexküll, Heidegger, Merleau-Ponty, and Deleuze* (Albany: SUNY, 2008).

Buck-Morss, Susan, *The Dialectics of Seeing: Walter Benjamin and the Arcades Project* (Cambridge, MA: The MIT Press, 1991).

Cache, Bernard, 'Geometries of Phàntasma', in *Projectiles* (London: AA Publications, 2011), 74–90.

Cache, Bernard, 'George L. Legendre in Conversation with Bernard Cache', *AA Files* 56 (2007): 8–19.

Cache, Bernard, 'Plea for Euclid', in *Projectiles* (London: Architectural Association, 2011), 31–59.

Canguilhem, Georges, 'Machine and Organism', in *Incorporations*, ed. Jonathan Crary and Sanford Kwinter, trans. Mark Cohen and Randall Cherry (New York: Zone Books, 1992), 45–69.

Cassirer, Ernst, *Rousseau, Kant, Goethe: Two Essays* (Princeton: Princeton University Press, 1970 [1945]).

Chemero, Anthony and Michael Silberstein, 'After the Philosophy of Mind: Replacing Scholasticism with Science', *Philosophy of Science* 75 (January 2008): 1–27.

Chemero, Anthony and Rob Withagen, 'Naturalising Perception: Developing the Gibsonian Approach to Perception along Evolutionary Lines', *Theory and Psychology* 19 (2009): 363–89.

Churchland, Paul M., *Plato's Camera: How the Physical Brain Captures a Landscape of Abstract Universals* (Cambridge, MA: The MIT Press, 2012).

Clark, Andy, *Being-There: Putting Brain, Body and World Together Again* (Cambridge, MA: The MIT Press, 1998).

Clark, Andy, *Surfing Uncertainty: Prediction, Action, and the Embodied Mind* (Oxford: Oxford University Press, 2016).

Colebrook, Claire, 'Creative Evolution and the Creation of Man', *The Southern Journal of Philosophy* 48 (2010): 133–46.

Colebrook, Claire, *Deleuze and the Meaning of Life* (London: Continuum, 2010).

Colebrook, Claire, 'Derrida, Deleuze and Haptic Aesthetics', *Derrida Today* 2, no. 1 (2009): 22–43.

Colebrook, Claire, 'Futures', in *The Cambridge Companion to Literature and the Posthuman*, ed. Bruce Clarke and Manuela Rossini (Cambridge: Cambridge University Press, 2016), 196–208.

Colebrook, Claire, 'Postmodernism Is a Humanism: Deleuze and Equivocity', *Women: A Cultural Review* 15, no. 3 (2004): 283–307.

Colebrook, Claire, *Sex after Life: Essays on Extinction*, Vol. 2 (London: Open Humanities Press, 2014).

Colebrook, Claire, 'Sexuality and the Politics of Vitalism', keynote lecture at the *7th European Feminist Research Conference: Gendered Cultures at the Crossroads of Imagination, Knowledge and Politics* (Utrecht, 4–7 June 2009).

Colebrook, Claire, 'Who Comes after the Post-Human?', in *Deleuze and the Non/Human*, ed. Jon Roffe and Hannah Stark (New York: Palgrave Macmillan, 2015), 217–34.

Coole, Diana and Samantha Frost, *New Materialisms: Ontology, Agency, and Politics* (Durham, NC and London: Duke University Press, 2010).

Corner, James, 'The Agency of Mapping: Speculation, Critique and Invention', in *Mappings*, ed. Dennis Crosgrove (London: Reaktion Books, 1999), 231–52.

Crary, Jonathan, 'Eclipse of the Spectacle', in *Art after Modernism: Rethinking Representation*, ed. Brian Wallis (New York: New Museum of Contemporary Art, 1984), 283–94.

Deacon, Terrence W., *Incomplete Nature: How Mind Emerged from Matter* (New York and London: W. W. Norton & Company, 2012).

Debaise, Didier, 'The Dramatic Power of Events: The Function of Method in Deleuze's Philosophy', *Deleuze Studies* 10, no. 1 (2016), 5–18.

Debaise, Didier, *Nature as Event: The Lure of the Possible* (Durham, NC and London: Duke University Press, 2017).

Debaise, Didier, 'What Is Relational Thinking?', *INFLeXions* 5: *Milieus, Techniques, Aesthetics* (2012): 1–11.

DeLanda, Manuel, '1000 Years of War', in *CTheory*, ed. Arthur and Marilouise Kroker (2003), <www.ctheory.net/articles.aspx?id=383> (accessed 5 April 2020).

DeLanda, Manuel, *Assemblage Theory* (Edinburgh: Edinburgh University Press, 2016).

DeLanda, Manuel, 'Deleuze and the Use of Genetic Algorithms in Architecture', in *Architectural Design: Contemporary Techniques in Architecture*, ed. Ali Rahim (Academy Press, 2002), 9–13.

DeLanda, Manuel, 'Deleuze in Phase Space', in *Virtual Mathematics*, ed. Simon Duffy. (Manchester: Clinamen Press, 2006), 235–47.

DeLanda, Manuel, 'Deleuze, Materialism and Politics', in *Deleuze and Politics*, ed. Ian Buchanan and Nicholas Thoburn (Edinburgh: Edinburgh University Press, 2008), 160–77.

DeLanda, Manuel, 'Deleuzian Ontology: A Sketch', presented at *New Ontologies: Transdisciplinary Objects*, University of Illinois (30 March 2002), <www.situ ation.ru/app/j_art_1078.htm> (accessed 15 October 2018).

DeLanda, Manuel, *Intensive Science and Virtual Philosophy* (London and New York: Continuum, 2002).

DeLanda, Manuel, 'Materialism and Politics', in *Deleuze: History and Science*, ed. Wolfgang Schirmacher (New York and Dresden: Atropos Press, 2010), 29–49.

DeLanda, Manuel, 'Materiality: Anexact and Intense', in *NOX Machining Architecture*, ed. Andrew Benjamin and Lars Spuybroek (London: Thames & Hudson, 2004).

DeLanda, Manuel, *A New Philosophy of Society: Assemblage Theory and Social Complexity* (New York: Continuum, 2006).

DeLanda, Manuel, 'Nonorganic Life', in *Incorporations*, ed. Jonathan Crary and Sanford Kwinter (New York: Urzone, 1992), 129–67.

DeLanda, Manuel, *Philosophy and Simulation: The Emergence of Synthetic Reason* (London and New York: Continuum, 2011).

DeLanda, Manuel, 'Uniformity and Variability: An Essay in the Philosophy of Matter', presented at the Doors of Perception 3: On Matter conference, Netherlands Design Institute, Amsterdam (1995), <www.t0.or.at/delanda/matterdl.htm> (accessed 5 April 2020).

Deleuze, Gilles, *Cinema 1: The Movement-Image*, trans. Hugh Tomlinson (London: The Athlone Press, 1986 [1983]).

Deleuze, Gilles, *Cinema 2: The Time-Image*, trans. Hugh Tomlinson and Robert Galeta (London: The Athlone Press, 1989 [1985]).

Deleuze, Gilles, 'Coldness and Cruelty', in *Masochism*, trans. Jean McNeil (New York: Zone Books [1967] 1989), 9–138.

Deleuze, Gilles, *Cours Vincennes*, 'Anti-Oedipe et Mille Plateaux' (27 February 1979), trans. Timothy S. Murphy, <www.webdeleuze.com/textes/186> (accessed 5 April 2020).

Deleuze, Gilles, *Cours Vincennes*, 'Sur Kant: Synthesis and Time' (14 March 1978), trans. Melissa McMahon, <www.webdeleuze.com/textes/66> (accessed 5 April 2020).

Deleuze, Gilles, *Cours Vincennes*, 'Sur Leibniz' (4 April 1980), trans. Charles J. Stivale, <www.webdeleuze.com/textes/50> (accessed 5 April 2020).

Deleuze, Gilles, *Cours Vincennes*, 'Sur Spinoza' (24 January 1978), trans. Timothy S. Murphy, <www.webdeleuze.com/textes/14> (accessed 5 April 2020).

Deleuze, Gilles, *Cours Vincennes*, 'Sur Spinoza' (17 February 1981), trans. Timothy S. Murphy, <www.webdeleuze.com/textes/38> (accessed 5 April 2020).

Deleuze, Gilles, *Cours Vincennes*, 'Sur Spinoza: The Actual Infinite-Eternal, the Logic of Relations' (10 March 1981), trans. Simon Duffy, <www.webdeleuze.com/textes/42> (accessed 5 April 2020).

Deleuze, Gilles, *Difference and Repetition*, trans. Paul R. Patton (New York: Columbia University Press, 1994 [1968]).

Deleuze, Gilles, *Empiricism and Subjectivity: An Essay on Hume's Theory of Human Nature*, trans. Constantin V. Boundas (New York: Columbia University Press 1991 [1977]).

Deleuze, Gilles, *Essays Critical and Clinical*, trans. Daniel W. Smith and Michael A. Greco (Minneapolis: University of Minnesota Press, 1997 [1993]).

Deleuze, Gilles, *The Fold: Leibniz and the Baroque*, trans. T. Conley (London and New York: Continuum, 2006 [1988]).

Deleuze, Gilles, *Foucault*, trans. Sean Hand (Minneapolis: University of Minnesota, 1988 [1986]).

Deleuze, Gilles, *Francis Bacon: The Logic of Sensation*, trans. Daniel W. Smith (London and New York: Continuum, 2003 [1981]).

Deleuze, Gilles, *Kant's Critical Philosophy: The Doctrine of the Faculties*, trans. Hugh Tomlinson and Barbara Habberjam (Minneapolis: University of Minnesota Press, 1984 [1967]).

Deleuze, Gilles, *The Logic of Sense*, trans. Mark Lester and Charles C. Stivale (New York: Columbia University Press, 1990 [1969]).

Deleuze, Gilles, *Negotiations, 1972–1990*, trans. Martin Joughin (New York: Columbia University Press, 1995 [1990]).

Deleuze, Gilles, *Nietzsche and Philosophy*, trans. Hugh Tomlinson (New York: Columbia University Press, 2006 [1962]).

Deleuze, Gilles, 'Postscript on the Societies of Control', *October* 59 (1992): 3–7.

Deleuze, Gilles, *Pure Immanence: Essays on A Life*, trans. Anne Boyman (New York: Zone Books, 2001), 25–33.

Deleuze, Gilles, *Spinoza, Practical Philosophy*, trans. Robert Hurley (San Francisco: City Lights Books, 1988 [1970]).

Deleuze, Gilles, *Two Regimes of Madness: Texts and Interviews 1975–1995*, trans. Amy Hodges and Mike Taormina (Los Angeles: Semiotext(e), 2006).

Deleuze, Gilles and Félix Guattari, *Anti-Oedipus*, trans. Robert Hurley, Mark Seem and Helen R. Lane (New York: Penguin, 2008 [1972]).

Deleuze, Gilles and Felix Guattari, *A Thousand Plateaus*, trans. Brian Massumi (Minneapolis: Minnesota University Press, 1987 [1980]).

Deleuze, Gilles and Félix Guattari, *What Is Philosophy?*, trans. Hugh Tomlinson and Graham Burchell (New York: Columbia University Press, 1994 [1991]).

Deleuze, Gilles and Claire Parnet, *ABC Primer*, overview by Charles J. Stivale, directed by Pierre-André Boutang (1996), <www.langlab.wayne.edu/Cstivale/D-G/ABC1.html> (accessed 5 April 2020).

Deleuze, Gilles and Claire Parnet, *Dialogues*, trans. Hugh Tomlinson and Barbera Habberjam (New York: Columbia University Press, 1987 [1977]).

Dennett, Daniel C., *Consciousness Explained* (Boston: Back Bay Books, 1991).

Dennett, Daniel C., *From Bacteria to Bach and Back: The Evolution of Minds* (London: Allen Lane, 2017).

Descartes, René, 'Treatise on Man', in *The Philosophical Writings of Descartes*, Vol. 1, trans. John G. Cottingham et al. (Cambridge: Cambridge University Press, 1985), 99–108.

Dijk, Hans van, 'Critical Project or the Project of Criticism?', in *The Architectural Annual 2003–2004*, ed. Henco Bekkering et al. (Rotterdam: 010 Publishers, 2005), 68–75.

Doevendans, Kees, 'Sustainable Urban Development and the Fourth Typology', in *Ecopolis: Sustainable Planning and Design Principles*, ed. Dimitra Babalis (Florence: Alinea Editrice, 2006), 31–8.

Dosse, François, *Gilles Deleuze and Félix Guattari: Intersecting Lives*, trans. Deborah Glassman (New York: Columbia University Press, 2010).

Doucet, Isabelle and Kenny Cupers, eds, *Agency in Architecture: Reframing Criticality in Theory and Practice*, Footprint 4 (Spring 2009), <https://journals.open.tudelft.nl/index.php/footprint/issue/view/374> (accessed 5 April 2020).

Dreyfus, Hubert L., 'Heidegger's Critique of Husserl's (and Searle's) Account of Intentionality', *Social Research* 1, no. 60 (Spring 1993): 17–38.

Dreyfus, Hubert L., *Skillful Coping: Essays on the Phenomenology of Everyday Perception and Action* (Oxford: Oxford University Press, 2014).

Dreyfus, Hubert L., *What Computers Can't Do* (Cambridge, MA: The MIT Press, 1972).

Dreyfus, Hubert L., *What Computers Still Can't Do: A Critique of Artificial Reason* (Cambridge, MA: The MIT Press, 1992).

Eagleton, Terry, *After Theory* (New York: Basic, 2003).

Eagleton, Terry, *The Ideology of the Aesthetic* (Oxford: Blackwell, 1990).

Edelkoort, Li, 'In Free Fall', in Ben van Berkel and Caroline Bos, *UN Studio – Unfold*, ed. Véronique Patteeuw (Rotterdam: NAi Publishers, 2002), 96–7.

Eisenman, Peter, 'From Object to Relationship II: Giuseppe Terragni casa Giuliani Frigerio', *Perspecta* 13/14 (1971): 38–61.

Engel, Heino, *Structure Systems* (Ostfildern-Ruit: Hatje Cantz, 1997).

Evans, Robin, *The Projective Cast: Architecture and Its Three Geometries* (Cambridge, MA: The MIT Press, 1995).

Evans, Robin, *Translations from Drawing to Building and Other Essays* (London: AA Documents 2, 2003 [1990]).

Ferry, Luc and Alain Renault, *French Philosophy of the Sixties: An Essay on Antihumanism* (Amherst: University of Massachusetts, 1990 [1985]).

Finnes, Sophie, *The Pervert's Guide to Cinema* (Vienna: Mischief Films, London: Amoeba Film, 2006).

Flaxman, Gregory, 'Introduction', in *The Brain Is the Screen: Deleuze and the Philosophy of Cinema*, ed. Gregory Flaxman (Minneapolis: Minnesota University Press, 2000), 12–15.

Flusser, Vilém, *The Shape of Things: A Philosophy of Design* (London: Reaktion Books, 1999).

Foster, Hal, ed., *Vision and Visuality* (Seattle: Bay Press, 1988).

Foucault, Michel, *The Order of Things: An Archaeology of the Human Sciences* (London: Routledge Classics, 2002 [1966]).

Foucault, Michel, *Society Must Be Defended: Lectures at the Collège de France, 1975–1976* (New York: Picador, 1997 [1976]).

Foucault, Michel, 'Theatrum Philosophicum', *Critique* 282 (1970): 885–908.

Foucault, Michel and Gilles Deleuze, 'Intellectuals and Power', in *Language, Counter-Memory and Practice*, ed. Donald F. Bouchard (Ithaca: Cornell University Press, 1977), 205–17.

Frichot, Hélène, 'Stealing into Gilles Deleuze's Baroque House', in *Deleuze and Space*, ed. Ian Buchanan and Gregg Lambert (Edinburgh: Edinburgh Press, 2005), 61–79.

Frichot, Hélène and Stephen Loo, eds, *Deleuze and Architecture* (Edinburgh: Edinburgh University Press, 2013).

Frichot, Hélène, Catharina Gabrielsson and Jonathan Metzger, eds, *Deleuze and the City* (Edinburgh: Edinburgh University Press, 2016).

Fukuyama, Francis, *The End of History and the Last Man* (New York: The Free Press, 1992).

Gibson, J. J., 'The Concept of the Stimulus in Psychology', *American Psychologist* 15, no. 11 (November 1960): 694–703.

Gibson, J. J., *The Ecological Approach to Visual Perception* (Hillsdale, NJ: L. Erlbaum, 1986 [1979]).

Gibson, J. J., *The Perception of the Visual World* (Boston: Houghton Mifflin, 1950).

Gibson, J. J., *Reasons for Realism: Selected Essays of James J. Gibson*, ed. Edward S. Reed and Rebecca Jones (Hillsdale, NJ: L. Erlbaum, 1982).

Gibson, J. J., *The Senses Considered as Perceptual Systems* (Boston: Houghton Mifflin, 1966).

Gibson, J. J. and Ernst Gombrich, 'Gombrich/Gibson Dispute', *Gombrich Archive* (1971–), <https://gombrich.co.uk/gombrichgibson-dispute/> (accessed 5 April 2020).

Gibson, William, *Neuromancer* (New York: Ace Science Fiction, 1984).

Gleick, James, *Chaos: Making a New Science* (New York: Viking Books, 1987).

Graafland, Arie, 'An Afterthought on Urban Design', in *Urban Asymmetries: Studies and Projects on Neoliberal Urbanisation*, ed. Tahl Kaminer, Miguel Robles-Durán and Heidi Sohn (Rotterdam: 010 Publishers, 2011), 274–85.

Graafland, Arie, 'Artificiality in the Work of Rem Koolhaas', in *Architectural Bodies*, ed. Michael Speaks (Rotterdam: 010 Publishers, 1996), 39–65.

Graafland, Arie, 'Looking into the Folds', in *The Body in Architecture*, ed. Deborah Hauptmann (Rotterdam: 010 Publishers, 2006), 138–57.

Graafland, Arie, 'On Criticality', in *Crossover: Architecture, Urbanism, Technology* (Rotterdam: 0101 Publishers, 2006), 688–703.

Graafland, Arie, *The Socius of Architecture: Amsterdam, Tokyo, New York* (Rotterdam: 010 Publishers, 2000).

Greenberg, Clement, *Art and Culture: Critical Essays* (Boston: Beacon Press, 1989).

Grossberg, Lawrence, 'Affect's Future: Rediscovering the Virtual in the Actual (in an interview by Gregory J. Seigworth and Melissa Gregg)', in *The Affect Theory Reader*, ed. Gregory J. Seigworth and Melissa Gregg (Durham, NC: Duke University Press, 2010), 309–38.

Grosz, Elisabeth, *Chaos, Territory, Art: Deleuze and the Framing of Earth* (New York: Columbia University Press, 2008).

Grosz, Elizabeth, *The Incorporeal: Ontology, Ethics, and the Limits of Materialism* (New York: Columbia University Press, 2017).

Guattari, Félix, *Chaosmosis: An Ethico-Aesthetic Paradigm*, trans. Paul Bains and Julian Pefanis (Bloomington: Indiana University Press, 1995 [1992]).

Guattari, Félix, *Chaosophy: Texts and Interviews 1972–1977*, ed. Sylvère Lothringer, trans. David L. Sweet, Jarred Becker and Taylor Adkins (Los Angeles: Autonomedia/Semiotext(e), 1995).

Guattari, Félix, 'Cracks in the Street', trans. Anne Gibault and John Johnson, *Flash Art* 135 (1987): 82–5.

Guattari, Félix, 'A Liberation of Desire', trans. George Stambolian, in *Soft Subversions: Texts and Interviews 1977–1985* (Los Angeles: Semiotext(e), 2009), 141–57.

Guattari, Félix, *Lines of Flight: For Another World of Possibilities*, trans. Andrew Goffey (London and New York: Bloomsbury Academic, 2016 [2011]).

Guattari, Félix, *Molecular Revolution: Psychiatry and Politics*, trans. Rosemary Sheed (London: Penguin, 1984 [1977]).

Guattari, Félix, 'The Postmodern Impasse', in *The Guattari Reader*, ed. Gary Genosko, trans. Todd Dufresne (Oxford: Blackwell, 1996 [1986]), 109–13.

Guattari, Félix, 'Les Quatres Inconscients' (13 January 1981), trans. Taylor Adkins, *Fractal Ontology* (2020), <https://fractalontology.wordpress.com/2020/04/12/new-translation-of-felix-guattaris-seminar-les-quatres-inconscients-13-01-1981/?fbclid=IwAR1_Yi1XEJ4_m2aCAMjMuQluusfve9evkA6FRX7-Bxr2hwRwWUB_-ZkaiNI&blogsub=confirming#subscribe-blog> (accessed 15 April 2020).

Guattari, Félix, *Schizoanalytic Cartographies*, trans. Andrew Goffey (London: Bloomsbury, 2013 [1989]).

Guattari, Félix, *The Three Ecologies*, trans. Ian Pindar and Paul Sutton (London: Continuum, 2008 [1989]).

Hage, Ghasan, 'The Open Mind and Its Enemies: Anthropology and the Passion of the Political', Inaugural Distinguished Lecture in Anthropology, *The Australian Anthropological Society* (8 December 2009), <www.themonthly. com.au/anthropology-and-passion-political-ghassan-hage-2230> (accessed 1 April 2013).

Hallward, Peter, *Out of This World: Deleuze and the Philosophy of Creation* (London: Verso, 2006).

Haraway, Donna J., *Staying with the Trouble: Making Kin in the Chthulucene* (Durham, NC and London: Duke University Press, 2016).

Harman, Graham, 'On the Undermining of Objects: Grant, Bruno and Radical Philosophy', in *The Speculative Turn: Continental Materialism and Realism*, ed. Levi Bryant, Nick Srnicek and Graham Harman (Melbourne: re.press, 2011), 21–40.

Hauptmann, Deborah and Andrej Radman, 'Northern Line', in *Deleuze and Architecture*, ed. Hélène Frichot and Stephen Loo (Edinburgh: Edinburgh University Press, 2013), 40–60. (Chapter 3 in this volume.)

Hauptmann, Deborah and Warren Neidich, eds, *Cognitive Architecture: From Bio-politics to Noo-politics* (Rotterdam: 010 Publishers, 2010).

Hauptmann, Deborah and Andrej Radman, eds, *Asignifying Semiotics: or How to Paint Pink on Pink*, *Footprint* 8/1, no. 14 (Delft: Architecture Theory Chair in partnership with Stichting Footprint and Techne Press, 2014), <https://doi. org/10.7480/footprint.8.1> (accessed 5 April 2020).

Hayles, Katherine N., *How We Became Posthuman: Virtual Bodies in Cybernetics, Literature, and Informatics* (London: The University of Chicago Press, 1999).

Hayles, Katherine N., *My Mother Was a Computer: Digital Subjects and Literary Texts* (Chicago: The University of Chicago Press, 2005).

Hayles, Katherine N., *The Unthought: The Power of the Cognitive Nonconscious* (Chicago and London: The University of Chicago Press, 2017).

Hays, Michael K., 'Critical Architecture: Between Culture and Form', *Perspecta* 21 (1984): 14–29.

Hays, Michael K., 'Ideologies of Media and the Architecture of Cities in Transition', in *Cities in Transition*, ed. Deborah Hauptmann (Rotterdam: 010 Publishers, 2001), 262–73.

Healy, Patrick, *The Model and Its Architecture* (Rotterdam: 010 Publishers, 2008).

Heft, Harry, *Ecological Psychology in Context: James Gibson, Roger Barker, and the Legacy of William James's Radical Empiricism* (Mahwah, NJ: L. Erlbaum, 2001).

Heidegger, Martin, 'Building Dwelling Thinking', in *Poetry, Language, Thought*, trans. Albert Hofstadter (New York: Harper and Row, 1971 [1951 lecture]), 145–61.

Herzogenrath, Bernd, *An [Un]Likely Alliance: Thinking Environment[s] with Deleuze|Guattari* (Newcastle upon Tyne: Cambridge Scholars Publishing, 2008).

Holl, Steven, Juhani Pallasmaa and Alberto Perez-Gomez, *Questions of Perception: Phenomenology of Architecture* (Tokyo: A+U, 1994).

Holland, Eugene W., 'Nonlinear Historical Materialism and Postmodern Marxism', *Culture, Theory and Critique* 47, no. 2 (2006): 181–96.

Hörisch, Jochen, *Theorie-Apotheke: Eine Handreichung zu den humanwissenschaftlichen Theorien der letzten fünfzig Jahre, einschließlich ihrer Risiken und Nebenwirkungen* (Frankfurt: Eichborn, 2005).

Horkheimer, Max and Theodor W. Adorno, *Dialectics of Enlightenment: Philosophical Fragments*, trans. Edmund Jephcott (Stanford: Stanford University Press, 2002 [1944]).

Hughes, Howard C., *Sensory Exotica: A World beyond Human Experience* (Cambridge, MA: The MIT Press, 2001).

Hui, Yuk, 'One Hundred Years of Crisis', *e-flux journal* 108 (April 2020), <www.e-flux.com/journal/108/326411/one-hundred-years-of-crisis/> (accessed 14 April 2020).

Hurley, Susan L., *Consciousness in Action* (Cambridge, MA: Harvard University Press, 1998).

Ingels, Bjarke, *Yes Is More: An Archicomic on Architectural Evolution* (Cologne: Evergreen, 2010).

Ingold, Tim, 'From Complementarity to Obviation: On Dissolving the Boundaries between Social and Biological Anthropology, Archaeology and Psychology', in *Cycles of Contingency: Developmental Systems and Evolution*, ed. Susan Oyama, Paul E. Griffiths and Russel D. Gray (Cambridge, MA: The MIT Press, 2001), 255–79.

Ittelson, William H., 'Environment Perception and Contemporary Perceptual Theory', in *Environment and Cognition* (New York: Seminar Press, 1973), 1–19.

James, Philip, *Henry Moore on Sculpture* (New York: Da Capo Press, 1992).

James, William, *The Principles of Psychology*, Vol. 1 and 2 (New York: Dover Publications, 1950 [1890]).

James, William, *The Will to Believe and Other Essays in Popular Philosophy* (Cambridge, MA and London: Harvard University Press, 1979 [1897]).

Jay, Martin, *Downcast Eyes: The Denigration of Vision in Twentieth-Century French Thought* (Berkeley: University of California Press, 1994).

Jones, Judith, 'Provocative Expression: Transitions in and from Metaphysics in Whitehead's Later Work', in *Beyond Metaphysics? Explorations in Alfred North Whitehead's Late Thought*, ed. Roland Faber, Brian G. Henning and Clinton Combs (Amsterdam and New York: Rodopi, 2010), 259–79.

Jullien, François, *The Propensity of Things: Toward a History of Efficacy in China* (New York: Zone Books, 1995).

Kahneman, Daniel, *Thinking: Fast and Slow* (New York: Farrar, Straus and Giroux, 2011).

Kaminer, Tahl, *The Idealist Refuge: Architecture, Crisis, and Resuscitation* (TU Delft doctoral dissertation, 2008).

Kandinsky, Wassily, *Point and Line to Plane*, trans. Howard Dearstyne (New York: Dover Publications, 1979 [1923]).

Kipnis, Jeffrey, 'Form's Second Coming', in *The State of Architecture at the Beginning of the 21st Century*, ed. Bernard Tschumi and Irene Cheng (New York: Montacelli Press, 2003), 58–9.

Kipnis, Jeffrey, 'Moneo's Anxiety', in *On Criticism, Harvard Design Magazine* (Fall 2005): 97–104.

Kipnis, Jeffrey and Reinhold Martin, 'What Good Can Architecture Do?' (The Harvard Graduate School of Design, 2010), <www.youtube.com/watch?v=HDo40Fr41os/> (accessed 5 April 2020).

Kipnis, Jeffrey, et al., '2015 Grad Thesis Prep Symposium', <http://sma.sciarc.edu/video/2015-grad-thesis-prep-symposium/> (accessed 4 May 2015).

Kittler, Friedrich A., *Literature, Media, Information Systems: Essays* (London and New York: Routledge, 2012 [1997]).

Klein, Felix. 'Vergleichende Betrachtungen über neuere geometrische Forschungen', *Mathematische Annalen* 43 (1893): 63–100, <http://eudml.org/doc/157672> (accessed 5 April 2020).

Koolhaas, Rem, *Delirious New York: A Retroactive Manifesto for Manhattan* (New York: Oxford University Press, 1978).

Koolhaas, Rem, 'Interview by Jennifer Sigler', *Index Magazine* (2000), <www.indexmagazine.com/interviews/rem_koolhaas.shtml> (accessed 5 April 2020).

Koolhaas, Rem, *S, M, L, XL*, ed. OMA with Bruce Mau (New York: Monacelli Press, 1995).

Koolhaas, Rem, 'Salvador Dali, the Paranoid Critical Method, Le Corbusier, New York', lecture at the Architectural Association, (London, 18 December 1976), <www.youtube.com/watch?v=HcnRzxQu27w> (accessed 5 April 2020).

Koolhaas, Rem and Hans Ulrich Obrist, interview with Robert Venturi and

Denise Scott Brown, 'Re-Learning from Las Vegas', in *Content* (Cologne: Taschen, 2004), 150–7.

Krasner, Lee, 'Interview with Dorothy Strickler' (1964) for the Smithsonian Institution Archives of American Art, <www.aaa.si.edu/collections/oralhis tories/transcripts/krasne64.htm> (accessed 5 April 2020).

Kubrick, Stanley (dir.), *2001: A Space Odyssey* (Stanley Kubrick Productions/ Metro-Goldwyn-Mayer, 1968).

Kugler, Peter N. and Robert Shaw, 'Symmetry and Symmetry-Breaking in Thermodynamic and Epistemic Engines: A Coupling of First and Second Laws', in *Synergetics of Cognition* (Heidelberg: Springer-Verlag Berlin, 1990), 296–331.

Kwinter, Sanford, *Architectures of Time: Toward a Theory of the Event in Modernist Culture* (Cambridge, MA: The MIT Press, 2001).

Kwinter, Sanford, 'A Discourse on Method (For the Proper Conduct of Reason and the Search for Efficacity in Design)', in *Explorations in Architecture: Teaching, Design, Research*, ed. Reto Geiser (Basel: Birkhäuser, 2008), 34–47.

Kwinter, Sanford, *Far from Equilibrium: Essays on Technology and Design Culture* (Barcelona: Actar, 2008).

Kwinter, Sanford, 'Flying the Bullet, or When Did the Future Begin?', in *Rem Koolhaas: Conversation with Students*, ed. Sanford Kwinter (New York: Princeton Architectural Press, 1996), 67–94.

Kwinter, Sanford, 'Hydraulic Vision', in *Mood River*, ed. Jeffrey Kipnis and Anetta Massie (Columbus, OH: Wexner Center for the Arts, 2002), 32–3.

Kwinter, Sanford, 'La Cittá Nuova: Modernity and Continuity', in *Architecture Theory since 1968*, ed. Michael K. Hays (Cambridge, MA: The MIT Press, 1998), 586–612.

Kwinter, Sanford, 'Landscapes of Change: Boccioni's "Stati d'animo" as a General Theory of Models', *Assemblage* 19 (1992): 52–65.

Kwinter, Sanford, 'Neuroecology: Notes toward a Synthesis', *The Psychopathologies of Cognitive Capitalism: Part Two*, ed. Warren Neidich (Berlin: Archive Books, 2014), 313–33.

Kwinter, Sanford, 'On Vitalism and the Virtual', in *Pratt Journal of Architecture: On Making* (New York: Rizzoli, 1992), 185–9.

Kwinter, Sanford, 'Sensing the Aerocene' (2016), <https://cargocollective.com/ sanfordkwinter/Sensing-the-Aerocene> (accessed 5 April 2020).

Kwinter, Sanford, 'Soft Systems', in *Culture Lab*, ed. Brian Boigon (New York: Princeton Architecture Press, 1993), 207–28.

Kwinter, Sanford, 'Who's Afraid of Formalism?', in *Phylogenesis: FOA's Ark*, ed. Michael Kubo and Albert Ferré with FOA (Barcelona: Actar, 2003), 96–9.

Laboria Cuboniks, 'Xenofeminism: A Politics for Alienation' (2015), <www.laboriacuboniks.net> (accessed 5 April 2020).

Lambert, Gregg, *In Search of a New Image of Thought: Gilles Deleuze and Philosophical Expressionism* (Minneapolis: University of Minnesota Press, 2012).

Langer, Susanne K., *Feeling and Form: A Theory of Art* (New York: Scribners, 1953).

Langer, Susanne K., *Philosophy in a New Key* (Cambridge, MA: Harvard University Press, 1957).

Lash, Scott, *Another Modernity: A Different Rationality* (Oxford: Blackwell, 1999).

Lash, Scott and Celia Lury, *Global Culture Industry: The Mediation of Things* (Malden, MA: Polity, 2007).

Latour, Bruno, 'A Cautious Prometheus? A Few Steps toward a Philosophy of Design (with Special Attention to Peter Sloterdijk)', keynote lecture for the *Networks of Design* meeting of the Design History Society (Falmouth, Cornwall, 3 September 2008), 1–13.

Latour, Bruno *The Pasteurization of France*, trans. Alan Sheridan and John Law (Cambridge, MA: Harvard University Press, 1988 [1984]).

Le Corbusier, *Toward an Architecture*, trans. John Goodman (Los Angeles: Getty Research Institute, 2007 [1923]).

Leroi-Gourhan, André, *Gesture and Speech*, trans. Anna Bostock Berger (Cambridge, MA: The MIT Press, 1993 [1964]).

Lessing, Gotthold Ephraim, *Laocoon: or, The Limits of Poetry and Painting*, trans. William Ross (London: Ridgeway, 1836 [1766]).

Lewontin, Richard, 'Organism and Environment', in *Learning, Development, and Culture*, ed. Henry C. Plotkin (Chichester: Wiley, 1982), 151–70.

Lewontin, Richard, *The Triple Helix: Gene, Organism, and Environment* (Cambridge, MA: Harvard University Press, 2000).

Livesey, Graham, ed., *Deleuze and Guattari on Architecture (Critical Assessments in Architecture, Volume II)* (London: Routledge, 2015).

Longo, Giuseppe, 'The Consequences of Philosophy', in *Site 0: Castalia, the Game of Ends and Means|Glass Bead* (2016), 1–12, <www.glass-bead.org/wp-content/uploads/the-consequences-of-philosophy_en.pdf> (accessed 5 April 2020).

Lord, Beth, 'Deleuze and Kant', in *The Cambridge Companion to Deleuze*, ed. Daniel W. Smith (Cambridge: Cambridge University Press, 2012), 82–102.

Lorraine, Tamsin, 'Living a Time out of Joint: Sense, the Event and the Time of

Aion', in *Between Deleuze and Derrida*, ed. Paul R. Patton and John Protevi (London and New York: Continuum, 2003), 30–46.

Lovelock, James, *Gaia* (New York: Oxford University Press, 1987).

Lury, Celia, 'Topology for Culture: Metaphors and Tools', *Colloquium 1: Thinking Topologically? A Topological Approach to Cultural Dynamics* (2007), <www.atacd.net/index.php%3Foption=com_content&task=view&id=107&Itemid=88.html> (accessed 25 May 2011).

Lynch, Kevin, *Good City Form* (Cambridge, MA: The MIT Press, 1984).

Lynch, Kevin, *The Image of the City* (Cambridge, MA: The MIT Press, 1960).

Lynn, Greg, *Animate Form* (New York: Princeton Architectural Press, 1999).

Lyotard, Jean-François, *Discourse, Figure*, trans. Antony Hudek and Mary Lydon (Minneapolis: University of Minnesota Press, 2011 [1971]).

Maas, Wietske and Matteo Pasquinelli, 'Accelerate Metrophagy (Notes on the Manifesto of Urban Cannibalism)', *DIS Magazine* (October 2014) <http://dis-magazine.com/dystopia/67349/manifesto-of-urban-cannibalism/> (accessed 5 April 2020).

Macapia, Peter, 'Interview with Bernard Cache in *Saint Ouen l'Aumône*' (June 2008), <www.adrd.net/crowdcast/video/11.html> (accessed 21 February 2010).

Mace, William M., 'James J. Gibson's Strategy for Perceiving: Ask Not What's Inside Your Head, but What Your Head's Inside of', in *Perceiving, Acting and Knowing: Toward an Ecological Psychology*, ed. Robert Shaw and John Bransford (Hillsdale, NJ: L. Erlbaum Associates, 1977), 43–65.

Mackay, Robin: 'Introduction: Three Figures of Contingency', in *The Medium of Contingency* (Falmouth: Urbanomic, 2011), 1–9.

Magnani, Lorenzo, *Abductive Cognition: The Epistemological and Eco-Cognitive Dimensions of Hypothetical Reasoning* (Berlin: Springer-Verlag, 2009).

Malabou, Catherine, *What Should We Do with Our Brain?*, trans. Sebastian Rand (New York: Fordham University Press, 2008).

Manning, Erin and Brian Massumi, 'Coming Alive in a World of Texture for Neurodiversity', in *Dance, Politics and Co-Immunity: Thinking Resistances/ Current Perspectives on Politics and Communities in the Arts*, Vol. 1, ed. Gerald Siegmund und Stephan Hölscher (Zürich and Berlin: diaphanes, 2013), 73–96.

Massumi, Brian, *99 Theses on the Revaluation of Value: A Postcapitalist Manifesto*, (Minneapolis: University of Minnesota Press, 2018).

Massumi, Brian, *Architectures of the Unforeseen: Essays in the Occurrent Arts* (Minneapolis: University of Minnesota Press, 2019).

Massumi, Brian, 'Building Experience: The Architecture of Perception', in *NOX*

Machining Architecture, ed. Andrew Benjamin and Lars Spuybroek (London: Thames & Hudson, 2004), 322–31.

Massumi, Brian, 'The Critique of Pure Feeling', seminar at the School of Criticism and Theory, Cornell University (2009), <www.arts.cornell.edu/sochum/sct/courses.html> (accessed 27 September 2009).

Massumi, Brian, 'The Diagram as Technique of Existence', from *Diagram Work*, ed. Ben van Berkel and Caroline Bos, special issue of *ANY (Architecture New York)* 23 (1998): 42–7.

Massumi, Brian, 'Immediation Unlimited', in *Immediation II*, ed. Erin Manning, Anna Munster, Bodil Marie Stavning Thomsen (London: Open Humanities Press, 2019), 501–43.

Massumi, Brian, 'National Enterprise Emergency: Steps toward an Ecology of Powers', in *Beyond Biopolitics: Essays on the Governance of Life and Death*, ed. Patricia Ticineto Clough and Craig Willse (Durham, NC and London: Duke University Press, 2011), 19–45.

Massumi, Brian, 'Of Microperception and Micropolitics', interview by Joel McKim, in *Inflexions: Micropolitics: Exploring Ethico-Aesthetics* 3 (2009): 1–20, <www.senselab.ca/inflexions/volume_3/node_i3/PDF/Massumi%20Of%20Micropolitics.pdf> (accessed 5 April 2020).

Massumi, Brian, *Ontopower: War, Powers, and the State of Perception* (Durham, NC: Duke University Press, 2015).

Massumi, Brian, *Parables for the Virtual: Movement, Affect, Sensation* (Durham, NC: Duke University Press, 2002).

Massumi, Brian, 'Perception Attack: The Force to Own Time', in *Theory After 'Theory'*, ed. Jane Elliott and Derek Attridge (New York: Routledge, 2011), 75–89.

Massumi, Brian, *The Power at the End of the Economy* (Durham, NC: Duke University Press, 2015).

Massumi, Brian, 'The Thinking-Feeling of What Happens', in *Interact or Die*, ed. Joke Brouwer and Arjen Mulder (Rotterdam: V2 Pub./NAi, 2007), 70–91.

Massumi, Brian, 'Transforming Digital Architecture from Virtual to Neuro: An Interview by Thomas Markussen and Thomas Birch', *Intelligentagent* 5, no. 2, (2006), <www.intelligentagent.com/archive/Vol5_No2> (accessed 25 May 2011).

Massumi, Brian, *A User's Guide to Capitalism and Schizophrenia* (Cambridge, MA: The MIT Press, 1992).

Massumi, Brian, 'The Virtual', Experimental Digital Arts lecture (EDA, 2000), <http://design.ucla.edu/eda/archive/serve.php?stream=/mnt/video/design/video/041700_massumi.rm> (accessed 21 February 2010).

Massumi, Brian, 'Virtual Ecology and the Question of Value', in *General Ecology: The New Ecological Paradigm* (London: Bloomsbury Academic 2017), 345–73.

Massumi, Brian, *What Animals Teach Us about Politics* (Durham, NC: Duke University Press, 2014).

Mau, Bruce and the Institute without Boundaries, *Massive Change: It's Not about the World of Design. It's about the Design of the World* (London: Phaidon, 2004).

McKim, Joel, 'Radical Infrastructure? A New Realism and Materialism in Philosophy and Architecture', in *The Missed Encounter between Radical Philosophy with Architecture*, ed. Nadir Lahiji (London: Bloomsbury, 2014), 133–49.

McLuhan, Marshall, *Understanding Media: The Extensions of Man* (Cambridge, MA: The MIT Press, 1994 [1964]).

Meillassoux, Quentin, *After Finitude: An Essay on the Necessity of Contingency*, trans. Ray Brassier (London and New York: Continuum, 2008).

Meillassoux, Quentin, 'Interview with Meillassoux', Steve Harris blog (2010), <http://steve-harris.blogspot.com/2010/02/interview-with-meillassoux.html> (accessed 25 May 2011).

Meillassoux, Quentin, 'Interview with Quentin Meillassoux', *After Nature* blog (2011), <http://afterxnature.blogspot.nl/2011/10/interview-with-meillas-soux-posted-for.html> (accessed 5 April 2020).

Meillassoux, Quentin, *Science Fiction and Extro-Science Fiction*, trans. Alyosha Edlebi (Minneapolis: Univocal Publishing, 2015).

Meillassoux, Quentin, 'Subtraction and Contraction: Deleuze, Immanence, and *Matter and Memory*', *COLLAPSE III: Unknown Deleuze [+ Speculative Realism]* (November 2007): 63–107.

Merleau-Ponty, Maurice, *Phenomenology of Perception*, trans. M. Colin Smith (London: Routledge Classics, 2003 [1945]).

Michaels, Claire F. and Claudia Carello, *Direct Perception* (Englewood Cliffs, NJ: Prentice-Hall, 1981).

Morton, Timothy, *The Ecological Thought* (Cambridge, MA: Harvard University Press, 2010).

Morton, Timothy, *Ecology without Nature: Rethinking Environmental Aesthetics* (Cambridge, MA: Harvard University Press, 2007).

Morton, Timothy, 'Objects as Temporary Autonomous Zones,' *Continent* 1, no. 3 (2011): 149–55.

Moure, Gloria, *Duchamp* (Madrid: Sala de Exposiciones de la Caja de Pensiones, 1984).

Nealon, Jeffrey T., 'Beyond Hermeneutics: Deleuze, Derrida and Contemporary

Theory', in *Between Deleuze and Derrida*, ed. Paul R. Patton and John Protevi (New York: Continuum, 2003), 158–68.

Nealon, Jeffrey T., *Foucault beyond Foucault: Power and Its Intensifications since 1984* (Stanford: Stanford University Press, 2008).

Negarestani, Reza, *Cyclonopedia: Complicity with Anonymous Materials* (Melbourne: re.press, 2008).

Negarestani, Reza, 'Frontiers of Manipulation', Speculations on Anonymous Materials symposium (2014), <www.youtube.com/watch?v=Fg0lMebGt9I/> (accessed 5 April 2020).

Negarestani, Reza, *Torture Concrete: Jean-Luc Moulène and the Protocol of Abstraction* (New York: Sequence Press, 2014).

Neidich, Warren, 'Neuropower: Art in the Age of Cognitive Capitalism', in *The Psychopathologies of Cognitive Capitalism: Part One*, ed. Arne De Boever and Warren Neidich (Berlin: Archive Books, 2013), 219–66.

Noë, Alva, *Is the Visual World a Grand Illusion?* (Thorverton: Imprint Academic, 2002).

Nöe, Alva, *Out of Our Heads: Why You Are Not Your Brain, and Other Lessons from the Biology of Consciousness* (New York: Farrar, Straus and Giroux, 2009).

Nöe, Alva, 'You Are Not Your Brain', interview by Gordy Slack (2009), <http://socrates.berkeley.edu/~noe/an_interviews.html> (accessed 22 June 2012).

Novak, Marcos, 'Alloaesthetics and Neuroaesthetics: Travel through Phenomenology and Neurophysiology', *Journal of Neuro-Aesthetic Theory* 4 (2005), <www.artbrain.org/neuroaesthetics/novak.html>.

Odling-Smee, John, 'Niche Inheritance: A Possible Basis for Classifying Multiple Inheritance Systems in Evolution', *Biological Theory* 2, no. 3 (2007): 276–89.

Oosterling, Henk, 'Dasein as Design, or: Must Design Save the World?', *Premsela. org* lecture (2009), <http://finzhao.wordpress.com/2010/09/22/what-is-relational-design/> (accessed 5 April 2020).

Otero-Pailos, Jorge, *Architecture's Historical Turn: Phenomenology and the Rise of the Postmodern* (Minneapolis: University of Minnesota Press, 2010).

Oxvig, Henrik, Jan Bäcklund, Michael Renner and Martin Søberg, eds, *What Images Do* (Aarhus: Aarhus University Press, 2018).

Panofsky, Erwin, *Meaning in the Visual Arts* (Harmondsworth: Penguin, 1970).

Parisi, Luciana, *Contagious Architecture: Computation, Aesthetics and Space* (Cambridge, MA: The MIT Press, 2013).

Payne, Jason and Jesse Reiser, 'Chum: Computation in a Supersaturated Milieu', *Kenchiku Bunka* 53, no. 619 (1998): 19–26.

Peirce, Charles Sanders, *Collected Papers of Charles Sanders Peirce: The*

Electronic Edition 1994, reproducing Vol. I–VI, ed. Charles Hartshorne and Paul Weiss (Cambridge, MA: Harvard University Press, 1931–5).

Peirce, Charles Sanders, *Philosophical Writings of Peirce,* ed. Justus Buchler (New York: Dover Publications, 1955 [1903]).

Peirce, Charles Sanders, *Reasoning and the Logic of Things: The Cambridge Conferences Lectures of 1898,* ed. Kenneth Laine Ketner (Cambridge, MA: Harvard University Press, 1992), 242–68.

Pelbart, Peter Pál, *Cartography of Exhaustion: Nihilism Inside Out* (Minneapolis: Univocity Publishing, 2015).

Pisters, Patricia, *The Neuro-Image* (Stanford: Stanford University Press, 2012).

Plotnitsky, Arkady, 'Algebras, Geometries and Topologies of the Fold: Deleuze, Derrida and Quasi-Mathematical Thinking (with Leibniz and Mallarmé)', in *Between Deleuze and Derrida,* ed. Paul R. Patton and John Protevi (New York: Continuum, 2003), 98–119.

Plotnitsky, Arkady, 'Chaosmologies; Quantum Field Theory, Chaos and Thought in Deleuze and Guattari's *What Is Philosophy?*', *Paragraph* 29, no. 2 (2006): 40–56.

Polanyi, Michael, *The Tacit Dimension* (Garden City, NY: Doubleday, 1966).

Popper, Karl, 'The Bucket and the Searchlight: Two Theories of Knowledge', in *The Philosophy of Ecology: From Science to Synthesis,* ed. David R. Keller and Frank B. Golley (Athens: The University of Georgia Press, 2000), 141–6.

Prigogine, Ilya and Isabelle Stengers, *Order out of Chaos: Man's New Dialogue with Nature* (London: Heinemann, 1984).

Protevi, John, '4EA blog', <https://proteviblog.typepad.com/protevi/embod iedembeddedaffective_cognition/> (accessed 5 April 2020).

Protevi, John, 'Deleuze, Jonas, and Thompson: Toward a New Transcendental Aesthetic and a New Question of Panpsychism' (Montreal: SPEP, 2010), <www.protevi.com/john/NewTA.pdf> (accessed 5 April 2020).

Protevi, John, *Life, War, Earth: Deleuze and the Sciences* (Minneapolis: University of Minnesota Press, 2013).

Radman, Andrej, 'Architecture's Awaking from Correlationist Slumber: On Transdisciplinarity and Disciplinary Specificity', in *Footprint* 6, no. 10/11, ed. Deborah Hauptmann and Lara Schrijver (Delft: DSD in partnership with Stichting Footprint and Techne Press, 2012): 129–41. (Chapter 2 in this volume.)

Radman, Andrej, 'Ecologies of Architecture', in *Posthuman Glossary,* ed. Rosi Braidotti and Maria Hlavajova (London: Bloomsbury Academic, 2018), 117–20.

Radman, Andrej, 'Involutionary Architecture: Unyoking Coherence from

Congruence', in *Posthuman Ecologies: Complexity and Process after Deleuze*, ed. Rosi Braidotti and Simone Bignall (London: Rowman & Littlefield, 2019), 61–86. (Chapter 11 in this volume.)

Radman, Andrej, 'Sensibility Is Ground Zero: On Inclusive Disjunction and Politics of Defatalization', in *This Deleuzian Century: Art, Activism, Society*, ed. Rosi Braidotti and Rick Dolphijn (Leiden and Boston: Brill/Rodopi, 2014), 57–86. (Chapter 4 in this volume.)

Radman, Andrej, 'Space Always Comes After: It Is Good When It Comes After; It Is Good Only When It Comes After', in *Speculative Art Histories: Analysis at the Limits*, ed. Sjoerd van Tuinen (Edinburgh: Edinburgh University Press, 2017), 185–201. (Chapter 7 in this volume.)

Radman, Andrej and Stavros Kousoulas, 'Twenty Theses on Ecologies of Architecture', <https://d1rkab7tlqy5f1.cloudfront.net/BK/Over_de_faculteit/Afdelingen/Architecture/Architecture%20Theory/EoA/20Theses-EoA.pdf> (accessed 5 April 2020).

Radman, Andrej and Heidi Sohn, 'Preface: The Four Domains of the Plane of Consistency', in *Critical and Clinical Cartographies: Architecture, Robotics, Medicine, Philosophy*, ed. Andrej Radman and Heidi Sohn (Edinburgh: Edinburgh University Press, 2017), 1–20.

Rajchman, John, *The Deleuze Connections* (Cambridge, MA: The MIT Press, 2000).

Rancière, Jacques, *The Politics of Aesthetics: The Distribution of the Sensible*, trans. Gabriel Rockhill (London and New York: Continuum, 2004).

Rand, Ayn, *The Fountainhead* (New York: Signet, 1993 [1943]).

Raunig, Gerald, *Dividuum: Machinic Capitalism and Molecular Revolution*, Vol. 1 (Los Angeles: Semiotext(e), 2016).

Reed, Edward, *James J. Gibson and the Psychology of Perception* (New Haven: Yale University Press, 1988).

Reiser, Jesse and Nanako Umemoto, *Atlas of Novel Tectonics* (New York: Princeton Architectural Press, 2006).

Robertson, Alan, *Conrad Hal Waddington 1905–1975, Biographical Memoirs of Fellows of the Royal Society* 23 (1977).

Robinson, Kim Stanley, 'The Coronavirus Is Rewriting Our Imaginations', *The New Yorker* (1 May 2020), <www.newyorker.com/culture/annals-of-inquiry/the-coronavirus-and-our-future> (accessed 1 May 2020).

Roche, François, 'Alchimis(t/r/ick)-machines', <www.new-territories.com/roche%20text.htm> (accessed 5 April 2020).

Roche, François, 'Matters of Fabulation: On the Construction of Realities in the Anthropocene', in *Architecture in the Anthropocene: Encounters among*

Design, Deep Time, Science and Philosophy, ed. Etienne Turpin (Ann Arbor: Open Humanities Press, 2013), 197–208.

Roche, François, 'Reclaim Resi[lience]stance//......R²', *Log* 25 (2012): i–5.

Rocker, Ingeborg, 'Apropos Parametricism: If, in What Style Should We Build?', *Log* 21 (2011): 89–101.

Roden, David, 'A Post-Sellarsian Encounter' (2016), <https://enemyindustry. wordpress.com/2016/11/25/a-post-sellarsian-encounter/> (accessed 20 April 2020).

Rosen, Robert, *Essays on Life Itself* (New York: Columbia University Press, 2000).

Rossi, Aldo, *The Architecture of the City*, trans. Diane Ghirardo and Joan Ockman (Cambridge, MA: The MIT Press, 1982).

Rouvroy, Antoinette, 'Adopt AI, Think Later: The Coué Method to the Rescue of Artificial Intelligence' (2020), <https://doi.org/10.13140/ RG.2.2.33462.65601> (accessed 5 April 2020).

Ruyer, Raymond, *Neofinalism*, trans. Alyosha Edlebi (Minneapolis: Minnesota University Press, 2016 [1952]).

Ryle, Gilbert, *The Concept of Mind* (Chicago: The University of Chicago Press, 1949), 25–61.

Sauvagnargues, Anne, *Artmachines: Deleuze, Guattari, Simondon*, trans. Suzanne Verderber and Eugene W. Holland (Edinburgh: Edinburgh University Press, 2016).

Scheers, P. M. C., 'Structure, Supporting Structure and Dimensioning', lecture at TU Delft, 2002.

Schmid, Veronika and Ursa Vrhunc, 'Interview: Robert E. Somol', *Oris* 5, no. 2 (2003): 122–35.

Schrödinger, Erwin, *What Is life? The Physical Aspect of the Living Cell* (based on lectures delivered under the auspices of the Dublin Institute for Advanced Studies at Trinity College, Dublin, 1943), <www.whatislife.ie/downloads/ What-is-Life.pdf> (accessed 20 April 2020).

Schumacher, Patrik, 'Architecture's Next Ontological Innovation', in *Not Nature, Tarp – Architectural Manual* (New York: Pratt Institute, 2012).

Schumacher, Patrik, 'Parametricism with Social Parameters', in *The Human (Parameter): Parametric Approach in Israeli Architecture*, ed. Ionathan Lazovski and Yuval Kahlon (Tel Aviv: ZEZEZE Architecture Gallery, 2015).

Schumacher, Patrik, 'The Parametricist Epoch: Let the Style Wars Begin', *AJ – The Architects' Journal* 231, no. 16 (2010): 41–5.

Schumacher, Patrik, 'Patrik Schumacher, Promoter of Parametricism', interview by Flavien Onfroy, <http://artilinki.com/en/patrik-schumacher-crea tor-of-parametricism/> (accessed 15 October 2018).

Scott, Geoffrey, *The Architecture of Humanism* (New York: W. W. Norton, 1974 [1914]).

Sellars, John, 'Nomadic Wisdom: Herodotus and the Scythians', in *Nomadic Trajectories*, ed. John Sellars and Dawn Walker, *Pli* 7 (1998): 69–92.

Sennett, Richard, *The Craftsman* (London: Penguin Books, 2008).

Sennett, Richard, 'The Open City', in *Urban Age* (Berlin, November 2006), <www.urban-age.net/introduction/investigation/housingAndNeighbourhoods/> (accessed 15 October 2018).

Sennett, Richard, 'The Technology of Unity', in *Olafur Eliasson: Surroundings Surrounded. Essays on Space and Science*, ed. Peter Weibel (Karlsruhe: ZKM, 2000), 556–65.

Serres, Michel, 'Birth', in *The Five Senses: A Philosophy of Mingled Bodies* (New York: Continuum, 2008), 17–23.

Shannon, Claude E., 'A Symbolic Analysis of Relay and Switching Circuits', *Transactions of the American Institute of Electrical Engineers* 57, no. 12 (1938): 713–23, <https://doi:10.1109/T-AIEE.1938.5057767> (accessed 5 April 2020).

Shaviro, Steven, 'The Actual Volcano: Whitehead, Harman, and the Problem of Relations', in *The Speculative Turn: Continental Materialism and Realism*, ed. Levi Bryant, Nick Srnicek and Graham Harman (Melbourne: re.press, 2011), 279–90.

Shaviro, Steven, *Discognition* (London: Repeater Books, 2015).

Shaviro, Steven, 'Object-Oriented Philosophy', *The Pinocchio Theory* (2009), <www.shaviro.com/Blog/?p=712> (accessed 5 April 2020).

Shaviro, Steven, *Universe of Things: On Speculative Realism* (Minneapolis: University of Minnesota Press, 2014).

Shaviro, Steven, *Without Criteria: Kant, Whitehead, Deleuze, and Aesthetics: Technologies of Lived Abstraction* (Cambridge, MA: The MIT Press, 2009).

Sheets-Johnstone, Maxine, ed., *The Corporeal Turn: An Interdisciplinary Reader* (Exeter: Imprint Academic, 2009).

Sheets-Johnstone, Maxine, *The Primacy of Movement* (Aarhus: Aarhus University, Department of Philosophy, 1999).

Shields, Rob, *Spatial Questions: Cultural Topologies and Social Spatialisations* (London: Sage, 2013).

Shklovsky, Victor, 'Art as Technique', trans. Lee T. Lemon and Marion J. Reis, in *Russian Formalist Criticism: Four Essays* (Lincoln and London: University of Nebraska Press, 1965 [1917]), 3–24.

Simondon, Gilbert, 'Genesis of the Individual', trans. Mark Cohen and Sanford

Kwinter, in *Incorporations*, ed. Jonathan Crary and Sanford Kwinter (New York: Zone Books, 1992 [1964]), 297–319.

Simondon, Gilbert, *On the Mode of Existence of Technical Objects*, trans. Cécile Malaspina and John Rogove (Minneapolis: Univocal Publishing, 2017).

Simons, Jon, *Foucault and the Political* (London and New York: Routledge, 1995).

Sloterdijk, Peter, 'Atmospheric Politics', in *Making Things Public: Atmospheres of Democracy*, ed. Bruno Latour and Peter Weibel (Cambridge, MA: The MIT Press, 2005), 944–51.

Sloterdijk, Peter, 'Foreword to the Theory of Spheres', in *Cosmograms*, ed. Melik Ohanian and Jean-Christophe Royoux (New York: Lukas & Sternberg, 2005), 223–41.

Sloterdijk, Peter, *In the World Interior of Capital*, trans. Wieland Hoban (Cambridge: Polity, 2013).

Smail, Daniel, *On Deep History and the Brain* (Berkeley: University of California Press, 2008).

Smith, Barry, 'The Objectivity of Taste and Tasting', in *Questions of Taste: The Philosophy of Wine*, ed. Barry Smith (Oxford: Signal Books, 2007), 41–78.

Smith, Barry, 'Values in Contexts: An Ontological Theory', in *Inherent and Instrumental Values: Excursions in Value Inquiry*, ed. G. John M. Abbarno (Lanham, MA: University Press of America, 2015), 17–29.

Smith, Christopher and Andrew Ballantyne, 'Flow: Architecture, Object and Relation', *Architectural Research Quarterly* 14, no. 1 (2010): 21–7.

Smith, Daniel W., 'Deleuze's Concept of the Virtual and the Critique of the Possible', *Journal of Philosophy: A Cross Disciplinary Inquiry* 4, no. 9 (2009): 29–42.

Smith, Daniel W., *Essays on Deleuze* (Edinburgh: Edinburgh University Press, 2012).

Smith, Daniel W., 'The Inverse Side of the Structure: Žižek on Deleuze on Lacan', *Criticism* 46, no. 4 (2004): 635–50.

Smithson, Robert, *Robert Smithson: The Collected Writings* (Los Angeles: University of California Press, 1996).

Somol, Robert, 'Dummy Text, or The Diagrammatic Basis of Contemporary Architecture', in *Diagram Diaries* (New York: Universe Publishing, 1999), 6–25.

Speaks, Michael, 'Folding toward a New Architecture', in Bernard Cache, *Earth Moves: The Furnishing of Territories* (Cambridge, MA: The MIT Press, 1995), vxiii–xx.

Spencer, Douglas, *The Architecture of Neoliberalism: How Contemporary*

Architecture Became an Instrument of Control and Compliance (London and New York: Bloomsbury Academic, 2016).

Spencer, Douglas, 'The Critical Matter of the Diagram', in *Relational Skins: Chronicling the Works of Diploma Unit 12 at the AA School London*, ed. Holger Kehne and Jeff Turko Spencer (London: Lulu, 2009).

Spinoza, Baruch, 'Letter 62 (P03) to G. H. Schuller or Schaller (The Hague, October 1764)', <www.faculty.umb.edu/gary_zabel/Courses/Spinoza/Texts/ Spinoza/let6258.htm> (accessed 5 April 2020).

Spuybroek, Lars, interview by Arjen Mulder, 'The Aesthetics of Variation', in *Interact or Die*, ed. Joke Brouwer and Arjen Mulder (Rotterdam: V2 Pub./ NAi, 2007), 132–51.

Spuybroek, Lars, *The Architecture of Continuity: Essays and Conversations* (Rotterdam: NAi Publishers, 2008).

Spuybroek, Lars, 'Machining Architecture', in *NOX Machining Architecture*, ed. Andrew Benjamin and Lars Spuybroek (London: Thames & Hudson, 2004), 6–13.

Spuybroek, Lars, 'Motor Geometry', *Architectural Design* 68, no. 5–6 (1998): 48–55.

Spuybroek, Lars, *The Sympathy of Things: Ruskin and the Ecology of Design* (Rotterdam: V2 Pub./NAi, 2011).

Stengers, Isabelle, 'The Challenge of Ontological Politics', in *A World of Many Worlds* (Durham, NC: Duke University Press, 2018), 83–111.

Stengers, Isabelle, 'An Ecology of Practices', in *Cosmopolitics* (Minneapolis: University of Minnesota Press, 2010).

Stengers, Isabelle, 'The Symbiosis between Experiment and Techniques', in *The Politics of the Impure*, ed. Joke Brouwer, Arjen Mulder and Lars Spuybroek (Rotterdam: V2_Publishing, 2010), 14–45.

Stenner, Paul, 'Deep Empiricism', lecture at the Topological Approach to Cultural Dynamics conference, subtitled Changing Cultures: Cultures of Change (Barcelona, 9–12 December 2009).

Stern, Daniel N., *The Interpersonal World of the Infant: A View from Psychoanalysis and Developmental Psychology* (New York: H. Karnac, 1985).

Stiegler, Bernard, *Technics and Time, 1: The Fault of Epimetheus*, trans. Richard Beardsworth and George Collins (Stanford: Stanford University Press 1998).

Stotz, Karola, 'Why Developmental Niche Construction Is Not Selective Niche Construction: And Why It Matters', *Interface Focus* 7: 20160157 (2017), <http://doi.org/10.1098/rsfs.2016.0157> (accessed 5 April 2020).

Tafuri, Manfredo, 'L'architecture dans le boudoir', in *The Sphere and the*

Labyrinth: Avant-Gardes and Architecture from Piranesi to the 1970s, trans. Pellegrino d'Acierno and Robert Connolly (Cambridge, MA: The MIT Press, 1987), 267–90.

Tafuri, Manfredo, 'Toward a Critique of Architectural Ideology', in *Architecture Theory Since 1968*, ed. Michael K. Hays (Cambridge, MA: The MIT Press, 1998), 6–35.

Taylor, Mark C., 'Coevolutionary Disequilibrium (the Efficient Market Hypothesis)', in *The State of Architecture at the Beginning of the 21st Century*, ed. Bernard Tschumi and Irene Cheng (Montacelli Press, 2003), 80–1.

Thelen, Esther and Linda B. Smith, *A Dynamic Systems Approach to the Development of Cognition and Action* (Cambridge, MA: The MIT Press, 1994).

Tomkins, Silvan, *Exploring Affect: The Selected Writings of Silvan S. Tomkins*, ed. E. Virginia Demos (Cambridge: Cambridge University Press, 1995).

Toscano, Alberto, *The Theatre of Production: Philosophy and Individuation between Kant and Deleuze* (Basingstoke: Palgrave Macmillan, 2006).

Tuinen, Sjoerd van, 'Deleuze: Speculative and Practical Philosophy', in *Genealogies of Speculation: Materialism and Subjectivity since Structuralism*, ed. Armen Avanessian and Suhail Malik (London and New York: Bloomsbury, 2016), 93–114.

Tuinen, Sjoerd van, ed., *Speculative Art Histories: Analysis at the Limits* (Edinburgh: Edinburgh University Press, 2017).

Turner, Scott J., 'Extended Phenotypes and Extended Organisms', *Biology and Philosophy* 19 (2004): 327–52.

Turpin, Etienne, 'Who Does the Earth Think It Is, Now?', in *Architecture in the Anthropocene: Encounters among Design, Deep Time, Science and Philosophy*, ed. Etienne Turpin (Michigan: Open Humanities Press, 2013), 3–10.

Turvey, Michael T., 'Perception: The Ecological Approach', in *Encyclopedia of Cognitive Science* (New York: Nature Publishing Group, 2003), 538–41.

Turvey, Michael T., 'Theory of Brain and Behaviour in the 21st Century: No Ghost, No Machine', in *Language and Cognition 2003–2004, University Seminar #681* (New York: Columbia University, 2004), 57–70.

Uexküll, Jakob von, 'A Stroll through the Worlds of Animals and Men: A Picture Book of Invisible Worlds', *Instinctive Behavior: The Development of a Modern Concept*, ed. and trans. Claire Schiller (New York: International Universities Press, Inc., 1957), 5–80.

Uexküll, Jacob von, *Theoretical Biology* (New York: Harcourt, 1926).

Venturi, Robert, *Complexity and Contradiction in Architecture* (New York: Museum of Modern Art, 1966).

Venturi, Robert, Denise Scott Brown and Steven Izenour, *Learning from Las Vegas* (Cambridge, MA: The MIT Press, 1972).

Vidler, Antony, 'The B-B-B-Body: Block, Blob, Blur', in *The Body in Architecture*, ed. Deborah Hauptmann (Rotterdam: 010 Publishers, 2006), 131–7.

Vidler, Anthony, 'The Third Typology', in *Architecture Theory since 1968*, ed. Michael K. Hays (Cambridge, MA: The MIT Press, 1998 [1977]), 284–94.

Viveiros de Castro, Eduardo, 'Cosmological Deixis and Amerindian Perspectivism', *Journal of the Royal Anthropological Institute* 4, no. 3 (1998): 469–88.

Waddington, Conrad Hal, *The Strategy of the Genes* (New York and London: Routledge, 2014 [1957]).

Waddington, Conrad Hal, *Tools for Thought* (New York: Basic Books, 1977).

Wachowski Siblings (dir.), *The Matrix* (Warner Bros. Pictures, 1999).

Wark, McKenzie, *Molecular Red: Theory for the Anthropocene* (London and New York: Verso, 2015).

Watson, Janell, *Guattari's Diagrammatic Thought: Writing between Lacan and Deleuze* (New York: Continuum, 2009).

Wexler, Brian, 'Neuroplasticity, Culture and Society', in *The Psychopathologies of Cognitive Capitalism: Part One*, ed. Arne de Boever and Warren Neidich (Berlin: Archive Books, 2013), 185–218.

Whitehead, Alfred North, *The Concept of Nature* (Ann Arbor: Ann Arbor Books, 1957 [1920]).

Whitehead, Alfred North, *Process and Reality: An Essay in Cosmology*, ed. David Ray Griffin and Donald W. Sherburne (New York: The Free Press, 1978 [1929]).

Wigley, Mark and Jeffrey Kipnis, 'The Architectural Displacement of Philosophy', in *Pratt Journal of Architecture: Form, Being, Absence* (1988), 4–8.

Wigley, Mark, *The Architecture of Deconstruction: Derrida's Haunt* (Cambridge, MA: The MIT Press, 1993).

Wigley, Mark, 'The Translation of Architecture, the Production of Babel', in *Architecture Theory since 1968*, ed. Michael K. Hays (Cambridge, MA: The MIT Press, 1998), 658–75.

Williams, James, 'Deleuze's Ontology and Creativity: Becoming in Architecture', *Pli* 9 (2000): 200–19.

Williams, James, *Gilles Deleuze's Philosophy of Time: A Critical Introduction and Guide* (Edinburgh: Edinburgh University Press, 2011).

Wilson, Colin St. John, 'Classical Theory and the Aesthetic Fallacy', in *The Other Tradition of Modern Architecture* (London: Academy Editions, 1995).

Wolfe, Charles T., 'De-Ontologizing the Brain: From the Fictional Self to the

Social Brain', *CTheory: 100 Days of Theory*, ed. Arthur and Marilouise Kroker (2007), <www.ctheory.net/articles.aspx?id=572> (accessed 5 April 2020).

Wolfe, Katharine, 'From Aesthetics to Politics: Rancière, Kant and Deleuze', *Contemporary Aesthetics* 4 (2006), <https://quod.lib.umich.edu/c/ca/7523 862.0004.012/--from-aesthetics-to-politics-ranciere-kant-and-deleuze?rgn =main;view=fulltext> (accessed 5 April 2020).

Wolfendale, Peter, *Object-Oriented Philosophy: The Noumenon's New Clothes* (Falmouth: Urbanomic, 2014).

Worringer, Wilhelm, *Abstraction and Empathy*, trans. Michael Bullock (Cleveland: Meridian, 1967 [1907]).

Zaera-Polo, Alejandro, 'Politics of the Envelope: A Political Critique of Materialism', *Archinet* 17 (2008): 76–105.

Žižek, Slavoj, *Disparities* (London and New York: Bloomsbury Academic, 2016).

Žižek, Slavoj, *Event: Philosophy in Transit* (London: Penguin Books, 2014).

Žižek, Slavoj, 'Lacan between Cultural Studies and Cognitivism', *UMBR(a): A Journal of the Unconscious* 4 (2000): 9–32.

Žižek, Slavoj, *Pandemic! COVID-19 Shakes the World* (New York and London: OR Books, 2020).

Žižek, Slavoj, 'Remarks on Occupy Wall Street', *Log* 25 (2012): 118–20.

Zourabichvili, François, 'Six Notes on the Percept (On the Relation between the Critical and Clinical)', in *Deleuze: A Critical Reader*, ed. Paul R. Patton (Cambridge, MA: Blackwell, 1996), 188–216.

Zuboff, Shoshana, *The Age of Surveillance Capitalism: The Fight for a Human Future at the New Frontier of Power* (London: Profile Books, 2019).

Index